MODERN NORWEGIAN LITERATURE
1860–1918

MODERN NORWEGIAN LITERATURE
1860-1918

BY

BRIAN W. DOWNS

*Formerly Master of Christ's College and
Professor of Scandinavian Studies in the
University of Cambridge*

CAMBRIDGE
AT THE UNIVERSITY PRESS
1966

PUBLISHED BY
THE SYNDICS OF THE CAMBRIDGE UNIVERSITY PRESS

Bentley House, 200 Euston Road, London, N.W. 1
American Branch: 32 East 57th Street, New York, N.Y. 10022

©

CAMBRIDGE UNIVERSITY PRESS
1966

Printed in Great Britain at the University Printing House, Cambridge
(Brooke Crutchley, University Printer)

LIBRARY OF CONGRESS CATALOGUE
CARD NUMBER: 66-18662

CONTENTS

Prefatory Note *page* vii

Map of Norway, showing the principal places mentioned in
the text viii

1   Preliminary 1

2   Bjørnson 17

3   Ibsen before 1884 43

4   Elster and Lie 65

5   Kielland and Amalie Skram 80

6   Garborg and other Landsmaal Authors of his Time 99

7   Ibsen after 1882 116

8   The Norwegian Theatre: Gunnar Heiberg 133

9   The New Men of the 'Nineties 146

10   Kinck and Hamsun 165

11   The New Century 189

12   Coda 209

General Notes 215

Bibliographical Appendix 262

Index 271

v

PREFATORY NOTE

THE main portion of this study is intended for readers of English. English titles of books are given throughout. On first mention, except an incidental one, I have given the Norwegian title in addition and affixed a dagger (†) when there is an English translation; where there is no translation of titles, it may be assumed that they are proper names of persons or places. I have also given quotations in English, except in a very few instances when it seemed to me that my prose paraphrase could do no justice whatever to a verse-original.

Certain inconsistencies in spelling and nomenclature may be excused by changes in usage over the last hundred years: an obvious instance is the name for the Norwegian capital, now Oslo, but Christiania (or Kristiania) over the whole of the period under discussion; I have deferred to English prejudices in the use of capital letters in titles and in preferring forms like *paa* to *på* wherever possible.

The notes which appear as footnotes are predominantly biographical. The General Notes, pp. 215 ff., to which attention is drawn in the main portion, are intended primarily for the professed student, who may be assumed to have knowledge of Norwegian and Danish.

The Bibliographical Appendix is a guide to further reading in the subject and confines itself to works of a general or comprehensive character. Commentaries on more specialized points are indicated at appropriate places among the Notes.

I have to thank my former colleague Dr Ronald Popperwell who has carefully gone through my typescript and saved me from many blunders, and Dr Harald Tveterås, Chief Librarian of the University Library of Oslo, who generously put its facilities at my disposal.

B. W. D.

vii

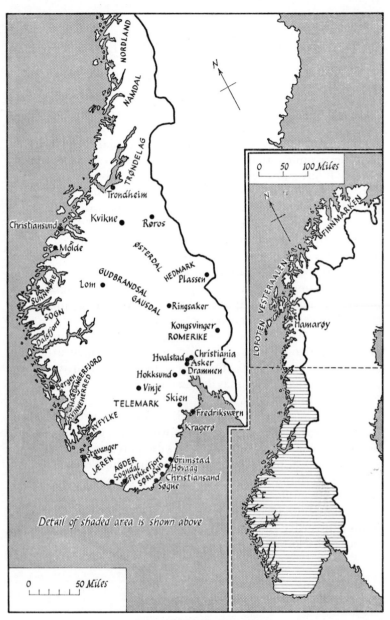

Norway, showing the principal places mentioned in the text.

I

PRELIMINARY

(1) *The new Norway*

AN ample social and political history of the Norwegian people
during the period with which this study deals would be out of
place in it. For describing the development of their literature
in a satisfactory manner it will be necessary, however, to sketch
in certain features of the background before which writers
worked rather more fully than would be appropriate in a history
of other countries at the same epoch; and the account will have
to go somewhat further back in time so as to account for the
existence of these features.

The new Kingdom of Norway was created by an upsurge of
national will in 1814, amid highly unpropitious conditions. The
country, never a rich one,[1] had suffered great privations during
the Napoleonic wars, so that for a generation or more the main
energies of its ablest citizens were directed to making it viable.[2]
The independence believed to have been gained was found to
be restricted by the personal union of the crown with that of
Sweden on which the Powers had insisted; and although that
independence had been guaranteed by these Powers, Norway's
liberal constitution, framed under the impulses of a revolutionary movement, was not calculated to win their enthusiastic
support in the years of the great reaction after Waterloo. To
poverty and the sense of frustration induced by an imperfect
revolution, was added the consciousness of being left isolated in
an unfriendly world.

Particularly unsatisfactory were Norway's relations with its
nearest neighbours. As the Norwegians were well aware, most
Swedes looked on Norway as a compensation for the loss of
Finland and were eager to take any opportunity for asserting
their seniority in the new partnership. The unequal nature of
the relationship could not be denied, the king not merely living
in far-away Stockholm,[3] but also directing the foreign affairs of

his two kingdoms through his foreign minister, invariably a Swede. There were as good as no personal relations between the two countries: a British resident in Norway during the eighteen-thirties remarked[1] that he met more Englishmen than Swedes. A sign of recognition might on occasion be interchanged between a Swedish and a Norwegian *savant* or man of letters, but there could be no question of establishing a common front in the cultural field; the linguistic difference prohibited anything like the literary continuum that had obtained between Denmark and Norway in the eighteenth century.

Vis-à-vis Denmark the position was of quite a different order. History ensured that personal and commercial relations were a good deal closer than they were with Sweden, the former from reasons about to be discussed, the latter because Denmark lay on the route to much of the rest of Europe. For something near 300 years up to 1814 Norway had been governed from Copenhagen virtually as a Danish colony. This was now of course a thing of the past, nor did the Danes at any time contemplate anything like a war of revenge for the rights they had lost. But they had left a legacy, which many of the legatees would have designated a *damnosa hereditas*. It lay primarily in the sphere of governmental activity. The forms of administration which had to be taken over in 1814 were those of a foreign rule, and the administrators themselves were, in two ways, more than half foreign. Many of them were Danes by birth, some of whom finally settled in the country to which they had been ordered and founded families there; and the native administrators—those in the top ranks at least—had begun to qualify for their careers by graduating at the University of Copenhagen. To Copenhagen the latter, like their Danish colleagues, had looked not alone for their directives, but also, in a greater or smaller degree, as to their 'spiritual home'. It was not until 1811 that as one of its gestures of appeasement towards its restive colony the Danish government founded a Norwegian university.[2]

All this might seem merely a matter of the civil service. But that term had a very wide connotation. Judges, bishops and parochial clergy, medical officers of health (who in vast tracts of the country were the only available doctors), professors, headmasters and teachers of secondary schools were all civil servants. Even the cabinet ministers of the new kingdom, owing their appointment and continuance in office to the Crown and, until 1884, to the Crown alone, having no seat in Parliament, were in effect the permanent secretaries of their respective departments. The bureaucracy was not only numerous and pervasive, but extremely powerful. For there was little to counterbalance it. Parliament, the Storting, might be elected on the broadest franchise in Europe, but it was weak (moreover, members of the civil service, other than those in the central offices, were eligible); apart from a very few rich merchants, shipping magnates and mine-owners,[1] the middle classes in trade and industry remained, until well after the middle of the nineteenth century, as insignificant in influence as they were in numbers; for centuries there had been hardly any territorial aristocracy.[2] And if one takes a close look at the convivial parties of rural 'gentry' described in Norwegian novels as late as 1900 one finds that they were preponderantly made up of the local sheriff, the county-court judge, the headmaster of the nearest grammar school and their more presentable aides, together with an occasional military or naval officer—all servants of the state—with their families and the families which their predecessors had left behind.

We may thus speak of an Establishment in a quite literal sense, an oligarchy powerful by virtue not only of its functions, but also of the attraction it exerted on would-be recruits still outside the charmed circle, and, not least, through the general culture and ethos of its members. And that culture and that ethos were Danish in origin.

Resentment and hostility were naturally roused as well as emulation and took practical forms. Much of the political history of Norway throughout the nineteenth century is a running fight between Establishment and its enemies.[3] The political opposition, organized and unorganized, derived and long sustained such strength as it possessed from the country-interest: in usual parlance the Bønder or Peasants.[4] The division between the inner circle and those outside it, the antagonism of Establishment versus Opposition thus reflects another deep cleavage in the national life, that of Town versus Country. Not least for the bearing it has on its literature, it should always be remembered that this outwardly placid country was for long stretches of time riven and unhappy.

(2) *Culture in the new Norway*

The cultural aspect of this division deserves closer attention. The Establishment, the inner circle, the prominent citizens of the towns—all, in fact, who 'set the tone'—continued to cling fast to their Danish heritage; the drawing-rooms, libraries, clubs, societies, the musical and dramatic entertainments of Christiania or Bergen were replicas of those of Copenhagen. It could scarcely be otherwise in the new Norway's early days. For where was distinctively Norwegian music? Where were Norwegian painting and sculpture? Where was Norwegian literature, since the surviving handful of Norway-born authors who had adorned the literary scene in Denmark[1] during the years around 1800 had all but fallen dumb—at a time, too, when Danish poetry and drama had entered on an era of remarkable florescence?

Such questions were asked not only by the ironical and complacent to whom their heritage gave all they wished. There were others who felt them as a mortifying challenge, notably among the generation that had come to maturity in the new Norway and no longer sought a spiritual home in Copenhagen. These latter asked political questions too, and many of them, with protest and brawling, took every opportunity to express their resentment at the doubly alien rule—the Swedish king, the 'Danish' administrators—imposed upon them. The protesters and brawlers became known as the Patriots,[2] and they found an eminent champion and spokesman in Henrik Wergeland (1808–45), whose turbulent career may be said to have begun in 1828. It was an extremely variegated one: a student at the University of Christiania and a candidate for the Christian ministry, Wergeland was not only a copious and richly endowed poet, but also an acknowledged leader of opinion as well as of activist gangs. By way of answer to the nagging questions about Norwegian culture, it was his aim to seek out in history and the neglected lore of the countryside other sources

4

for it than those cherished by the Establishment and, having found them out, through speeches, newspapers, pamphlets and compilations, to make them known, vivify and foster them.[1]

Wergeland was an easy first among the Norwegian authors of his day and has remained a name to conjure with, not just with the *literati*, but in the nation at large. His vast publicist's activity firmly established among his compatriots the ascendancy, if not of the agitator-poet, at any rate of the man of letters who actively concerns himself with general social and political issues, whose opinions about them receive serious notice and whose imaginative works can be construed as contributions to their elucidation. *Tendens*, as the Norwegians call it—propaganda, tendentiousness or, at least, a 'palpable design on the reader'—has, thanks largely to Wergeland's example,[2] become more thoroughly engrained in Norwegian belles-lettres than in the literature of any other country. It is a word that will of necessity often recur in these pages. In some measure, the *tendens* of a Norwegian author is, almost always, an essential element in his literary aims, achievement and reputation.

(3) *National Romanticism*

The ideals and labours of Wergeland and his associates were among the chief driving forces behind the general movement known as *National-Romantiken* or *Nasjonalromantikken* (National Romanticism)[3] which gathered momentum in the eighteen-thirties and predominated in virtually the whole cultural sphere for some thirty years. Its name accurately represents its nature, implying an appreciation and cultivation of all the nation's (non-material) resources in the romantic spirit of wonder, *pietas* and admiration, with almost exclusive regard for what was claimed as peculiar to Norway alone. Only a few of its manifestations can be mentioned. A school of painters[4] came into existence to evoke the natural beauties or starkness of the Norwegian landscape and the lives of those who dwelt amid it. Musicians collected the melodies of the countryside and based their own compositions upon them.[5] The interests of the latter were closely allied to those of the folk-lorists, among whom Asbjørnsen and Moe won immense fame at home and abroad with their *Norwegian Folk-Tales* and *Norwegian Fairy Stories*.[1] The academic historians,[2] the philologists and the archaeologists were drawn in. The medieval literature was read. A Society for the Preservation of Ancient Buildings was founded, and the restoration of Trondheim Cathedral, the greatest material vestige of the Middle Ages, became a matter of nation-wide concern.

By no means all the credit for launching and maintaining these activities, however, belongs to the Patriots. When these first burst upon the scene, their chauvinism, their violence and the crudity of their manners and writing at once called out a counter-opposition among their coevals, those young men who were destined to become the Establishment of the future and who were not averse to being dubbed the Party of Intelligence (*Intelligens-partiet*). The standard-bearer of this group was Johan Sebastian Cammermeyer Welhaven (1807–73), poet, critic and ultimately professor of Philosophy, on his embroiling himself in a notorious feud with Wergeland, the particulars of which it is unnecessary to set out here. But as, after some ten turbulent years, the ferocity of their feud began to abate, the Party of Intelligence, which particularly resented the arrogance of their opponents' assumption of the appellation 'the Patriots', since they themselves were equally committed to the cause of the nation's culture, could not fail to be drawn into the broad current of National Romanticism. Indeed, in those aspects of the movement concerned with the past, 'living' past and dead past, it was they who came to stand out most prominently.

For all the interests the two parties had in common, one point must, however, be made emphatically. The Patriots preached that the redemption of Norway must come from Norway alone. The Party of Intelligence, the children, broadly speaking, of the Establishment as they were to be the Establishment of the future, never ceased to protest against the Patriots' isolationism, to insist that Norwegian culture must remain in the general European stream and turn to account the heritage they had received from their immediate forbears as well as the hidden treasure which National Romanticism was bringing to light. And that meant, in the circumstances of the time, as jealous a preservation as possible of the Dano-Norwegian continuum.

This deep-going divergence was to come out into the open most strikingly in the field of language. The Danish of the old régime continued in use as the written language of the realm. The spoken language of the officials and their circles was likewise Danish,[1] tinged with certain variations in pronunciation and vocabulary. It was the accepted language of parliament, the law-courts, the university and schools, the stage and, broadly speaking, the pulpit. On the other hand, there were the common parlances of the streets and countryside, which, though originally derived from the same source as standard Danish, had developed through the centuries in their own way. They who habitually employed these parlances, when addressed in the official language and expected to answer in it, felt themselves confronted in a foreign language—the language, they could remind themselves, of the evicted conqueror. This was a state of things anomalous in the sight of many, intolerable to some.

The outcome of this resentment was the creation of the Landsmaal (Country Language), the work of a self-taught village schoolmaster of peasant stock from Sunnmøre, Ivar Andreas Aasen (1813–96). Aasen began a thorough study of the provincial dialects during the eighteen-thirties and published the outcome of his findings in *The Grammar of the Norwegian Folk-Language* (*Det norske Folkesprogs Grammatik*) and a *Dictionary of the Norwegian Folk-Language* (*Ordbog over det norske Folkesprog*) in 1848 and 1850 respectively, followed by a specimen Reader, a little musical comedy and a collection of lyrics, which make their appeal to rather simple tastes.[2] As its appellation indicates, the Landsmaal was based on the parlances of the countryside, those of western Norway in particular, eliminating such works and forms as had crept in from cultivated speech and reinforced by adaptations from medieval writings. Aasen's was a synthetic language, in the sense that it was one which no one had spoken or, before himself, had written. It was not, however, too wildly grotesque and amid the prevailing enthusiasm for everything national, especially when a long pedigree could be claimed for it, at once found devoted champions. Linguistic habits being at issue, it naturally met with a more than equivalent ridicule and aversion,[3] but, thanks mainly to Aasmund Olafsen Vinje—to whom we shall shortly return—it succeeded nevertheless in establishing itself as a literary language within a very few years of Aasen's publications.

We need not consider in detail the process by which Landsmaal became, subject to local option, the language of instruction in elementary schools and received more and more official recognition, until now, known as Nynorsk (New Norwegian), though still capable of rousing objurgation, it has gained equality of legal status with the rival that has developed fairly freely from the Danish or Dano-Norwegian of the old establishment and has received the appellations Bymaal (Town-Language) or Riksmaal (Language of the Realm) and now, officially, Bokmaal (Book-Language). Both are still in a state of flux, and, in accordance with the national spirit, there is much deviationism.[1]

While we have to speak of the country now having two languages—*both* Norwegian—fidelity to written Danish persisted for long; to all intents and purposes, Ibsen and those of his contemporaries who did not actually adopt the Landsmaal wrote in Danish. This vestige of the Dano-Norwegian continuum endured practically untouched for nearly a century after the political severance, fervently cherished by those who maintained it as a nexus with a wider civilization, even by that quintessential Norwegian patriot, Bjørnson.[2]

(4) *Norwegian literature 1814–50*

By a natural transition we now come to the history of belles-lettres. What did the new Norway, what did National Romanticism do for Norwegian literature? The blunt answer must be 'not very much'. The fact has been mentioned that there was no 'carry-over' in literature from the period before 1814 and that the lack of native writers immediately after 1814—a phenomenon such as is not infrequently seen after the establishment of a new polity[3]—was matter for disquieted remark. In the course of the preceding pages all the major imaginative writers there were before 1850 have been mentioned: the fiery Wergeland, author of some fine (and not particularly fiery) narrative poems, some exquisite lyrics and a vast, tedious epic *Creation, Man, Messiah (Skabelsen—Mennesket—Messias)*, who also strove for a foothold in the theatre; Welhaven, the writer of generally placid verse 'romances', of elegiacal short poems and of a beautifully turned cycle of polemical sonnets, *The Dawn of Norway* (*Norges Dæmring*), very serviceable, too, in his time and place as a literary historian and critic; Peter Christen Asbjørnsen (1812–85), a zoologist and botanist by profession, whose presentations of native folk-lore not only familiarized the world with Trolls, but did much to make literary prose, as was greatly needed, more vivid and supple.[1]

Despite the differences between them, all these three authors can be well and truly ranged in the general tradition of European Romanticism: Wergeland, both in character and achievement very like a belated *Stürmer und Dränger*; Welhaven, whose verse in a good translation would be thought that of a contemporary German poet such as Uhland; Asbjørnsen, the conscious follower of the Grimm brothers. The same may be said of the lesser *littérateurs* of their time, not very numerous or gifted, devoting themselves mainly to the short poem.

Somewhat above the ruck of these latter epigone Romanticists stands Andreas Munch (1811–84),[2] an able, conscientious and fairly prolific craftsman, who characteristically made admirable verse-translations. He is interesting chiefly on three extrinsic counts. He affords an extreme example of loyalty to the Dano-Norwegian continuum in that, during his fifties, he settled in Denmark and thereafter identified himself with Danish literature; he was the first Norwegian to have virtually no profession except authorship;[3] and he was that very rare bird in his time and place, a writer of plays[4] that enjoyed at least a *succès d'estime* in the theatre.

(5) *Synopsis of Norwegian literature after 1850*

A young Norwegian, then, who in 1850 harboured literary ambitions could look to no substantial native tradition for guidance: a small bulk of formal poetry, a handful of plays, not many more novels or short stories, equally flaccid,[5] a minimum of criticism beyond what was published in polemic intent.[6] In considering his predicament, however, reference must once more be made to the Dano-Norwegian continuum and to the generally flourishing state of Danish literature,

available to a young Norwegian much as it would be to a young
Dane. As a rule such a one would be familiar with some at
least of the works of Oehlenschläger, Ingemann and Grundtvig
among the grand old men still in the field, of J. L. Heiberg,
Hertz, Winter, Paludan-Müller and Hans Christian Andersen
among their distinguished successors; talk about Søren Kierkegaard might already have come to his ears. For definitely
'foreign' authors (generally to be had in Danish translations)
it is more difficult to lay down a rule.[1] The Swede Tegnér's *Fri-
thiofs Saga*, Scott, Byron and recent or fairly recent German
poets and playwrights, Schiller in chief, had a reasonably wide
circulation; the new English and French novelists, Dickens,
Lytton, Balzac[2] and, especially, Eugène Sue and the elder
Dumas were beginning to be known, and Scribe was becoming
the standby of the Christiania Theatre.[3]

At this epoch, a small group of budding authors was, in
fact, beginning to announce itself, and from their time onwards
notable contributions to the national literature appear in a
steady stream such as the annals of Norway could not have
recorded before. It may be convenient, therefore, to give here
a brief, somewhat diagrammatic sketch of the course of this
stream during the seventy-five years or so following their
début.

Wergeland had died in 1845, but the other authors named
continued moderately active for some years ahead. The spirit
of National Romanticism still prevailed. All except one of
the new writers—Camilla Collett (1813–95)—were in one way
or another strongly affected by it. The others of note are Henrik
Ibsen (1828–1906), Bjørnstjerne Bjørnson (1832–1910) and
Aasmund Vinje (1818–70), of whom the first two lived through
three literary generations.

The time of Vinje's departure from the scene is a critical
one. Up to then, the literature of Norway was essentially
Romantic; indeed, in the eighteen-sixties Romanticism, on the
decline almost everywhere else, seemed to have taken on a new
lease of life in this, its remotest outpost. But in the early eighteen-
seventies the *Moderne Gjennembrud* (Modern Break-Through),[4]
as it was called, marks as sudden and clean a break as literary
history can record, in the substitution, to put it baldly, of

Romanticism by Realism.[1] Ibsen and Bjørnson, almost veterans by now, became wholehearted converts, soon to be joined by Lie (1833–1908) and Kielland (1849–1906), who may be said to have made the Norwegian novel, and by Amalie Skram (1846–1905), who developed it further in the direction of Naturalism. Predominantly, moral preoccupations held first place in imaginative literature; the politically turbulent 'seventies and 'eighties were the heyday of *tendens*; prose drama and fiction became the favoured forms; there was scarcely any poetry of mark.

Another change took place about 1890, analogous with that observable in other countries at the same time. The writers now coming forward were often poets or, if not poets in the formal sense, concerned with the evocation of moods, reveries, the 'soul-life' of the individual and his private adventures, largely indifferent to the society around him. The new men drew older writers into their wake, notably Arne Garborg (1851–1924), who had attained notoriety as an almost extreme exponent of the realistic-social programme, and much has been said about the 'poetry' of Ibsen's last works, though its connexion with contemporary manifestations is tenuous and he had, in fact, himself heralded the coming change on turning away from narrowly social preoccupations after *An Enemy of the People* (1882).

The lyrical wind that set in at this time was a gentle one— no young Norwegian poet came near to rivalling in stature some contemporaries in, for instance, Sweden and the Low Countries—but it was persistent, and it has never since then died down. The liberation of fancy and imagination, however, of which the revival of verse was the most obvious symptom, the trend towards literary impressionism on the one hand and, on the other, to turn for subject-matter and setting away from 'the busy haunts of men' to the experience of solitary individuals or of isolated groups in the vast countryside, came to characterize more impressively the new prose-writers, among whom Knut Hamsun (1859–1952) and Hans Kinck (1865–1926) were the most eminent.

A novel feature of the literary scene in the eighteen-nineties is the comparatively large number of authors of medium pretensions and achievements who now entered the field; hitherto, in broad terms, the middle rank had shown very thin. Many of the tyros, novelists and playwrights, trod the trails blazed by Lie, Bjørnson and Ibsen, but in the best of them there was a vigour of movement or at least an exploratory bent that may be attributed to the general 'shake-up' occurring at the time of their emergence, the time when the new stars on the further horizon were Kipling, Maeterlinck, Rostand, Barrès, Fröding, Selma Lagerlöf, and the fame of older masters like Dostoievsky, Tolstoy and Nietzsche had spread abroad.

The shake-up makes the broad picture of Norwegian literature during the eighteen-nineties, relatively speaking, chaotic: youth and eld, experiment and tradition, neo-Romanticism and Naturalism jostle one another, though without undue acrimony. When, after some ten years, the prospect clears, the persistent toughness of the realistic strand becomes more apparent. The first decades of the twentieth century constitute indeed a notable flowering-time of the Norwegian novel, realistic and 'modern' as that of its pioneers had been, if more diversified and much less committed to 'causes' and 'programmes'.[1] For a time verse seemed to go into partial eclipse again, until, about 1906, a remarkable group of young poets came to supersede the effete survivors of the aesthetes of 1890. Like the prose-writers, most of them had given the measure of their talents before the end of the Great War and were to continue fruitful for a goodly time to come.

(6) Fru Collett and Vinje

In common with all delimitations of historical periods, this reasonably neat scheme smoothes over a few ragged edges. A sadly refractory one is the first. A new impressiveness undeniably came into Norwegian literature with the writers who made their début in the eighteen-fifties. But can one say with any precision just when it showed itself? 'Modern Norwegian Literature', a knowledgeable foreign observer declared,[2] 'begins with *Synnøve Solbakken*', published in 1857. A later, more specialized use of the adjective 'modern' might demand some year after the *Moderne Gjennembrud*. 1857, however, remains as good a one as any.

That, however, would involve some anomalies. Apart from the trifling one that *Synnøve Solbakken* just misses being its author Bjørnson's earliest venture into belles-lettres, it disregards also the short range of Ibsen's juvenilia, and it passes over a more 'modern' work than any that these two had written to date, namely Camilla Collett's novel *The Sheriff's Daughters* of 1855. Although Fru Collett lived for another forty years, *The Sheriff's Daughters* remained her one notable piece of imaginative writing; it is an isolated outlier, and for that reason may not improperly receive summary notice in this preliminary chapter. To do the same for Vinje is, admittedly, less defensible. For, pioneer as he was too, his real pioneering did not begin until two years after *Synnøve Solbakken*, and, in quantitative terms, he is more than anything a man of the 'sixties. But, an older man than Ibsen or Bjørnson and dying some forty years before them, he occupies a markedly different, senior position in literary history, in that he was unaffected by the great *Umwertung aller Werte* so characteristic of their development.[1]

We turn now to the first Norwegian novel of any stature, Camilla Collett's* *The Sheriff's Daughters* (*Amtmandens Døttre*), published in 1855—176 years after *The Princess of Cleves* and 114 years after *Pamela*.

Sheriff Ramm,[2] after whose three surviving girls *The Sheriff's Daughters* takes its title, is stationed in a thinly populated district far from the capital. There is scarcely any society, and what there is of it is notably deficient in young men who by any standard could be thought 'eligible', since these anticipate their eligibility by seeking their fortunes—and their wives—elsewhere. The brightest of the daughters, having missed her chance when she was sent to live for two years in Copenhagen, is, like her two elder sisters, thrown back on the family tutor-cum-secretary, this time a young man of intelligence, charm, some means and a face strikingly like that of Lord Byron. Sophie and Georg Cold genuinely fall in love with one another. By an unlucky chance, however, Sophie overhears a conversation between Cold and a visiting friend, intended to throw

---

* Jacobine Camilla Wergeland was born at Christiansand in 1813, the sister of Henrik Wergeland. After a notorious, one-sided passion for her brother's enemy, Welhaven, she married in 1841 Peter Jonas Collett, who left her a widow in 1851. Before *The Sheriff's Daughters* she had written a few short stories and sketches collected in *Fortællinger* (1861). In her latter days she was recognized as the foremost declared feminist of her country. She died in Christiania in 1895.

the latter's prying off the scent, and infers from it that she has been deceived in believing her passion to be returned. Before there is time to clear up the misunderstanding she goes off with her mother to stay with an elderly connexion, a rural dean, a widower with children, and, emotionally quite untouched, accepts his lukewarm proposal of marriage: her elder sister, Amalie, poorly and unhappily married though she is, has advised her that she cannot hope for anything better. Sophie and the rural dean go to the altar together with his entirely colourless curate and the youngest of the girls.

The Sheriff's Daughters is built on a grievance; the authoress called it a 'shriek'. Her point is not so much that girls like the Ramms are badly placed for finding husbands (to which the purpose of their lives is directed) as that their scope for falling in love is restricted, passion being the only true basis for marriage (and, one may refine, passion on the woman's part, almost irrespective of her partner's erotic temperature). This insistence on passion may be romantic at bottom, but, in the presentation it is entirely subdued to the realism of the rest. The middle-class rural *milieu* is firmly though not minutely depicted; the characters, but for Cold, are ordinary—the men mostly clods and the women often shrews—and faithfully exhibited as such. The style is level, correct and flat, heightened neither by grace nor by humour, the construction pedestrian, if adequate; the 'fatal misunderstanding' may just pass, and a dissipation of interest between the three girls is averted.

Fru Collett may have had none of the imaginative power of her contemporaries Emily and Charlotte Brontë, whose novels equally centred on passionate young women in bleak surroundings, but her pioneer work provided a worthy exemplar: twenty years were to elapse before it was rivalled.[1] Its preoccupation with 'the woe of women' set a tone which re-echoed through many a more distinguished work of later date and a host of lesser products.

Vinje's* signal service to Norwegian literature has been

---

* Aasmund Olafsen Vinje was born at Vinje in 1818, became an elementary schoolmaster and at the age of 32 began to study law at the University of Christiania, matriculating from the cramming establishment where Bjørnson and Ibsen were his contemporaries. But he did not graduate and until his death supported himself poorly by journalism, freelance lecturing and, for a time, a minor clerkship in a government office. He died of cancer in 1870.

alluded to in connexion with the rise of the Landsmaal. A cottar's son from Telemark, he became an enthusiast for it from the first. But it was not until 1858 that his enthusiasm took practical shape, when he started his periodical *The Dalesman* (*Dølen*) and adopted, with some variations of his own, the new language for it.[1] Nominally a weekly, it continued by fits and starts until the year of his death, and he wrote virtually the whole himself. Vinje published in it some lengthier pieces in prose and verse classifiable as 'imaginative literature', but the staple of *The Dalesman* is a series of periodical essays, akin to the innumerable Spectators of the eighteenth century. The ruling principle was to give country readers some idea of the current topics discussed in the towns—debates on education, folk-lore, the language question and politics, obituaries, notices of plays and philosophies—and at the same time to indicate to any town-dweller caring to read *The Dalesman* what these things looked like to such an interpreter.

The Dalesman essays were intended to be a link, a unifying agent, and at this juncture the Landsmaal was singularly fortunate in finding such an exponent with such an aim. Vinje was a countryman, mainly self-educated, interested in the folk from whom he sprang and not unconscious of his own talents; he was, however, anything but a bumptious rustic wiseacre. Angular though he might be and hard to get on with in his personal relations,[2] he had yet acquired a breadth of culture scarcely excelled by any one of his contemporaries: he was one of the first in his country to write about Darwin and the new positivistic philosophers; one of his books, on a sociological topic, was written in English;[3] and he cherished the ambition—never, alas, realized—of translating Homer into Landsmaal. He had scant sympathy with the aims and idols of the extreme nationalists and, knowing more about it than most of his contemporaries, never cried up 'peasant-culture'.

The 'double vision' necessitated by *The Dalesman*'s programme is equally evident in the style of its essays, conversational, varified, but predominantly ironic: among Vinje's favourite authors were Holberg, Sterne, Heine and the mordant Danish polemist Goldschmidt of his own time. The new, uncouth-looking Landsmaal he proceeded to fashion into an instrument of notable strength, flexibility, almost at times of subtility. His more imaginative writing, in which, like Heine, he liked to mingle prose and verse, showed it equally capable of beauty and tenderness. *Memories from a Journey in the Summer of 1860 (Ferdaminni fraa Sumaren 1860)*[1] is, outside drama, the finest piece of literature written by a Norwegian between Wergeland's death and Bjørnson's *Arnljot Gelline* of 1870.[2] After the *Dalesman* essays and the *Memories* no further proof was needed that the Landsmaal was equal to any literary task that might be entrusted to it. Vinje judged by European standards, and not least among his merits is that he saved Landsmaal literature from becoming, as it so easily might have remained if left in hands no more deft than Aasen's, irredeemably provincial.

BJØRNSON

(1) *Introduction*

DURING their lifetime Ibsen and Bjørnson were looked on at home and abroad as the Castor and Pollux of Norwegian literature. There was much argument about which of the two was the greater, and there still is. The argument is bedevilled by the fact that literary merit alone is not at issue. When, in the early years of the century, the Swedish Academy awarded the first Nobel Prizes for Literature, they gave one to Bjørnson, but never to Ibsen. Their terms of reference enjoined them to take 'idealistic tendency' into account,[1] and herein Ibsen was found wanting, many thinking, as some perhaps do today, that he represented an anarchic, pessimistic principle.

Factors such as these bulk especially large in the appraisal of Bjørnson. In deliberate judgements two distinguished contemporaries, both with a long, close knowledge of him and both eminently qualified to speak on literary matters, at once brought in non-literary considerations—and, having done so, arrived at diametrically opposite verdicts! Georg Brandes, the proponent of a wide cultural mission, like Bjørnson, as well as a critic of literature, concluded that his writing enshrined 'the best of his nature'. Ibsen, however, declared Bjørnson's life to be his best work, generously adding: 'And to realize himself in the whole conduct of his life is in my opinion the highest a man can attain to.'[2] While Ibsen's claims are based on his writings, Bjørnson's envisage the 'whole conduct of his life', in which the production of belles-lettres was only a fraction. An untiring publicist for over half a century, a political influence of immense power at a decisive epoch of his country's history, an outstanding man of the theatre, perhaps the greatest orator of his day in an age when oratory flourished, advocating great causes,[3] Bjørnson would still be one of Norway's national heroes, even if not a single poem, play or work of fiction had come from his pen. Posterity, on the whole, has come down on the side of Ibsen in this divergence of opinion, as in another sense it has come down on his side when it has been concerned to weigh literary merit alone. Ibsen remains a great power in the whole Republic of Letters. The same cannot be said of Bjørnson.

This implies no condemnation. No one now, I think, would concur in the verdict on Bjørnson of the American critic W. M. Payne, who in 1910, surveying a scene graced by Tolstoy, Ibsen and Carducci, pronounced him confidently 'primus inter pares';[1] but there might be a substantial measure of agreement with the opinion of another writer in English, Mr J. W. McFarlane, given half a century later: 'In his works he reached on occasions heights of sublimity unapproached by any other Norwegian writing in his century, Ibsen not excluded.'[2]

On the heights of sublimity or not, Bjørnson's work almost always commands attention. In part, though only in part, this springs from the fact that he was a pioneer. Through his peasant-tales he was the first to win recognition for the new Norwegian literature abroad.[3] The renascence of European drama in the latter part of the nineteenth century was due, it is usually accepted, mainly to the example of the two great Norwegian practitioners, Ibsen and him. Though by nearly five years the junior, he found himself the more quickly and in several respects acted as the pacemaker. The general background before which both projected their imaginings is more fully revealed in his than in Ibsen's. It is not unreasonable, therefore, that he should receive the prior consideration.

(2) *Bjørnson the Romantic*

On coming of age in 1853, Bjørnson* abandoned his plan of taking holy orders and broke off his studies at the University

* Bjørnstjerne Martinius Bjørnson was born, the son of a yeoman turned country parson, on 8 December 1832 at Kvikne in North Hedmark and had his schooling at Molde Middle School. Considerable portions of his life were spent abroad (1860–3 mainly in Italy, 1880–1 in the U.S.A., 1882–7 and from 1893 onwards repeatedly in Paris, the Tyrol or Rome, constant visits to Denmark). He was awarded an official pension for his services to literature in 1863. He died in Paris on 26 April 1910, after a paralytic stroke the year before. In 1858 he married

of Christiania. For three years or so he made a poor living by casual journalism, mostly critical, for the Christiania papers. One of them, in 1856, printed, without the author's name, the first[1] of his short stories of peasant life, 'Aanun', followed during the next four years by nine others of the same kind, which speedily made up one of the great household books of Norway, spread the author's fame abroad and established him as a worthy rival of the best among his predecessors in this line of writing, such as Steen Steensen Blicher, Jeremias Gotthelf, Berthold Auerbach and George Sand.[2]

The earliest tales are somewhat angular, but already in †*Synnøve Solbakken* of 1857[3] Bjørnson had attained to mastery in the genre. It is an ingenuous story about two farm-children, Synnøve and Thorbjørn, obviously intended for one another from childhood, but kept apart by a rowdy episode in Thorbjørn's lapse from grace in early manhood during a drunken brawl, and thereafter by his inability, from shame for his disgrace and the inveterate taciturnity of countrymen, to speak out; ultimately the parents take the business into their hands, and all ends as it should. The story, mainly told in the simple language[4] appropriate to the theme and characters, receives colour and relief on the one hand by the vivid descriptions of common episodes in village life and of the prosperous countryside in which it is set and, on the other, by the interpolation of lyrics.

The radiance of *Synnøve Solbakken* has cast its light over the remainder of these early tales. It would, however, be wrong to write them off as mere idylls. Bjørnson did not shrink from delineating the dark side of peasant life. In †*Arne* (1859), which shares the crown with *Synnøve Solbakken*, the story may be the edifying one of a country lad who works his way to sober usefulness and contentment in the place to which he has been born, as it is enriched with fine lyric passages in verse and prose; yet the human setting is anything but edifying —one of brutality, sub-human roistering and incontinence, scarcely veiled incest.

Karoline Reimers, a Bergen baker's daughter. Their son Bjørn became a distinguished man of the theatre, as actor, producer and first director of the National Theatre; their daughter Bergljot married Ibsen's son Sigurd.

Such indications of vice reveal a deliberate didactic purpose. In the firstling, 'Aanun'—a record, by the way, of almost unrelieved misery—it rose to the pitch of a direct address to village schoolmasters, reminding them of their responsibilities and warning them against the common fault of cutting their charges to pattern. Such crudity was soon avoided. Even in *Synnøve Solbakken*, however, an exemplary trend appears strongly, glorifying as it does the virtues of the peasantry—their industry, their sense of conscience and duty, their preference for deeds over words, their engrossment with church and family.

Such *tendens* may spoil the charm of *Synnøve Solbakken* for the over-sophisticated, and it caused annoyance at the time of its appearance: Vinje thought Bjørnson's peasant-tales the effusions of a town-dweller who did not know what he was talking about and his language, the Bryst-Norsk ('chest-Norse') on which he prided himself,[1] to be neither fish (Riksmaal) nor flesh (Landsmaal) nor good red herring. But to most the *tendens* was an added appeal. They saw in *Synnøve Solbakken* the high water-mark of National-Romanticism. Towards the end of the eighteen-fifties, nevertheless, that movement showed signs of decline; enthusiasm for the peasantry, particularly, had been badly damaged by the statistical demonstrations of the distinguished sociologist, Eilert Sundt, that their life was, in Hobbes's famous words, 'nasty, brutish and short'. And after 1860 Bjørnson wrote only one more peasant story in his old vein,[2] †'The Bridal Tune' ('Brude-Slaatten', 1872).

The social climate in general seemed to be turning harsher too. The opening of the first railway in Norway, in 1854, ushered in the new iron age, that of steam and competitive industrialism. The next short story Bjørnson was to write had the significant title †'The Rail Road and the Churchyard' ('Jernbanen og Kirkegaarden', 1866); it is laid in a community akin to those presented in the earlier stories; but the sun has gone in; there are no sentimental amours; the tale centres on the struggle for power in a parish council, issuing in the construction of a railway track over the narrow cells in which the rude forefathers of the hamlet sleep.

In the interval between the last of the *Synnøve Solbakken* group and this tale Bjørnson had directed his literary energies into another channel, that of drama. Unlike his Austrian contemporary, Anzengruber, he did not advance to modern social drama by way of plays about current rustic life. Instead, he addressed himself to the writing of historical plays, envisaging a collection to cover the period of civil strife in Norway during the twelfth and thirteenth centuries, much as Shakespeare had dealt with the comparable Wars of the Roses. Still in accord with the ideals of National Romanticism, he wished not only to provide his fellow-countrymen with a picture-gallery of their ancestors, but equally to bring out the vigour and richness of these ancestors' lives.

He came to historical drama by way of two somewhat trifling costume plays—†*Between the Battles* (*Mellem Slagene*, 1857) and *Limping Hulda* (*Halte-Hulda*, 1858)[1]—dramas of intrigue that happen to be set in bygone times, of which the theatrical idol of the day, Eugène Scribe, was the acknowledged master. The genuinely historical series began in 1861, by which time Bjørnson had turned his back on Scribe and put himself at the feet of Oehlenschläger, Schiller, Kleist and Shakespeare, exemplars of the earlier romantic theatre.[2] It comprises, strictly speaking, only two items, *King Sverre* (*Kong Sverre*, 1861) and †*Sigurd the Bad* (*Sigurd Slembe*, 1862); but there are three outliers, if one may so call them, the later, operatic *Sigurd the Crusader* (*Sigurd Jorsalfar*, 1872), *King Eystejn* (*Kong Eystejn*, not published till 1932) and †*Mary Stuart in Scotland* (*Maria Stuart i Skotland*, 1864).[3]

The last named remains the most widely known, largely because it is *not* on a Norwegian subject. Though lacking comic relief and kept in prose throughout (as far as dialogue is concerned), it is outwardly the most Shakespearean of his plays, by virtue of the frequent alternations of tone and focal interest and the multiplicity of personages and events, combining to evoke a whole turbulent society at a decisive point of its history. The essential stimulus to its composition, however, was Bjørnson's desire to round off, as it were, Schiller's *Mary Stuart*—which he highly esteemed—in showing how the temperament of the glamorous queen of Scots and past history, conditioned by that temperament, pointed to the tragic end that had been the German poet's concern.

Sigurd the Bad[1] is the tragedy of an obscure twelfth-century pretender to the Norwegian throne. It calls once more Schiller and Shakespeare to mind, the former by its division into three parts, like *Wallenstein*, the latter not merely by the general features which also characterized *Mary Stuart in Scotland*, but more essentially by its theme. In Sigurd, Bjørnson presented another and a greater Macbeth, the heroic figure of a barbarous age, Bellona's bridegroom indeed, but also *in esse* and *in posse* a wise, magnanimous statesman, conscious of his abilities and convinced of the legitimacy of his claim to royal station, whom the intrigues and perfidy of a degenerate court drive to armed revolt, fratricide, massacre and treason. The execution is worthy of the theme, whether judged for psychology or theatrical power. The majestic poetry of *Macbeth* is not equalled, but otherwise Bjørnson may here challenge comparison with the English master. A better play than *Mary Stuart in Scotland*, not alone for having more unmistakably a beginning, a middle and an end, it vies with Ibsen's *Pretenders* (of the following year) for the crown of Norwegian historical drama.

Occasional verse of a somewhat ceremonious character has always had a great vogue in the northern countries. Most of it, called forth by births, marriages and deaths, anniversaries and toasts, is domestic; but, the event or person to be celebrated being of sufficient importance, it can easily pass from the intimate to the public sphere. Of this kind Bjørnson was the master. In him, as Georg Brandes observed, one of the oldest strains of Scandinavian literature was revived, that of the chieftain who at the same time was his own court-poet. Unlike many court-poets one could name, he became also and remained the nation's 'household-poet'.

Bjørnson's poet-laureateship began with two poems of 1859, 'There lies a Land' ('Der ligger et land') and 'Yes, we love this Land' ('Ja, vi elsker dettet landet').[2] The opening of the latter strikes his keynote with quite startling clarity. The first word is an *affirmative*, the third grounds the affirmation in positive *love*, the fifth stresses that the love embraces the *whole* of Norway from its geology upwards; the great names in patriotic lore that follow, Harald, Haakon, Olav, Tordenskjold, Frederikshall, extend the purview in time as well as space. If after this the alumni of Christiania University needed a cantata or wished to do homage to Professor Welhaven, if Norwegian parliamentarians had the whim of greeting their Swedish confreres with a song, it was to Bjørnson, whatever the momentary height of his popularity, that they turned, and he was not only ready to oblige but kindled by their request. It came from his heart to demand in verse, always sonorous and straightforward, the inclusion of the Norwegian colours in a union jack of Sweden and Norway at one time and the sanctioning of a pure Norwegian flag at another, or to commemorate Nansen's adventurous disappearance into the polar pack-ice.[1]

But this kind of verse, considerable fraction of the whole though it may be, is not the only title to Bjørnson's fame as a poet. It is by no means always that he speaks with the big editorial We. The collected †*Poems and Songs* (*Digte og Sange*) published in 1870, he was minded at first to call *Songs* only, and in good measure they are in fact either songs to be sung in his plays or incidental lyrics in the tales, equally crying out for the musical setting that was speedily composed for them. It is significant how many of them are put into the mouths of imaginary persons, are dramatic projections—the leaning is evident even in one of the greatest of them, the lament of Bergliot,[2] which is a dramatic monologue comparable with those of Browning, amplified even by brief stage-directions. The intimate, purely personal lyric Bjørnson rarely attempted.[3]

What Norwegian criticism subsumes under the designation *episk* would seem to have been peculiarly congenial to him. His *œuvre*, as it happens, comprises only one noteworthy example of this kind: it is, however, not just noteworthy, but one of the lasting glories of the national literature ,†*Arnljot Gelline* (1870). As in *Sigurd the Bad*, Bjørnson took for his hero a minor historical figure whom he represented as a born leader thwarted and brutalized by (as he conceived it) injustice and persecution. To revenge himself he turns bandit and pirate, but redeems himself at last by bringing his crew of ruffians to help Olav, king and martyr, in the fatal battle of Stiklestad (1030), himself falling in the first onslaught. Through its curious aftermath Stiklestad ensured the conversion of Norway to Christianity, and a strongly religious strain runs through Bjørnson's poem:

Arnljot Gelline turns in revulsion against the savage deities of
his fathers, later renounces the religion of self-reliance which
was all that was then left him and ultimately receives baptism
at the hands of the royal saint. For this there is adequate
warranty in Bjørnson's source, the *Olafssaga*, but a sentimental
admixture, closely linked with the religious, is free invention.
It turns on the fair young heiress Ingered, whom in pursuit of
his vengeance Arnljot, having murdered her relatives, abducts
and (one must presume) ravishes, with the twofold result
that he and she become deeply enamoured and she feels compelled to expiate her fall in a nunnery.

The triple interest, heroic, religious and sentimental, charac-
terizes the three great nineteenth-century poems of the neighbouring peoples, which Bjørnson knew well and plainly aimed
to emulate: the Dane Oehlenschläger's *Helge*, the Swede
Tegnér's *Frithiof's Saga* and the Finn Runeberg's *King Fjalar*.[1]
In all four works the hero is a pagan of the remote northern
past who is converted to a new moral code, Christian or near-
Christian, loads himself with what he then comes to recognize
as sin and atones for it. Bjørnson excelled his rivals in bringing
out, both as regards character and event, the barbarism of the
times in which the stories are laid. For this he was helped
powerfully by the rejection of conventional poetic diction in
favour of a harsh style, to which echoes from the Sagas and
from popular speech contributed much, by his unsophisticated,
if greatly varied, metrical forms, based more often on alliteration
than rhyme, and by the electrifying vitality of most of his
episodes.[2]

(3) *Prelude to change*

Had Bjørnson died immediately after the publication of *Arnljot
Gelline* and *Poems and Songs*, he would have been mourned as a
great Romantic taken away at the height of his powers. All
his best work had fallen into three categories particularly
favoured by those who are also so labelled, and the spirit
informing it had been recognizably akin to theirs. Among his
neo-pastoral tales, the historical dramas and the 'poetry' in
its restricted sense, ranging from personal effusions to something
near to the epic, there had, however, appeared two 'sports',

not of great value in themselves, but calling for notice as giving a premonition of his equally eminent achievements in very different fields: a two-act play, *The Newly Wed* of 1865, and a story of intermediate length, *The Fisher Lass* of 1868.

It is not strictly accurate to call † *The Newly Wed (De Nygifte)*[1] the first 'modern' Norwegian play, since the time presumed for the action of the earliest play produced by a native author under the new régime, Bjerregaard's *Adventure in the Fells* (1825), and Ibsen's *St John's Eve* and *Love's Comedy* had been the present; but, lacking all their romantic trappings—peasant costume, open-air scenery, music, dancing, verse-dialogue— it looks and sounds like one more obviously than they did. It is in fact a drawing-room play. More than that, it is a problem-play, turning on the matrimonial frictions set up by a young wife's devotion to her parents carried to such an excess as dangerously to scant her husband of the attentions he thinks due to him. The embodiment of the theme is anything but brilliant; the happy ending in all-round reconciliation is brought about, most improbably, by the heroine's bosom friend, who not only makes a third on the wedding journey, but also composes a novel, which recounts some awful consequences of marital neglect and which she reads aloud to stir the bride's conscience. Dialogue and characterization are equally flat, though there is some mild humour at the expense of the heroine's self-complacent parents, who, for instance, think it quite in order for her and her husband to keep away from an evening party in their honour because Mamma has a bit of a cough. All the same, a distinguished Danish critic, looking back on the Copenhagen *première*, commends it as 'the first play which put questions and doubts into the bourgeoisie of that generation'.[2]

† *The Fisher Lass (Fiskerjenten*, 1868) leads on from Bjørnson's peasant-tales to his later fiction in a curious broken-backed way.[3] After opening, in a village community by the sea, with the troubles of a young wench who contrives to get herself engaged to three youths at the same time, the scene then abruptly changes and, with it, the theme. Petra the Fisher Lass is violently driven out of her home for her scandalous behaviour and has all her previous entanglements broken off in consequence. She finds a lodging with some kindly people in Bergen,

where she recovers from her shock and, enraptured by seeing her first play, Oehlenschläger's highly romantic *Axel and Valborg*, determines to become an actress; but her application to join the local troupe is refused. In the rural dean's parsonage to which she then betakes herself she seriously prepares herself for the stage, so that the story can end by her making her début in *Axel and Valborg*, with a good likelihood of also making a match with the worthiest of her admirers.

(4) *Bjørnson's 'problems'*

'A singer's vocation is the prophet's', Bjørnson asserted.[1] His vaticinations, his *tendens*, his 'problems' therefore call for consideration at this point, when his outlook and his art were showing radical changes, the romantic turning realist. The discussion may move a good distance away from literary history, but, while focused on Bjørnson, it serves likewise to display the stage on which all Norwegian writers during his long lifetime not merely moved, but, often enough, also assumed speaking parts.

The Newly Wed was already a problem-play. The second part of *The Fisher Lass* became a problem-novel, informed, however, by a personal urgency such as had not been operative in the tepid little drawing-room comedy. Much of it reads like a tract which the eighteenth century would have entitled 'On the Lawfulness of the Player's Calling'. Through the conversations of Petra, the rural dean and a liberal-minded friend of theirs the author was, however, settling a crucial *crise de conscience* of his own. When the three concluded that the stage could serve good ends as well as bad and that Petra's urge to become an actress—that abomination of the strait-laced—was of God, Bjørnson could apply the same liberating syllogism to himself, the director of playhouses and the author of feigned histories, dramatic or narrative: 'The Fisher Lass! Why that is me myself'.[2]

That Art need not conflict with Religion was a principle of vital moment to him at a time when, devout Christian as he was, inherited puritanic doubts were calling his whole *raison d'être* in question.

Bjørnson owed his liberation to the great Danish reformer Bishop Grundtvig—priest, poet, scholar and educator—whose undogmatic, hopeful message, based on love, brotherly and divine, and on the continuous operations of the Word, came to Norway at the time that the moral atmosphere had turned harsh and divinity had received an access of minatory gloom through the doctrines associated with another Danish prophet, Kierkegaard—the time, in fact, of Ibsen's *Brand*. For some years it seemed as if Bjørnson was destined to become the Elisha to Grundtvig's Elijah. This expectation was however falsified, partly for political reasons,[1] but more decisively through the development of his religious thinking, which led him to protracted controversies on Christian dogma and ultimately to the position where (in 1878) he publicly announced his severance from the Church, as a 'Free Thinker, no longer believing in the divinity of Christ'. The searing inward strife that induced his apostasy is mirrored in his dramatic master-piece, *Beyond Our Powers*, Part I (1883), and the short story 'Dust' (1882). A theist, nevertheless, Bjørnson always remained, a fundamentally religious man; and to the end of his life he acknowledged 'old Grundtvig's' as the profoundest influence he had undergone.[2]

It had an immediate bearing on his political activity, which could now be deployed with renewed vigour.[3] The syllogism that had justified Art could have infinite implications. For the disciple of Grundtvig politics meant the expression of the will of the whole people, enlightened and guided by the peremptory promptings from on high which those who had received them were in duty bound to proclaim. It was not for nothing that Ibsen intended to give to the play ultimately known as *The League of Youth*, in which Bjørnson saw himself lampooned, the title of 'Our Lord and Co.'. As Gladstone was accused of believing that the ace of trumps he had up his sleeve had been put there by God, so Bjørnson left the impression that he was the Almighty's accredited political agent in Norway.

The League of Youth appeared in 1869, the year after *The Fisher Lass*. That was a crucial year in the political history of Norway, for it saw the formation of the Party of the Left, the *Venstre*, whose cohering principle was opposition to the old bureaucratic Establishment, ultimately consummated by the introduction of parliamentary government fifteen years later. Bjørnson never stood for Parliament, but, during the years of constitutional strife and for some time after, he served the democratic *Venstre* as its unwearying and most formidable publicist and its conscience—which, by an extension that seemed self-evident to his congeners, was equivalent to the conscience of the nation. As he was Norway's ungarlanded laureate, Bjørnson came to be looked on as Norway's uncrowned king.

The clearest reflexion of his political views in his imaginative writing is the play of *The King* (1877), which, in a manner horrifying to timid souls, exhibited his hostility to 'Stockholm', the power inherent in the half-alien monarchy, from which, allied with the bureaucracy at home, the old régime derived its own. The exposure of lesser abuses which might be laid to its charge—*The Editor* (1874), for instance, or *The New System* (1879)—could also count as grist to the mill. Of a different order of impressiveness is *Paul Lange and Tora Parsberg* (1898), inspired by a tragedy enacted on the political scene during the unhappy years of disunion and disillusion when the victorious Party of the Left—always an uneasy alliance between intellectual radicals and the basically reactionary country interest—lost the coherence that it had been Bjørnson's most signal achievement to maintain for nearly two decades.[1]

After the broad issues of religion and politics, there are two others to be considered, which, though narrower in scope and more specific than these, were not only 'burning questions' for Bjørnson's contemporaries too, but also in their different ways had a more obvious relevance to his imaginative writing.

The first of these is the wrangle known as *Sædelighedsfejden* or The Morality Feud. A protracted controversy and a highly ramified one, its seeds were sown in the late 'seventies—Bjørnson's play about divorce, †*Leonarda*, and Ibsen's *Doll's House*, of the same year (1879), being the most vital. The 'Feud' itself, however, dates from Bjørnson's †*Gauntlet* of 1883,[2] in which at one and the same time the heroine smacked her lover across the face with her glove and the author threw down a deliberate challenge to 'respectable' society. The play in question revolves round an innocent young lady's discovery that, in erotic affairs, her fiancé is less innocent than she, and its implicit and explicit arguments advanced the doctrine of a rigid single standard of sexual morality for men and women. Bjørnson pursued the theme first in his novel *The Flags are Out in Town and Harbour* and, pushed to its extreme, in a lecture with which he stumped all the northern lands and which he provocatively advertised as on 'Monogamists and Polygamists'.

The Feud was, as has been said, a highly ramified one. It was provoked by a debate on marital obligations (which Ibsen's *Ghosts* came to acerbate in 1881); it had a link even with the long parliamentary debates on the novelist Kielland's state pension, which was the proximate cause of the *Venstre*'s disintegration; and, towards its end it became entangled with the *Bohêmefejde* (the 'Bohemia' feud),[1] mainly centred on mere lechery. As an author, Bjørnson was not involved in the latter. But it placed him between two fires. The *tendens* of *A Gauntlet* had rallied to his side the puritans who brought about the prosecution of two of the 'Bohemia' novelists; but, nauseated though he might be by their revelations, he could not, as an unflinching advocate of free speech, refrain from inveighing against the action taken against them by an ostensibly Liberal government. None the less, his own puritanism had alienated many of his radical friends, among them notably Georg Brandes.[2]

The Danish critic's name leads on to the last head under which general 'problems' are to be considered in this section, namely Bjørnson's place in *Det moderne Gjennembrud*, the Modern Break-Through, or The Break-Through to Modernity.[3] Its focal point was the inaugural lecture[4] which Georg Brandes, all afire with the ideas of Sainte-Beuve, Taine and John Stuart Mill, gave in the university building of Copenhagen on 3 November 1871. The thesis therein propounded was that literature had lost itself in a world of dreams, make-believe, nostalgia and vague, metaphysical speculations and had resigned its essential function of projecting into imaginative forms ideas and ideals through which men and women could determine their values and regulate their behaviour in the world they were actually living in. The heart of its positive doctrine was the dictum: 'That in our days literature is alive is shewn by its submitting problems to debate.'[1] As for the kind of problems that should be so submitted and that in fact had been submitted by advanced writers abroad Brandes instanced Byron and Feuerbach on religion, Proudhon on property, George Sand on marriage, the younger Dumas on irregular relationships between the sexes and Augier on social relations more generally.

Brandes's challenge raised at once an uncommon stir in all the literary circles of the North.[2] In Denmark and Sweden, at least, a new inspiration was overdue; it was only too manifest that for long no authors of comparable stature had come forward to replace the great men, now all dead or dying, who had been the glory of their Romantic literature and that those carefully walking in their footsteps had nothing of interest to offer.

In Norway, as Brandes himself allowed, the situation was different. Three great Romantic poems, which no one could stigmatize as dreamy, etiolated or imitative, had been published in the last few years—Ibsen's *Brand* and *Peer Gynt*, Bjørnson's *Arnljot Gelline*—and their authors were in the prime of life. For all that, in Norway too a change took place, more sudden and more striking even than in the sister-countries. After they had published their collected poems in 1871 and 1870 respectively, these two all but gave up writing verse; it became palpable that they were concentrating their energies on depicting the society of their day and submitting its problems to debate, and they were soon seconded by others doing the same. The stimulus from Brandes cannot be gainsaid; we know that all these authors had heard the call from the Copenhagen lecture-room and that for Ibsen it was an immediate, shattering experience.

This cannot be said of Bjørnson. He and Brandes had known of one another's activities since the middle 'sixties, but, as late as 1872, Brandes, for Bjørnson, was just a nasty little Jew-boy;[3] later they were fairly close friends until the divergence of their views on polygamy wrought a breach never to be fully healed. In their copious correspondence,[4] though always suspicious of one another's basic values, they were constantly exchanging ideas and encouragement. Besides giving him good critical advice on his work as it was advancing, Brandes lauded Bjørnson as one of the champions of his Break-Through, and Bjørnson, convinced that all great writers showed *tendens* in their work,[1] appreciated its necessity and importance. There is a distinct echo of Brandes's famous dictum in what he said of *The King*: 'When I wrote this play my principal aim was to extend the limits of free debate.'[2] But it induced in him no such *crise de conscience* as he had undergone over the composition of *The Fisher Lass*. Already there and in *The Newly Wed* he had been groping his way towards his later manner, and long before 1871 he had heard a good deal more about the founding fathers of Brandes's philosophy than just their names.[3] His mind and art would have developed, perhaps more slowly, as they did, if Brandes had never come to his notice. It is interesting that, as far back as 1855, he had, in a piece of journalism, forecast that the future of literature lay with 'naturalism'.[4]

(5) *Bjørnson's drama after 1871*

Surprise may be felt today at finding the name of Émile Augier in Brandes's list of models for the new literature. While, however, the playwrights of the almost forgotten Common Sense School (*L'Ecole de bon Sens*), in which Augier held high place, were flourishing, they not only supplied all the theatres of the Western world, but were also well received by the critics. What at this time particularly attracted Brandes to them was their declared hostility to the wildly Romantic drama of Victor Hugo and the criticisms of society which they conveyed through their relatively sober and realistic plays of contemporary life.[5]

So when, after collecting his *Poems*, publishing *Arnljot Gelline* and finishing off *Sigurd the Crusader*, Bjørnson turned away from Romanticism, it was natural that, as a man of the theatre thoroughly familiar with the plays of Augier and his associates,[6] he should advance in their tracks. *A Bankruptcy*, *The Editor* and *The King* mark the first steps.

†*A Bankruptcy* (*En Fallit*, 1875)[7] presents first the crash of a

provincial business man from speculation and the near-fraudulent means he adopted for disguising his true position, and then his conversion to honest practices through the devotion of his family, his confidential clerk and the lawyer who originally uncovered his misdoings. To the main story is closely tied the sub-plot of the clerk's love for his employer's daughter, who at first disdains him, but, brought round to the recognition of his finer qualities, herself makes the proposal of marriage which ends that business. This was the most unconventional thing in the play, but an audience of the time could easily assimilate it and the other slightly unusual features—the provincial scene, the discussion of money-matters, an incursion of furious workmen—when together with them they had before them the familiar figures of a repentant sinner, his sick wife, their humbled proud daughter, her lowly admirer and the fortune-hunter who jilts her sister.

† *The Editor* (*Redaktøren*, 1875)[1] carries heavier guns. Its tone is sombre throughout; it involves a death on the stage; the causer of the dramatic 'mischief', moreover, may be left contrite, but there is no guarantee that he has reformed. He is the editor of a conservative newspaper whose venomous animadversions on a liberal candidate for parliament bring on the fatality alluded to. There is *tendens* here of a different order from that of *A Bankruptcy*. It is not only that the liberal stalwarts are presented in a uniformly favourable light, while their opponent is a villain, and that a Gallio among their friends has the dangers of political indifference sharply brought home to him, but Bjørnson's militant puritanism even peeps out in the somewhat complicated plotting devised for bringing down the catastrophe: if a certain man-servant had not been a devotee of the bottle, it would not have occurred. This fortuitous circumstance, however, does not invalidate the thesis for which Bjørnson wrote his play, that when the press abandons the discussion of principles and resorts to personalities it engenders a reign of terror with consequences that may be of the most sinister kind—a thesis which received point from the identification, immediately made, of the unnamed editor with Friele, the redoubtable power behind the Christiania *Morgenblad*.

The Editor marked an advance in realism both of dialogue and character-drawing, but it could not equal the popularity of *A Bankruptcy*. The pillorying of a well-known contemporary precluded its acceptance by the respectable Christiania Theater; and though malfeasances of the press were not confined to Norway—Augier had exposed them on the stage in *The Brazen* (*Les Effrontés*)—the field of *The Editor*'s activities seemed too provincial to rouse in foreign audiences the indignation requisite for counterbalancing the lack of superficial 'entertainment value'. The printed book, however, made a stir for showing that in his imaginative writings as well as in his other doings Bjørnson had become a Dangerous Man.

This became more glaringly evident in the next play, as Bjørnson was so well aware in advance as to envisage a first edition in English translation. That, however, came to nothing, and † *The King* (*Kongen*) was published, in 1877, in the original text.[1]

In this new play he flew very high, at nothing lower than the institution of kingship, in particular the constitutional variety developed during the nineteenth century. The main criticism implied in it was twofold: that it was still surrounded by too much feudal pomp, etiquette and religious aureole, setting an impenetrable barrier between the king and the vast majority of his subjects; and that the shrunken amount of responsible duty left him reduced his stature to that of the chairman of an insurance company, primarily concerned to insure the directors and their friends against threats to their monopolistic power. The positive side of his thesis, which in effect called for the short-term presidency of a hard-working administrator on the Swiss model, made it clear, not least to the ruling monarch, that this dangerous power behind the Party of the Left was working for the establishment of a Republic in Norway.

The investing of Bjørnson's theme was entirely fictitious, however. He presents as his hero a rather commonplace, slightly degenerate young man who comes to realize the nature of his office as Bjørnson sees it. The realization is effected through two persons: one, a young schoolmistress, the daughter of a notorious radical, with whom he falls in love during a masked ball, who returns his love, infuses him with her ideals and becomes against all the opposition of the Court engaged to him; the other an influential, liberal-minded business man, who became his friend when they were serving together in the navy, and who brings him into contact with subjects of his outside Court circles. He sees visions of popular kingship as well as of a cosy home. The play ends in catastrophe—brought about by means more melodramatic than Bjørnson had so far employed in his modern dramas: the fiancée falls dead on seeing the phantom of her father, the friend is killed in a grotesque duel he foolishly consents to fight. These two fatalities occur almost simultaneously. The shock of them, the shattering of his visions, his realization of complete loneliness and unfitness for any decent mode of life now open to him, drive the king to suicide.

The abundance of movement, the magnitude of the subject no less than the tragic outcome and the two accidents leading up to it make 'good theatre'; the improbability of these accidents granted, the whole of the story so far described keeps well within the limits of modern social drama à la Augier. Bjørnson has now perfected his dialogue, economical and idiomatic; the numerous characters are clearly differentiated, the public and private themes in mesh, sympathy for the king as a man admirably offsetting the indignation at the basic causes for his predicament that Bjørnson intended to rouse. One element in *The King*, however, is quite alien to the usual well-constructed *pièce-à-thèse*. That is a series of verse intermezzi, effective enough in themselves, between the acts of the earthly drama in which, somewhat after the manner of a Greek chorus, disembodied spirits are introduced, commenting on and apparently affecting its course—the device Hardy was to use in *The Dynasts*, but Bjørnson never again.

At irregular intervals during the next thirty-two years Bjørnson wrote eleven more plays, all in prose, all theatrically effective, all embodying a thesis of the author's or at least intended to convey what the eighteenth century called 'an useful moral'. Besides *A Gauntlet*, already sufficiently dealt with in connexion with the *Sædelighedsfejde*, only three of them can be singled out for special notice here: *Beyond Our Powers, Geography and Love* and *Paul Lange and Tora Parsberg*.[1]

At the opposite extreme to *A Gauntlet* stands †*Geography and Love* (*Geografi og Kjærlighed*, 1885). In the thick of the earnest debate over the former, Bjørnson indulged himself in a frolic, a high-spirited comedy, farcical enough while just keeping within the bounds of credibility. A professor of Geography is shown getting what he thinks he wants, complete freedom to devote himself to his researches without interference from his womenfolk, but finding that the Eveless fortress into which he has converted his house is anything but an earthly paradise, so that, in the end, he has to come to terms with the enemy. Delighted audiences recognized in the ebullient hobby-horse rider Professor Tygesen someone uncommonly like the author himself, giving himself a public admonition to be flexible and accept reasonable compromises.

A different Bjørnson is put on the stage in †*Paul Lange and Tora Parsberg* (*Paul Lange og Tora Parsberg*, 1898), the Bjørnson who was his Party's conscience. A tragedy, based on events ten years back, when from public duty he had brought about the disgrace of his former friend and ally, the Liberal politician Richter,[1] the play is one of his masterpieces. The integration of the public and private action is even closer than in *The King*, notably in the splendid second act, in a political drawing-room, when the long-sustained, mounting excitement and indignation at Paul Lange's last speech in Parliament is quelled by the coming of the hostess Tora Parsberg with the request to hand her in to dinner. Bjørnson never handled a crowded scene better, never made debate, whether in a crowd or—as in the quiet Acts I and III—between two persons, more effective in dramatic terms. Though he presented himself in Arne Kraft, it is remarkable that Bjørnson never came near to turning his play into either a self-justification or a lecture on politics. A 'fable' from real life is treated with complete artistic integrity.

For all its equally fine embodiment in a dramatic action, †*Beyond Our Powers* (*Over Ævne I*, 1883)[2] has, from the title onwards, *tendens* as a prime ingredient. Written with the same emotional involvement as *Paul Lange and Tora Parsberg*, it comes from the author's pen at the culmination of his long and agonizing religious wrestling. It amounts to a denial of the supernatural, through the failure of a reputed miracle-worker by means of prayer to heal his paralytic wife. Theme and story are magnificently invested: first and foremost through the character of the central figure, a sincere, humble clergyman, free of all cant and self-deception, and at the same time a devoted, understanding husband and father, killed by the realization of limits to his powers just when for a brief moment he believes that they have bent Heaven to his purposes. Then there is the twofold setting: on the one hand, the poor country parsonage isolated amid threatening forces of nature, and, on the other hand, a vast concourse of folk (tactfully kept out of sight, but not out of hearing), attracted both by the 'miracles' that have been performed and the miracle that is expected, including a party of clergymen, reverently and on occasion humorously treated, who discuss miracles from various standpoints. And lastly there are the strong, but legitimate theatrical effects—organ-music, hallelujahs, church-bells and the like—with the fatal collapse of Pastor Sang and his wife at the acme of their hopes. Much as he disliked pietism and all its ways, Georg Brandes was forced to admit: 'Bjørnson never did anything finer—nor Ibsen either.'[1]

(From the first, Bjørnson planned to complement the negative aspect of his theme with a more positive counterpart. That was ultimately attempted in *Beyond Our Powers*, Part II (1894), and far from successfully: the field is removed from religion to a rather naïve sociology, and, if the title is again to be interpreted by the action, the inference must be that to solve differences between employers and employees by direct action is also Beyond Our Powers. Lacking all the human interest that makes the strength of Part I, it is no more than a melodrama about an industrial dispute—done much better by Galsworthy in *Strife*—interesting only because its schematic personages and arguments adumbrate some of the methods and ideas of the later Expressionist dramatists).[2]

Among Bjørnson's plays, then, three are outstanding: *Sigurd the Bad, Beyond Our Powers* (Part I) and *Paul Lange and Tora Parsberg*, all on weighty themes pursued with immense power to a tragic end. At their centre stand in clear lineaments memorable personages, affording first-rate acting opportunities.

They move amid a large, fluid and animated company of well-marked, credible minor figures who contribute to what is perhaps these plays' greatest strength, the convincing solidity of their social setting. The scenario is carefully and economically constructed to keep the focus steadily on the main theme and to preserve dramatic tension throughout.

The remainder of Bjørnson's plays fall a good deal below the standard of his great three, save for these workmanlike qualities, which, admirable as they are, towards the end of his career often constitute their principal recommendation. It is commonly said that Bjørnson's work is deficient in psychological penetration; and it is certainly true that it was never his aim, nor was it his unconscious achievement, to explore any of the characters he projected to the deeps that Ibsen plumbed. In themselves the personages in these lesser plays— and consequently their predicaments—rouse no vital interest; Professor Tygesen may *amuse*, but he does not interest. On the other hand, the sound construction does not build up to those *scènes-à-faire* whose sheer theatrical power renders other criteria of judgement irrelevant. The fairest comparison here would be, not with Sardou or Ibsen, but still with Émile Augier, his fellow in sincerity, liberality, courage and honest workmanship.

A last small point: Bernard Shaw gave special praise to Ibsen for inventing the drama of discussion.[1] The credit for the innovation, which Shaw himself adopted with such signal success, might go to Bjørnson rather than to Ibsen. The scene in *Getting Married* which is nothing but a round-table colloquium on marriage is strikingly anticipated in *Leonarda* (1879), where a number of persons go through the same exercise, also under the chairmanship of a bishop.

(6) *Bjørnson's fiction after 1871*

On turning again to the writing of novels, Bjørnson took much longer to find a manner suited to his new utilitarian ideal than that he had so quickly evolved for his plays.[2] So disappointing were †*Magnhild* (1877), and †*Captain Mansana* (*Kaptejn Mansana*, 1879) that Georg Brandes recommended him to take lessons in the contemporary French school of fiction. He complied, but with small profit. The bases of their Naturalism were abhorrent to him—its determinism, its insistence on the lustful beast of prey in man, its justification for dwelling on squalor and corruption on grounds both scientific and aesthetic.[1] It was not until he had been given congenial native examples of a middle-of-the-road realism by Lie and Kielland, now at the height of their powers, that he was able to work out the synthesis of truth-to-life, *tendens* and imaginative appeal to which he aspired.

Lie and Kielland were novelists in the English tradition, in the same broad sense as Bjørnson the dramatist was in the Augier tradition; and Bjørnson, who had followed up his course in French with one on English literature, is equally to be ranged in it. Superficially, this shows in Bjørnson's two most substantial novels, of which the earlier, † *The Flags are out in Town and Harbour* (*Det flager i Byen og paa Havnen*), appeared in 1884, with its somewhat rambling construction, the relatively large number of persons whose interlocking fortunes are related in some detail, the boisterousness of its humour and its lapse into theatricality.[2]

The propaganda in the book is also of English inspiration. Bjørnson, whose reading of books in English in the years just before the publication of *The Flags are Out* was by no means confined to fiction,[3] had been deeply impressed by Herbert Spencer's *Education*, and—to the degree in which *Little Dorrit* is a diatribe against the civil service—his novel is a tractate on that subject. It is a somewhat confused one, since it is the education of the *male* in sexual ethics that the author of *A Gauntlet* had at heart, while it is now a *girls'* school, teaching Hygiene in its 'advanced' syllabus and encouraging free discussion among its pupils, round which he built his story and, as a summary will show, the effect of its programme was, in a cardinal point, singularly unsuccessful.

Nevertheless, Bjørnson was happily inspired in his setting. He liked the company of young girls, seems to have won their confidence and had an uncommon talent in delineating them. His Nora, Tora, Tinka and Milla, who form the headmistress's 'general staff', are all admirably done; they give *The Flags are Out* a freshness and gaiety that cover over its unevennesses and doctrinal anomalies and make it the most generally liked of Bjørnson's novels, With the predominance of the feminine element a story likely to win the habitual novel-reader lay to hand. One of the girls had to 'get into trouble'. Over-sexed and impetuous Tora (who acts like a complete little fool throughout) is gotten with child by a wealthy and licentious naval lieutenant, who thereupon proposes to make a match with rich, vain Milla—and Milla, though fully aware of her friend's predicament (in outline at least), is quite amenable, being as unaffected by her education on the best Bjørnsonian principles as Tora. The upshot is a scene in the grand tradition of melodrama; the unmarried mother flings herself and her babe before the altar at the fashionable wedding for which all the flags are out in town and harbour. The intimation, to wind up with, that the future of his odd school is assured through the betrothal of the headmaster to the steadiest of his girls comes as an anti-climax of an equally bizarre character.

The wedding-scene, however, Bjørnson having thrown all *tendens* to the winds, carries everything off, its sinister kernel completely overlaid by its pulsating life and a good deal of deliberate fun that has no trace of cynicism about it: the German organist, with his fee partly in his pocket, but mostly down his gullet, making a mess of the music, and, among the smart, scandalized congregation, the old hypocrite Riis with his wife (from Bjørnson's *New System*), Consul Bernick (from Ibsen's *Pillars of Society*) singing the hymns like a young cockerel learning to crow, and, by the side of her unfaithful husband, adulterous Fru Garman (from Kielland's *Garman & Worse*) than whom none is louder in lauding holy wedlock.

On God's Paths (*Paa Guds Veje*, 1889) contains a bravura piece, comparable with this, the description of a provincial ball—hot, stuffy, a little dowdy and surrounded by a fringe of animality, but full to bursting with the energy and joy of the participants—not altogether integrated with the rest. It too, like *The Flags are Out*, has a loose kind of prologue,[1] making a gap of perhaps twenty years between the first chapters and the others. But since it rounds out three of the principal characters by showing them as children, it fits into the general

scheme more smoothly; and in structure and the fuller realization both of its theme and of the personages through whom
it is worked out *On God's Paths* surpasses its predecessor. It
should indeed be ranked among the outstanding examples of
typically Victorian fiction.

Religion, as the title suggests, is now at issue: more narrowly,
Lutheranism in Norway at the time of writing, which in
essence differed little from its counterparts among the easier
bourgeoisie throughout the western world. Its stale traditions,
dwindled to little more than a regard for church-going respectability, bring about the alienation of old friends, the clergyman
Ole Tuft and his wife Josefine on the one hand, and the free-
thinking doctor Edvard Kallem (Josefine's brother) on the
other. Worse than that, the former are held responsible for
the death of the latter's wife Ragni. Having a 'past'—no more
heinous than her divorce from her first, utterly abominable
husband—Ragni is an easy target for some quite unjustifiable
scandal which the Tufts do nothing to denounce, though they
are under the greatest obligations to the doctor for having
saved the life of their child. Shock occasioned to Ragni by
learning of the scandal and of her bad ex-husband's coming
to settle nearby brings on galloping consumption, of which
she dies. Josefine, her sense of justice not completely stifled by
her husband's narrow code, realizes the difference between
the free-thinker's Goodness and her own Grundyish Badness,
and, overwhelmed by remorse, all but commits suicide. She is
saved, however, by her brother and her husband (whose
conscience has been similarly moved), and the surviving three
agree in all amity to walk the paths of open-minded righteous-
ness and beneficence together: 'Where good folk walk, there
are God's Paths.'

It is commonly accepted that, once he had worked out a
satisfactory manner, Bjørnson wrote only two novels, *The Flags
are Out* and *On God's Paths*. †*Mary* (1906) might well be added
to the number. Bjørnson called it a 'Fortælling', using that
very useful intermediate term for which there is no good
English equivalent, and it usually goes into the class of his
short stories. Short it certainly is: but with its pregnant style,
lucid, dramatic dialogue and elimination of transitional

passages, Bjørnson contrived to pack into some 55,000 words a story covering a considerable stretch of time and introducing a goodly number of personages that, handled in the broader manner of his two undoubted novels, might have run to twice its length.

The smarter technique accords well with the vivid, impetuous Norvego-American heroine, Bjørnson's most complex 'character'. She, strikingly beautiful, intelligent, sovereign in her demeanour, but egoistic and sensual, is the heiress to a considerable fortune and to the estate of an old-established family of merchants and landowners among whose ramified members the story is played out. To one of these, a piano-playing young military officer who turns diplomat (danger signals to a reader of Bjørnson!), she becomes engaged. The marriage, however, has to be postponed when her father falls critically ill on news of great financial losses. The night before an indefinite and probably lengthy separation from Jørgen Thiis, Mary, without any solicitation or expectation on his part, gives herself to him. Finding herself pregnant, she travels to her lover to arrange for a speedy wedding. In a splendid short scene in a Stockholm street, Jørgen's obvious unwillingness to commit himself any further before her 'business affairs' are settled and, concurrently, his ill-treatment of his dog open Mary's eyes to his fundamental selfishness and cruelty. She breaks off the engagement without disclosing her condition. Eventually, she sees no way out but to do away with herself in a manner that would indicate an accident: suicide is to her more honourable than forced marriage to a cad. However, a woman doctor in the family (where Jørgen's character is better known than it had been to Mary) has tumbled to the trouble, its cause and possible outcome, and Mary is rescued by yet another relative, one of the great-hearted 'bears' beloved of Bjørnson, who has had to be let into the secret, conveys to her without any interchange of words that he does know it, that he loves her and, so to speak, 'forgives'. Fortunately, her sensuality has long been stirred by him, and a happy marriage between them is assured.

Some particulars of *Mary* were foreshadowed in the short story †'Mother's Hands' ('Mors Hænder', 1892), notably the figures of the spoiled society beauty and the great-hearted bear of a man who proves her salvation. 'Mother's Hands' is one of a group of tales which Bjørnson collected and published as *New Stories* (*Nye Fortællinger*, 1894). The more memorable among these contrast strongly with the early bucolic stories, not merely by the shift in milieu, but also by a corresponding gain in delicacy of perception and style. The name of Turgeniev indeed, is often and justly brought into criticisms of †'Dust' ('Støv', 1882). Even here, however, the author's didacticism peeps out. 'Dust' is in effect a parable on the danger of believing in angels. Similarly, †'Mother's Hands' preaches the doctrine of Work, while †'Absalom's Hair' warns against sensuality. But such undercurrents merely ripple the surface. The artistry by which they are merged with description and character-portrayal place the *New Stories* among the finest of their kind in a literature that, since *Synnøve Solbakken*, has been very rich in them.

Bjørnson's fiction shows a development—to which his last plays offer something of a parallel[1]—a growing preoccupation with artistic form, to which a counterpart can be seen in his public activity. As the doughty old cudgel-player became the advocate of universal arbitration, so, in the sphere of private morals, his imperatives lost their categorical nature. *Mary* proves how far the uncompromising author of *A Gauntlet* had advanced to the recognition that circumstances alter cases. His heroine may have been lucky after all, but Bjørnson clearly thinks that she deserved to be. Tolerance triumphed in the end.

3

IBSEN BEFORE 1884

(1) *Juvenilia*

IBSEN* took longer to find his feet than Bjørnson, his junior by nearly five years, whose *Synnøve Solbakken* established him as a leading figure in Norwegian literature before he was twenty-five. It was not until the year after *Synnøve Solbakken* that with *The Vikings in Helgeland* (1858), published in his thirty-first year and eight years after his formal début as an author, Ibsen gave unmistakable evidence of his powers. The plays he had written before had marked him as a promising purveyor of theatrical entertainment, though (with one exception) they did not meet with much favour either when new or later.

Ibsen's six juvenilia[1] all, however, have points of interest, largely extrinsic. The first of them, *Catiline* (*Catilina*, 1850)— three acts almost wholly in blank verse—which the young author founded on texts prescribed for his matriculation examination, betrays a bent towards the dramatic form and understanding of its potentialities somewhat remarkable in a lad from the country with no native models to guide him; where freely invented, the plot is constructed round a man under cross-fire from two women, the situation already to which in his

---

* Henrik Johan Ibsen was born in the small town of Skien on 20 March 1828, the son of a thriving merchant, whose failure in business not long afterwards cast an enduring blight on the family. After indifferent schooling, young Henrik became a pharmacist's assistant at Grimstad and six years later, in the spring of 1850, moved to Christiania intending to become a university student. This came to very little; for eighteen months afterwards he accepted a post as 'house-poet' and (later) stage-manager at the new Norske Theater in Bergen. This he held for 5½ years, going on to the directorship of the Møllergate theatre in Christiania, until it failed in 1862. In 1864 he left Norway and, partially supported by a parliamentary pension from 1866 onwards, made his home first in Italy and then in Germany. Royalties from his works and shrewd investments eventually made him well-to-do, and he received many decorations, which he liked to display. In 1891 he settled in Christiania where he died, a paralytic, on 23 May 1906. In 1858 he married Susannah Thoresen, the daughter of a Bergen clergyman, who survived him and by whom he had one child, Sigurd Ibsen (1859–1930), politician and author.

maturity he was to have frequent recourse; and the theme, even if in a sense forced upon him, illustrated a sympathetic concern with rebels against the established order on which for long his reputation was to be grounded.

With *The Warrior's Barrow* (*Kjæmpehøjen*, one act in verse), Ibsen found his way on to the stage when it was produced, for three performances in all, at the Christiania Theater on 26 September 1850; and to it he owed the appointment which kept him as resident dramatist to the Norske Theater at Bergen: for its setting, in the Viking Age, admirably conformed to his employers' National-Romantic aims. This is equally true of the four new plays with which Ibsen honoured his contract: *St John's Night* (*Sancthansnatten*, 1853), a phantasia having a good deal in common with Shakespeare's *Midsummer Night's Dream* and giving a foretaste of the topical satire which was to be fully developed in *Love's Comedy* and *Peer Gynt*; *Lady Inger of Østraat* (*Fru Inger til Østerraad*, 1855); and two pieces which through music, costume, motifs taken from folk-lore conjured up a 'medieval ballad atmosphere', *The Feast at Solhaug* (*Gildet paa Solhaug*, 1856), which was its author's first success, and its weaker replica,[1] *Olaf Liljekrans* (1857).

Lady Inger altogether lacks the fantastical and poetic elements prominent in the other three Bergen plays.[2] Nevertheless, it fitted into the National Romanticists' programme well enough, taking its subject from the patriotic history of the expiring Middle Ages, an episode in the Norwegians' last attempt to shake off the Danish yoke. The episode in itself is obscure, and the play Ibsen made out of it is a very tenebrous affair, all played out by night, involving through disguises and intrigues much groping for identifications, motives and intentions and ending in the murder of a son at the instigation of his unwitting mother, who then runs mad. It is, however, the most impressive of these early plays, chiefly for the skill, learned from Scribe, with which Ibsen cast into theatrical form his complicated, indeed over-abundant, material. All the same it cannot be ranked higher than respectable melodrama.

(2) *Ibsen's Christiania plays 1858–64*

The Vikings in Helgeland (*Hærmændene paa Helgeland*, 1858),[1] completed after Ibsen had left Bergen, resembles *Lady Inger* superficially in a number of ways—its preference for scenes of night and mirk, the superabundance of matter, including a good deal of violent action both on and off the stage, a large number of participants, the concentration of interest upon the principal woman among them and its near-tragic end. But it has a greater 'weight', to use Ibsen's own term,[2] which effectually takes it out of the category of costume drama. That weight makes itself felt in four things: the terse, sometimes gnomic dialogue, skilfully and appropriately adapted to theatrical use from the Icelandic sagas; the consistency with which the atmosphere of a heroic age is maintained; the characterization of the villainess-heroine Hjørdis; and the intricately compacted construction organically bound up with this.

In *The Vikings of Helgeland* some of the action still arises from misconstruance *à la* Scribe of events not actually presented. Such instances of *qui-pro-quo*, however, are firmly made subservient to the psychological core which is hedged by no ambiguity. The fatal mistrust and strife between the two bands of Vikings who meet in Helgeland, it quickly becomes apparent, is the work of Hjørdis, who seemingly has no delight but mischief, the bloodier the better—best of all if it can involve her pacific husband, Gunnar. The grounds of her ferocious, but unformulated discontent are revealed in two stages—first to others, at last to Hjørdis herself. She has, quite literally, married the wrong man. It was not Gunnar who, years ago in Iceland, paid the price for her possession by killing the polar bear at her bower door, but, by proxy for him, his friend Sigurd, who now comes into her life again, accompanied by his wife Dagny. Hjørdis, both personally and publicly humiliated as the object of a fraudulent deal, resolves that one of the two men must be eliminated, so that, she thinks, she may be assured of getting the better of them, the true hero, for her mate. Sigurd makes it plain that though he is prepared to fight Gunnar, he will not do so to the end proposed by Hjørdis: he has become a Christian and his marriage to Dagny is indissoluble. Thus finally frustrated, Hjørdis kills Sigurd and disappears from the scene.

The continued interaction between the happenings far away in the past and what is enacted in the present affords the first full example in Ibsen's works of the 'analytic technique' with which he made himself one of the supreme masters of stage-craft. The dramaturgy of all the great modern plays from the second half of his active life (except *An Enemy of the People*) is grounded upon it. It is nowhere more apparent—to some tastes it may even be overworked there—than in the first of them, *Pillars of Society*, where three complicated old stories, of amorous intrigue, family finance and commercial enterprise have to be unravelled for setting out the situation in Consul Bernick's household; and not merely for setting it out, but in the process also advancing its piece-by-piece development to crisis and solution. The *Oedipus Rex* of Sophocles and Shake-speare's *Hamlet* are there to remind us that Ibsen did not invent a retrospective technique.[1] The distinctive achievement of his formally most characteristic dramas was to exhibit *ab initio* the infection of guilt or error in the psyche of their leading personages and, with marvellous economy, unfold the process by which, long before the rise of the curtain, the germs of guilt and error had been implanted and proliferated, often inducing a true deterioration of mind and conditioning the characters for the predicament the action of the play forces upon them.[2] For this the unwitting sinner Oedipus and the initially innocent Hamlet afford no precedent.

The diffuser action of *The Pretenders* (*Kongs-Emnerne*, 1864)[3] hardly brings the analytic technique into play. But the end it was made to subserve is equally patent. Hettner, the German critic, whose *Modern Drama* Ibsen had known since its publica-tion in 1852, had insisted that to be of more than local or trivial appeal a historical drama must also be a psychological drama. In embodying Hettner's doctrine Ibsen created the last great historical play in the rich Shakespeare-inspired line going back to the days of Goethe's youth. In a series of highly variegated scenes, public, semi-public and private, its overt aim is to show (veraciously enough) the process by which King Haakon IV made himself supreme over his rivals and, another Richmond, put an end to the barbarous civil wars which had rent Norway as the Wars of the Roses were to rend England in a later century.

The vital element, however, resides in the characters of the three contestants for power, all of the blood-royal: that of Haakon himself; that of Bishop Nikolas, essentially a self-centred, barren intriguer; and that of Earl Skule. It is the last which is most deeply probed. Hitherto Haakon's subject, Skule has himself proclaimed king by a powerful party of dissidents, but is unable to follow up the initial victory he wins in the field and virtually runs on Haakon's sword. The crucial point is Skule's faltering when the ball is at his feet. Pondering too closely upon the event, he has come to doubt whether the game is worth the candle. He can exercise power, but only through the collection of ruffians in his train, who will do no more than perpetuate the massacres and rapine of the past century, while he sees Haakon, clear-eyed and resolute, both possessed of and able to actualize the 'kingly thought' of creating a united nation where previously there had at best been no more than a centralized state. It may be thought that guilt and deterioration are no very obvious factors in Skule's tragedy. Hesitation is not a crime. But a liegeman has turned against his king, and his heart-searchings make him less and less fit to take his place.

With rare optimism Ibsen allows the man with a good mission to prevail. The question of a man's mission in life, its prerogatives and its terrible hazards was to be canvassed in almost all his subsequent works; and as deeply as Bjørnson in *The Fisher Lass* he pondered on his poetic vocation. Doubter as he was, like Earl Skule, he could not doubt that. Yet, should his 'call' bring want, even shame on those for whom it was his duty to provide, ought he not to silence it and settle down, for instance, in the steady post in the Customs that was his for the asking?

Brand, next to follow, was to be the supreme working out of the general problem. But it had provided a strand already in the play that had come between *The Vikings in Helgeland* and *The Pretenders*, *Love's Comedy* (*Kjærlighedens Komedie*, 1862)— a slighter one, but more closely tied than *Brand* to the author's own predicament. For its hero, Falk, is a poet, determined to be a poet, and egoistically seeing everything else in his life as subordinate to this call. The girl of his heart, Svanhild, who is equally in love with him, realizes this, and he loses her in consequence. For all the high spirits of *Love's Comedy*, Ibsen said that, at the time he wrote it, he was desperately concerned to disburden himself of the theme and the mood. He never did quite disburden himself, and *Love's Comedy* cannot have helped him much. Falk, attractive lover though he may be, is a light-weight; there is nothing to show that he is a poet of any account or that, when at the end he goes off on tour with an all-male glee-party, he will ever be heard of again. An interesting point, however, is the resolution he has come to in the collapse of his love-affair: his poetry henceforth shall be 'lived', in other words, the energy and aspirations he intended to put into verse can and shall go into action. The light-weight's idea may, at this juncture, have been his creator's, but was soon discarded.

Love's Comedy was originally to be called after its heroine, Svanhild.[1] The scenes in which she is prominent are seriously treated; reticent though she is, no one can doubt the reality of her passion, and in her love-encounters with Falk the verse rises to heights of undeniable beauty. Elsewhere, however, the metrical quirks, the sparkle and the wit, together with the surrounding gaiety of the scene, the music, the bustle, antics and talk of the lesser characters (and those of Falk, for that matter), may remind him who reads *Love's Comedy* in C. H. Herford's brilliant version of the libretti of W. S. Gilbert. Ibsen shows himself as anything but the solemn owl shied at by orthodox critics in later years. He could not only be a scintillating versifier, but also, for all to whom irony is not allergic, a humorist.

In *Love's Comedy* the humour is good-natured enough, at times farcical. It fastens on the grotesque side of middle-class courtship amid its inevitable chorus of vigilant mamma, facetious or coy family friends and noisy celebrations. There is, none the less, satire in it, satire with a sting.[2] It shows up the sentimental identification of erotic play, even passion, with matrimony and, in so doing, links the broad fun with the graver story of Svanhild and Falk. For Svanhild has a second admirer, the elderly, rich, kindly business-man Guldstad, who pretends to no infatuation and whose straightforward offer of a *mariage de convenance* she ultimately accepts. This transfer of her loyalty is managed with great understanding and delicacy, not derogating in the least from her firm, fine character, so that the last word of the comedy, 'Hurrah', can leave no bitter taste in the mouth. At the same time, it is a riposte on the romantic prepossession underlying *The Sheriff's Daughters*, as a pointed reference[1] makes explicit. Svanhild and Falk are the counterparts of Camilla Collett's heroine and hero, but Svanhild is given the full, free choice of a mate and, having it, puts passion behind her and opts for steady affection.

(3) *1866–73*

National Romanticism with two capital letters was on the wane in the eighteen-sixties, as Bjørnson's career showed. After *The Pretenders* Ibsen too moved further and further away from a movement to which he had perhaps never been wholeheartedly committed. From the forms of Romanticism in the wider sense, however—and some of its motifs too—he was not to break for some time yet. The nine-year period following on 1864, the year when he uprooted himself from his native land, was punctuated by the publication of five books by him, of which *The League of Youth* (1869) is a robustious, up-to-the-minute prose farce, but all the others, on the face of them, the work of a great romantic writer: *Brand* (1866), *Peer Gynt* (1867), the collected *Poems* (1871) and *Emperor and Galilean* (1873).

First and foremost stand *Brand* and *Peer Gynt*. Both would be defined by Polonius as 'epical-dramatical',[2] lengthy poems presented in dialogue (or soliloquy) with 'stage-directions' and, in spite of these and the essentially scenic character of all their episodes, not written for the stage, alike also in their verse-structure of loose, rhymed paragraphs and the combination of the grotesque and comic with the moving and the grim. They form complements to one another, a contrasting diptych, as it were, the one half by Jean-qui-pleure and the other by Jean-qui-rit, centred on two figures whose characters and fortunes contrast as completely as the tones of their background —Norway of the fjords and glaciers in *Brand*, Norway of the rich dales and infinite spaces in *Peer Gynt*.[1]

Brand[2] is a young clergyman, whose heroism in rowing out through a howling storm to shrive an anguished sinner induces his native village to invite him to its vacant pulpit. He cannot refuse the call. For two guiding principles his training for the ministry have implanted in him: the active and inexorable might of the First Person of the Trinity, and the demand made on man to do his duty in that station of life to which it may please God to call him. His mission henceforth is exemplary as well as hortative. To the duty laid upon himself he sacrifices the tender young wife he has taken and their infant son— victims as they become of the merciless physical and moral climate of their home—and also all the worldly possessions he inherits from his mother, to whom, on her death-bed, he has refused absolution since she has withheld the earnest of repentance he demanded.

That demand had been to give All or Nothing, the same that Brand puts also on his wife in compelling her to part with the last mementoes of their dead baby to a beggar, from which in the service of his God he himself never flinches and which in the end he endeavours to impose on his flock when, as a proof that their worship of that God is 'in spirit and in truth', he induces them to abandon their homes and the new church he has built for them and go with him on a pilgrimage to a chimerical Sinai. But here they break; they turn and stone him; and he is broken too. Through supernatural promptings it is revealed to him, and he is convinced, that in his demands he has neglected one thing needful, Charity. The *Deus Caritatis* sweeps him to himself in a down-rush of his Sinai's rock and ice.

A summary of *Brand* reads like that of a revivalist tract. Carried away by the poetry and compulsive power of what had gone before, humanists overlooked the end. Ibsen certainly intended no Kierkegaardian parable.[3] His purpose he clearly defined in two pronouncements: the first, the purely literary aim, to portray 'an energetic personality', whose clerical status was immaterial; the second, written into an official petition to the Crown, to make his people 'think greatly'.

The energetic personality undoubtedly gave an example of thinking greatly in one sense, and he made a host of others think greatly in another sense too and give robust expression to their thoughts. In uncounted pulpits and newspapers of every northern country Ibsen's characters and ideas became the subject of passionate argument. There was less of this, quite naturally, when the lighter *Peer Gynt*[1] appeared. Even if Peer could show himself brisk and purposeful enough when it suited his book, he could scarcely qualify as an 'energetic personality', and the essential thing about him is that, from temperament and convenience, he preferred to 'go round about' and certainly he did not 'think greatly'. In the diptych the man of no principle fronts the man of iron principle. If for any reason, however, we feel like condemning the one, it by no means follows that we are to approve the other; there is a curious resemblance about their latter end: failure and futility.

Ibsen used occasionally to refer to later plays of his as his 'tom-fooleries'; but there was no such sardonic irony in his begging readers of *Peer Gynt* to take it as a 'frolic'. The chances and changes of a play-boy's life-story follow swift on one another in a highly coloured kaleidoscope: scenes of bustle and rough fun, such as those of the village wedding of Act I and in the Hall of the King of Dovre, when Peer struggles with the Trolls, or in the lunatic asylum of Cairo to which he is consigned; the episode of a travelling tycoon's fooling by a second-rate dancing-girl; 'theatrically' effective incidents as that in which Peer pushes his fellow-survivor from shipwreck to his death or, in a phantasy congenial to both, drives his dying mother to Soria-Moria castle; witty interchanges of a not too recondite sort between Peer and the Devil (disguised as a missioner), or the ominous Button-Moulder who eventually is to 'melt him down' in the hope of using the material for something better. Offsetting such diversions, there are the scenes to which Solveig —waiting, girl and old woman, all her life for the return of her 'boy'—gives a great, simple beauty, and, over all, the supple mastery of Ibsen's verse.

But Ibsen would not be Ibsen if the pantomime, the tension and the beauty were not shot with satire. Not too blatant to jar on the rough-and-tumble of the Dovre King's court or the

Cairo alienist's establishment, there are some pretty shrewd digs at some of the prevailing nationalism's pet hobby-horses, its cult of 'ye olde Norroway' (the unsavoury Trolls) and of the 'aboriginal' Landsmaal (the mad philologist who wants to reduce Malabarese to the purity of the ancestral ape-language).[1] Nor, seductive, mercurial, inexhaustibly imaginative though he made him, was Ibsen taken in by his hero any more than Shakespeare was by Falstaff.

The contrasting portraits of the man of principle who sacrifices all to his mission and the man with no principles and no mission were eventually partnered by a third in even greater proportions. The 'world-historical' drama *Emperor and Galilean* (*Kejser og Galilæer*, 1873)[2] is the study of a man who has a 'call', responds to it with all the energy of Brand, and ultimately goes against it. Constantine the Great's nephew Julian, a Christian to begin with, abjures his faith; on becoming emperor he reinstates the pagan cults and, finding them as unsatisfactory as Christianity, undertakes the conquest of the world for the purpose of founding a Third Empire, not that of State or Church, only to perish more wretchedly even than Parson Brand. For his mission has just sickered away in the desert sand where he meets his final defeat, and he is succeeded by a Christian general.

Mr Wilson Knight extols[3] *Emperor and Galilean* as 'the greatest dramatic document of its century', and Ibsen always gave it a high place among his works. His predilection may in part be attributed to the sheer magnitude of the subject, inflated by the interest attaching to the great historical revolt against Christianity at a time when inferences drawn from biblical criticism and scientific discoveries were launching a new one.[4] It may also be explained by his pride in working on a definite, highly esteemed dialectical scheme, Hegel's celebrated doctrine of thesis (here paganism) and antithesis (Christianity) issuing in synthesis (the 'Third Empire'). But, in fact, the synthesis is neither achieved nor elaborated, scarcely adumbrated. As already the earliest searching critique complained,[5] all its ten acts revolve round the Third Empire, and in the end we know no more about it than we did at the beginning.

Ibsen's preparatory work had been long and thorough. In

spite of his 'little Latin and less Greek', he had immersed himself in the historical sources at his disposal:[1] a distinguished classical historian in Cambridge used to advise his pupils that for obtaining a general picture of the fourth century they could do no better than begin with *Emperor and Galilean*. As a scenario, too, it is satisfactory: the selection from the great mass of material to illustrate not only the forces with which Julian had to grapple, but also the development of his character is skilfully made, with the speculative matter economically integrated, and there is plenty of variety and movement in the separate incidents. But, as the cohering spark is feeble, a corresponding lack of vitality marks the characterization of the hero. Personally he may be, as history presents him, unattractive; but in his time and place, nurturing his world-shaking project, he should have stood out as a towering personality whose fall would be experienced as a crashing catastrophe. Instead, when his end comes, it is an almost unalloyed relief to everyone on or off the stage. One cannot resist the feeling in the second half that Ibsen's vast subject, brooded over for ten years or so, had begun to bore him. He saw he had come to the end of a chapter.

The chapter comprised also his collection of Poems. For a quarter of a century he had turned out a fair body of them, middling or short in length—hereinafter called 'poems' *tout court*—of which he published a rigorous selection, *Digte*, in 1871. Five of the items in it were songs from his plays; otherwise no material connexion between the poems and the dramas appears.[2] The craftsman and his preoccupations, however, are unmistakably the same, and if the poems had stood alone they would still have ensured for their author a place of honour in Norwegian literature.

High rhetoric he shunned, nor did he compete with Bjørnson in the cantata style. Otherwise, however, he kept well within the range of contemporary poetry, revolutionary neither in his style nor, basically, in the kind of theme he approached; and that range allowed for considerable variety. Besides the songs already mentioned, the 1871 volume[3] comprises prologues written for theatres with which he was associated and other occasional verse, interesting largely for the personalities and events that had truly stirred him (e.g. the old Intelligence Party's great statesman and economist Schweigaard, J. L. Heiberg and his actress-wife, the assassination of President Lincoln); there are essays in the latter-day ballad style (e.g. 'In Aakershus') and, closely related to them, the semi-heroic narrative poem on the Norwegian pilot Terje Vigen.

The most memorable and characteristic of the poems are, broadly speaking, of two kinds, the elegiac and the satirical, as disparate as *The Vikings in Helgeland* and *Love's Comedy*, even if a tinge of irony in some pensive lines occasionally brings them near to one another.

The first of these groups shows Ibsen plainly following in the footsteps of Welhaven, whose habit of mind was akin to his own and from whom he quickly learned an unemphatic, outwardly simple, though carefully pondered, style, economical without aridity. A few of these poems are purely lyrical; in most, however, description and mood are conjured up to convey a wider-reaching sentiment, as in the most ambitious of them, 'Paa Vidderne' ('On the Fells');[1] here Ibsen presents a man who takes to the solitary life of a sportsman on the moors until he has detached himself so completely from all human relations that he can watch from afar with nothing more than aesthetic appreciation the procession taking his sweetheart to her wedding and the fire that consumes his home and his mother.[2] Briefly to illustrate the elegiac variety one may take 'Borte' and 'Brændte Skibe' in Garrett's translations:

Gone

The late, last guest
    To the gate we followed;
Good-bye—and the rest
    The night-wind swallowed.

House, garden, street,
    Lay tenfold gloomy,
Where accents sweet
    Had made music to me.

It was but a feast
    With the dark coming on;
She was but a guest,—
    and now, she is gone.

Burnt Ships

To skies that were brighter
    Turned he his prows;
To gods that were lighter
    Made he his vows.

The snow-land's mountains
    Sank in the deep;
Sunnier fountains
    Lulled him to sleep.

He burns his vessels,
    The smoke flung forth
On blue cloud-trestles
    A bridge to the north.

From the sun-warmed lowland
    Each night that betides,
To the huts of the snow-land
    A horseman rides.

The satirical note is sometimes struck softly, almost demurely, in what seems an ordinary good-humoured context, for instance in 'Well-grounded Faith' ('Troens Grund'), when an old body congratulates herself at the time of the German threat to the north in 1863–4 that her soldier-boy is absolutely safe, since it is the *Norwegian* army he is enlisted in; it swells into full force in the 'Balloon-Letter to a Swedish Lady' ('Ballonbrev til en Svensk Dame'), where the coruscations of complex or deliberately 'forced' rhymes, colloquial or absurdly coined expressions and irreverent topical references that marked *Love's Comedy* insinuate the poet's views on Bismarck's militaristic state. As a short example one may quote 'To my Friend the Revolutionary Orator', with its notorious last line:

They say I'm becoming conservative;
No; still in my life-long creed I live.

Your changing pawns is a futile plan;
Make a sweep of the chess-board, and I'm your man.

Was never but one revolution unfaltering
That was not marred by half-hearted paltering.

To that, all since were but idle menaces.
I allude, of course, to the Deluge in Genesis.

Yet Lucifer tripped, even then; by a later ship
Came Noah, you remember, and seized the dictatorship.

Let us go, next time, to the root of the matter.
It needs men to act as well as to chatter.

You deluge the world to its topmost mark;
With pleasure I will torpedo the Ark.[1]

(4) *Ibsen and the challenge from Brandes*

When, after twenty-five years of literary production, Ibsen finished off *Emperor and Galilean*, the image he presented to the world was that of a great Romantic poet and dramatist. If parallels were drawn or influences imputed, it fell natural to adduce authors like Oehlenschläger, Johan Ludvig Heiberg, Hertz, Goethe,[2] Paludan-Müller or Welhaven. But, long after them though he came, Ibsen was clearly no mere camp-follower, no epigone. Like his even younger colleague Bjørnson, he retained the fire and independence, the polemical spirit (readily passing into the satirical) that had informed masters of Romanticism's heroic age, such as Shelley, Byron, Hugo, Wergeland or Heine, and which, as far as more recent Norwegian literature was concerned, had energized the critical element in the new writing of the eighteen-fifties.

To the strength of this element Ibsen's authorship had borne abundant testimony. Not only, however, had he shown himself a critic of the world in which he moved, he was equally a critic of himself. As has been seen, the 'call' had preoccupied in work after work, the 'mission' of personages as diverse as Falk, King Haakon, Brand, Peer Gynt and Julian the Apostate; but he had not succeeded in settling the vital question of his own.

It was while Ibsen was labouring on *Emperor and Galilean* that Georg Brandes sent him his famous introductory lecture. Its challenge made a greater impact on him than on Bjørnson.[3] He had, for one thing, been living abroad for eight years, fairly solitary, and had not been prepared for it as Bjørnson had been. Furthermore, the direct references Brandes made to himself touched him on that tenderest of spots, the doubts about his purpose in life and the means of realizing it. Through a work of art like *Brand* he had wished to make his people 'think greatly', and now a well-wisher had told him that its moral, if put into practice, would 'lead half mankind to starve to death from love of the Ideal'.[1] Brandes's demonstrations, he wrote to him, 'set a yawning gulf between yesterday and today'. Put crudely, they made him see 'yesterday' as Romanticism and 'today' as something not merely quite different from, but even opposed to it; and at the same time the positive programme for literature they advanced, that of helping to clarify problems of immediate concern to men and women of the day and presenting them in a familiar environment, seemed to offer him at last a solution for his personal problem, the reconciliation of the aesthetically and morally significant. Ibsen braced himself to the new 'call'. It meant an end to reconstructions of ancient Byzantium; it even meant, as Brandes put it, shooting his Pegasus.[2]

But it meant also some hard thinking about ways and means, harder than one might have expected, since Ibsen had before him not only the foreign exemplars recommended by Brandes, but soon also two native plays embodying his programme, Bjørnson's *Bankruptcy* and *Editor*. More than that, Ibsen had himself, already in 1869, launched out on a realistic prose play of modern life with *The League of Youth*,[3] an ingenious and amusing light comedy about the choosing of a member of Parliament in a rural constituency, such as might have taken place during the Storthing elections of that year.

Looking back on *The League of Youth*, however, under the admonitions of the new 'call', Ibsen may well have judged the 'local situation'—one of the stock phrases in the play that became proverbial—there presented to be too parochial, the technique too close to farce for repetition and the moral merely negative and trivial ('Don't vote for a Stensgaard'). Five years of cogitation after hearing Brandes's challenge, three years of planning and replanning, drafting and redrafting were to elapse before he had worked out to his satisfaction something that would conform to the new programme and might beat the author of *A Bankruptcy* at his own game.

(5) *The Ibsenite plays*

The English coined the term 'Ibsenite' to designate a work of literature which carried on the face of it the intention of working for moral reform by exposing the conventional hypocrisies that stood in its way. The four plays which within the span of five years Ibsen was now to give to the world and establish his fame in it are those which exemplify the term: *Pillars of Society*, *A Doll's House*, *Ghosts* and *An Enemy of the People*.

Pillars of Society (*Samfundets Støtter*, 1887)[1] followed Bjørnson's *Bankruptcy* in revolving round a piece of commercial malpractice. The central personage, Consul Bernick, owner of a shipyard in a small seaport, sends a vessel to sea which he knows to be unseaworthy. He not only knows that she is unseaworthy, but hopes that she will prove so: she is to have on board a man, his own brother-in-law, who, possessing incriminating evidence against him, has announced his intention of making it known. The action is complicated and sharpened by the discovery, after the ship has weighed anchor, that the consul's only son is on board as a stowaway.

The play does not end tragically, however, nor even exactly in the villain-hero's being called to account. His foreman,[2] always uneasy about the shoddy way in which he has been compelled to patch up the 'Indian Girl', stops her at the twelfth hour; the would-be informer is mollified; Bernick, an opportunity presenting itself, stands up before his fellow-citizens and confesses his misdeeds (or some of them). Although his audience are dismayed by his voluntary disclosure, it has won back the confidence Bernick had lost in the family circle, and one may reasonably suppose that a man of his undisputed ability and wealth will continue to prosper, even after he has persuaded himself that honesty is the best policy.

How can this story be interpreted as a constructive criticism of society consonant with the new Brandesian programme? What is one to make of its title? The answers are not quite straightforward. A rogue practises his roguery and gains the esteem of the community; when the roguery—not quite unsuspected—is exposed, that esteem is withdrawn. But Bernick has a case, and a not altogether specious one: his enterprise ensures the livelihood of countless families: and in the world of affairs even results that redound to the public good cannot always be obtained by open dealing; and in answer to his sister-in-law's question why he and men like him arrogate to themselves the title of 'Pillars of Society' he retorts that there are none better. A community with a criminal like Bernick for its corner-stone shares his guilt when it turns the blind eye. Stress may be laid on the fact that it is here a small, restricted community— an argument for the early critics of Ibsen who sneered at this provinciality;[1] but it needs no great ingenuity to illustrate the syllogism, as he would have called it, in fields of any magnitude. Dishonesty is dishonesty, whether practised in Grimstad or Wall Street, hypocrisy remains hypocrisy, and the remedy 'to let in some fresh air', which Bernick's sister-in-law Lona Hessel prescribes, is general as well as specific.

Bernick and his associates are pillars made of flesh and blood. But at the end of the play the ground is shifted. Taking up Lona Hessel's jibe—'your society is a society of bachelor-souls; you have no eyes for womanhood'—Bernick declares: 'I have learnt *this* in these days; it is you women who are the pillars of society.' To which she retorts: 'Then you have learnt a poor wisdom, brother-in-law. No, no; the spirits of Truth and Wisdom—these are the Pillars of Society'.

The resounding moral of this curtain-line is not the only similarity the play has with the old-established German-Austrian Volksstück,[2] familiar to Ibsen from his Dresden days, and, to judge by what has been said of *Pillars of Society* so far, it does not seem to mark any signal advance beyond *The League of Youth* or the naïvety of *A Bankruptcy*. An advance there is, however, bringing it nearer to the famous masterpieces of later years than it stands to *The League of Youth*. It lies in its profounder moral probing, its more genuine verisimilitude and the technical mastery which combines these elements in an artistically effective whole. The three-hours' traffic of the stage does not merely compress the four-day crisis that brings Bernick to the brink of the abyss; through the 'analytic technique', the process is revealed by which Bernick became the man he was and found himself in the predicament from which murder beckoned as the only escape. Fifteen years is the span of this process, originating in the comparatively venial deceit Bernick had practised when he allowed both his firm's financial straits and the paternity of his ward to be imputed to his absent brother-in-law. These and other revelations ensured by the analytic technique subserve in masterly manner the dramatic demands for compactness and surprise, and, at the same time, demonstrate the cancerous power of 'the lie' in a more literal sense than Ibsen's characters were apt to use elsewhere.

Formally, Ibsen's next two plays are notable for their greater concentration, with the gradual elimination of the old-fashioned elements *Pillars of Society* had in common with the Volksstück and the like. *A Doll's House* still comprises a sub-plot (Fru Linde and Krogstad); but there are only eight speaking parts, three of them quite tiny, and the pre-history is focused on one event only. *Ghosts* reduces the number of characters to five, there is neither sub-plot nor an 'interfering agent' (like Lona Hessel or Fru Linde) who deliberately works for a show-down; the action is compressed into some twelve hours.

The one event in the 'pre-history' of *A Doll's House* (*Et Dukkehjem*, 1879)[1] conditioning the action is a forgery perpetrated by Nora Helmer to procure a holiday for her sick husband, Torvald; it put her into the clutches of a blackmailer (Krogstad), who comes to have a particular reason for holding the threat of exposure over her, since he wants her help to secure for him, as a measure of social rehabilitation, a post in the bank to which Torvald has just been appointed director when the action begins. Her intercession failing, Nora, after days of agony, has to make a full confession. Instead of understanding and compassion—let alone, as she had romantically hoped, a readiness to take the guilt on himself—her confession calls forth from her husband nothing but fury and obloquy. At this point the blackmailer is induced to relent (by Nora's confidante, Fru Linde). Helmer immediately turns round and proposes, as far as his relations with his wife are concerned, to go on as if nothing had happened. But Nora cannot. In her agony and her husband's reactions she has realized that she knows neither the man with whom she has been co-habiting and whose love she believed assured by her own nor the world they live in; and, though it means leaving her home and children too, she goes out into the night to learn.

Much of this is drawing-room melodrama, almost in the boulevard manner—her flirtation, for instance, with her admirer Dr Rank in the hope of borrowing enough money to redeem the forged bill, or the scene of her rehearsing, at the height of her despair, her great parlour-trick, the tarantella danced in Neapolitan costume. The endless discussion provoked by the play sometimes turned on the verisimilitude of the action itself—notably the question whether the 'squirrel' and 'song-bird', as which Nora is first introduced, could by any possibility have turned into the dialectician who so ably argues her case in the formal show-down with her husband at the end.

That in itself could scarcely cause scandal. But scandal there was, basically on two counts. The first was the invasion in depth of a terrain which drama, that most 'public' of literary forms, had so far only rarely and in a very gingerly manner approached and which it was devoutly hoped that the critical spirits of the age would pass by, the Sanctuary of matrimonial intimacies. The second was the defence, implied in the whole tenour of the play and proclaimed by Nora herself, of every human being's right to act on private judgement in the teeth of conventional beliefs, however strongly buttressed by almost universal acceptance and even law. The right-minded saw in Ibsen, hitherto the hope of Norway's stern, unbending Tories, not only a violator of decency, but also an anarchist throwing a bomb as devastating as that impossible Bjørnson's *King*. With a shudder they remembered the 'torpedo under the Ark'.[1]

Something more must, very briefly, be said here on what for a long time made Ibsen an object of abhorrence, not in Norway alone, in a word his alleged Anarchism (then a topic of general concern, like the Bolshevism of a later age). To premise: Ibsen was anything but a doctrinaire: 'my business', he said,[2] 'is to ask questions, not to answer them'. He took part in no public debates, he belonged to no school, whether of Bakunin or John Stuart Mill, shunned and suspected all 'movements', horrifying a dinner-party given in his honour by an association for advancing the Women's Cause by declaring that he did not know what the Women's Cause was. Even in the 'Ibsenite' plays no specific reform is advocated or even hinted at: no one in *Pillars of Society* calls for a Board of Trade inspection of all out-going vessels; Nora Helmer's 'hard case' is no plea for amending the paragraphs of the Criminal Code relative to forgery.

Freedom, to be sure, was an objective for which he strove as passionately as the professed anarchists. But the difference between them is clearly seen in his growl[1] about people who only want to take liberties, but do not care in the least about liberty. Order, *arche* was an indispensable condition of *his* freedom for every individual to develop his talents and personality, which his art could assist in promoting by the exposure of the obstacles in its way raised by vested interests, obsolete beliefs and practices or inherited superstitions.

Ibsen's enemies were right in bracketing his feminism with the anarchism they scented. Comically though he despised Mill for taking ideas from his wife, he stood fundamentally on the ground taken in *The Subjection of Women*:[2] in its advancement to true liberty the human race was calamitously hobbled when one half of it was denied the facilities, even the right, to develop and exercise for the common good its latent capacities. In saying that he did not know what the Women's Cause was, Ibsen implied that it was the same thing as the Cause of Mankind.

A favourite topic in the debates that raged over *A Doll's House* was the question of Nora Helmer's future. A common view was that she went back to her husband pretty soon. This possibility Ibsen himself took up in *Ghosts, a Domestic Drama (Gengangere, et familjedrama,* 1881),[3] making it the cardinal event in the pre-history of the play. Helene Alving had run away from her husband too and had been promptly returned to him by the man with whom she sought refuge. She had come to terms, *her* terms, with her crapulous libertine of a husband; she had come to know him and the world she lived in, and is now shown, twenty-five years older, ten years a widow, living on her country estate, superintending the building of an orphanage for abandoned children which is to be her late husband's memorial, keeping abreast in her loneliness with what is going on and being thought in the great world.

The action begins when her only child Osvald, whom she sent abroad to escape both the pernicious example of his father and the frustrating environment of his home, comes back after many years. He is 'the spit and image'[1] of the late Captain Alving at his age, and, by a brilliant variant of the retrospective technique, the scene in which the latter began the seduction of a housemaid twenty years or so ago is re-enacted when Osvald makes amorous approaches to his mother's present maid-companion, Regine. Mrs Alving brings this affair into the open at once, acquiesces in Osvald's passion and is prepared to countenance his marriage with the girl, to the horror of her friend Pastor Manders. For it involves incest: Regine, as she and Manders know, is the offspring of Osvald's father and the housemaid of yore.

That consummation is averted. Osvald is a very sick man. Regine gets wind of it and sheers off. He is, as he confesses to his mother, suffering from an incurable venereal disease which will in time reduce him to idiocy. He extracts from her the promise that when this stage is reached she will give him the poison he carries with him. The play ends, after the destruction by fire of Captain Alving's double-edged memorial, with the supervening of the penultimate stage in Osvald's affliction and his mother's groping in his pockets for the deadly drug.

Ghosts was in the fullest sense a shocking play. So great was the scandal it raised that censorships formal and informal forbad its public performance for long years. All the subsidiary elements were outrageous: seduction in the matrimonial home, bastardy, the barter of a discarded mistress, a proposed incestuous marriage, the nature of Osvald's disease, the suggestion that something like a brothel should be set up with Pastor Manders's blessing. Not only did such things make the author an embarrassment, a liability to his well-wishers,[2] but the whole tenour of the play was a smack in the face to the most fervent of them, the true-blood Ibsenites: light and air were seen to be no guaranteed prophylactics—enlightenment, good intentions altruistically and resolutely pursued did not suffice to lay the ghost of Captain Alving. Above all there was the spectacle of a woman who was prepared to kill her only son and, one must presume, did kill him.

But it is this culminating horror that raises the 'domestic drama' of Helene Alving to a height where it challenges comparison with two of the acknowledged masterpieces of tragedy. The country-house Medea, who acts not from disprized love or *Schadenfreude*, is a more pitiable, more tragic figure than Euripides's barbaric heroine; like another Oedipus she has pinned her faith to the saving power of knowledge and truth and yet has not eluded an uncontrollable fate—a fate that in good nineteenth-century terms has taken on the guise of heredity.

Against the thesis common virtually to all critics of *Ghosts* that wrongs, if they involved unsavoury details, should be kept decently quiet and, equally, against 'the damned compact liberal majority' that by its silence had disowned him, Ibsen turned with unusual alacrity in *An Enemy of the People* (*En Folkefiende*, 1882).[1] 'Zola', he once said,[2] 'goes down into the sewer to take a bath; I do so in order to scour it.' He confessed to the sewer, and his new play almost literally brought it on to the stage. It is a hard-hitting, admirably constructed comedy, without any complicated 'pre-history' or involution of plot, showing how the insanitary conditions of the hydropathic establishment on which a small resort is founding its prosperity is publicly exposed by its officer of health, Dr Thomas Stockmann; and how for his pains vested interests and constituted authorities have him voted An Enemy of the People, damaged in body and estate and hounded from his post. It abounds in lively, even uproarious scenes, public and domestic, and in first-class acting parts of all sizes and ranges. Its lesson may be grim, but it is not utterly pessimistic. Something, after all, will *have* to be done about the Baths, and the effervescent, extravert Dr Stockmann may be left with his head bloody, but certainly unbowed. This amalgam of Ibsen and Bjørnson will live to fight another day.

4

ELSTER AND LIE

(1) *Two writers of transition*

IT has been suggested before that if they had died in 1873, at the ages of 40 and 45 respectively, the authors of *Synnøve Solbakken*, *Sigurd the Bad* and *Arnljot Gelline* and of *Brand, Peer Gynt* and *Emperor and Galilean* would have been set down in literary histories as distinguished representatives of the Romantic movement, groping now and then, it is true, towards the Realism that was to supersede it. The powerful impulses that then mastered them split their literary careers into two clear-cut halves; to sum them up as 'writers of transition', suggesting a certain gradualness, might therefore be misleading. Better so called are two men who made their effective débuts[1] at just about the time that Ibsen and Bjørnson came to the parting of the ways: Kristian Elster, short-lived, and Jonas Lie, who had nearly four decades of active authorship before him. A little early experimenting allowed for, one cannot discern any abrupt change of course in these. Their art was realistic in intention and effect, they were steady observers and critics of the contemporary society which mostly provides its matter, as was to be expected of a new writer of their time; but their *tendens* was muted, their technique and the reflective, often melancholy atmosphere disengaged by their imaginings kept something faintly old-fashioned. A lover of *Great Expectations* or Turgeniev's *Fathers and Sons* could have happily gone on reading their books without experiencing the shocks and distaste that *A Doll's House* or *The King* would have made him suffer.

(2) *Kristian Elster*

It was accordingly appropriate that the first piece of fiction published by Kristian Elster (1841–81)* should appear, in

* Kristian Mandrup Elster was born at Overhalla in Namdalen, the son of a minor official, in 1841. On the strength of studies in Germany, he qualified as a

1871, in the Copenhagen magazine *For Idé og Virkelighed*,[1] a 'bridge' periodical, as its title—baldly to be translated 'For the Ideal and Reality'—announces. 'En Korsgang' ('A Calvary') is a well-knit short story of a case of conscience in an elderly God-fearing peasant-woman on her discovering that her son has committed murder, in order to rob his victim. She has to fight her problem out for herself and finally denounces him to the police. There is no melodrama, but the firm, understanding delineation of Salbjørg's circumstances, character and terrible predicament justifies the title of the tale, which strikes a note both deeper and fuller than the most sombre of Bjørnson's peasant tales.[2]

Elster's two stories to attract the greatest attention (though it was not much) were the novels *Tora Trondal* (1879) and *Farlige Folk* (*Dangerous People*, 1881).[3] In 'A Calvary' his preoccupation had been religious, closely interwoven though Salbjørg's duty to her neighbour might be with her duty to God. The hero of *Tora Trondal* is a zealous curate, but the novels move more immediately on the moral and social plane.

Begun as a conventional story of a broken engagement with the usual modicum of complicating intrigue, *Tora Trondal* is well articulated: structurally, in fact, the best novel written so far in Norway. The total effect, nevertheless, remains somewhat confused. This is not only because during the eight years or more in which it was incubating Elster had, under the impulse of Georg Brandes's teaching,[4] changed his objective from more or less plain narrative to social criticism, but also because in the final form he designed to show as ripples in the backwater of a small country community—the lordly sheriff and his flashy chief assistant, the easy-going parson and his hot-gospelling new curate, their womenfolk and better-class neighbours—the eddies and cross-currents set up by the gales of the greater world outside. In miniature, therefore, muffled, overlapping, at times misunderstood or only guessed at, we have put before us all the antagonisms dividing Norway at

government forester, with headquarters from 1873 in Trondheim, where he died of pneumonia in 1881. He married in 1874. Kristian Elster, the author of the six-volume *Illustrert Norsk Literatur-Historie* (1927–37), was one of his children. Besides what is mentioned elsewhere, Elster wrote the short stories 'En fremmed Fugl' (1884) and 'Kjeld Horge' (1884).

this epoch: between the fat, prosperous Eastland (where the scene is laid) and the Westland, whose harshness and poverty are embodied in the curate-hero, between his call to a life of service and the superficial aestheticism which the parson's daughter has imported from Christiania drawing-rooms, between the notables of the district and their humbler neighbours, the peasants, for whose political and cultural aspirations these notables harbour nothing but contempt mingled with fear; even the language-question raises its head.

In *Dangerous People* 'tendens' becomes clearer. It tells of Arne and Knut Holt, father and son, the former a small-scale entrepreneur, the latter a qualified medico who returns from travel and experiences abroad to practice in his home-town. Both are earnest, reflective natures, devoted to one another, keeping themselves very much to themselves, yet profoundly concerned with and well informed about the society around them, its great contrasts of fortune and opportunity, arrogance on the one side and wretchedness on the other. The Consul Bernicks of their small trading seaport[1] label them Dangerous People for their independence and unconcealed sympathy with the under-dog. One of the stormy elections of the 'seventies pending, Knut decides to stand for Parliament, naturally on a liberal platform, and all the local magnates' latent hostility towards him and his father breaks forth. It would probably have been unavailing, if, at the height of the campaign, a wild woman of the pampas had not turned up, whom Knut had met on his travels and whom he believed lost at sea after she had seduced him and made him promise her marriage. His candidature becomes impossible. He goes through with the marriage, in honour bound, and leaves the town. His father dies, a broken man. The liberal cause is killed stone dead.

The fortuitous irruption of the *femme fatale* constitutes the obvious and damaging weakness of the story. But there is much to counterbalance it. The elderly agnostic Arne Holt, resigned to passivity so as not to spoil his beloved son's chances, and Knut, who equally holds his fire, knowing that to be effective propaganda must be underpinned by understanding and patience, completely win the reader's faith. Though the brevity of the novel allows for little detailed description, there had, at

67

the time that *Dangerous People* was written, been no presentation in Norwegian literature of a community so full and authentic. And, while the author's bias is plain enough, that presentation remains conspicuously fair. The established order is not vicious throughout. When at the height of the electoral campaign old rumours of Arne Holt's commercial unsoundness are revived, two upright conservatives, who have no reason to favour his son, come forward to contradict them, and Knut finds an affectionate ally in the daughter of one of the 'old houses', whom he could reasonably have been expected to marry. The only animus to break through is against the clergy[1]—it had already appeared in 'A Calvary', where by a sanctimonious evasion her parish-priest wriggles out of giving the least help to Salbjørg—and their religion: a parson prevents a rich young man's making an honest woman of the poor girl he has gotten with child, and the most fraudulent bankrupts in the town are the most pious.

His demonstration of the frailty of the good cause, as Elster esteems it, colours the whole with a pessimistic tinge, which his fairness and sympathy make melancholy rather than indignant or bitter. *Dangerous People* can be construed as a call to action only in the oblique manner in which Turgeniev's novels became so. The generic resemblance to Turgeniev, which Georg Brandes detected already in *Tora Trondal*,[2] is indeed patent; it appears also in the contrast between the patrician girl Cornelia, straightforward and resolute, and the ultimate ineffectiveness of the two men.

(3) *Lie's career*

Jonas Lie (1833–1908),* who, somewhat curiously, had been publicly hailed by Bjørnson as the coming laureate of North

* Jonas Lauritz Idemil Lie was born at Hokksund, 30 miles west of Christiania, on 6 November 1833, the son of a lawyer who became a *Sorenskriver* (county-court judge). Going up to the University of Christiania, where Bjørnson and Ibsen were his contemporaries and friends, he graduated (1858) with first-class honours in law. On marrying his first cousin Thomasine Lie, he practised as an attorney at Kongsvinger (1860–8). Involved in the timber-speculations then rife, he went bankrupt and thenceforward earned his living as an author, mainly abroad (Italy, Germany and Paris, 1871–5 and 1878–1905). Parliament voted him a pension in 1874. When sounded in 1905, he declined to be considered for

Norway before he had printed a line of imaginative prose, saw, like Elster, his first story printed in *For Idé og Virkelighed*: 'By Lake Enare' ('Ved Enaresjøen,' 1870), a silly little tale of a youth who drowns himself under the spells which, for his infidelity, his Lapp sweetheart has laid upon him. The more substantial †*Visionary* (*Den Fremsynte*) of the following year it was that gave him his real start, rather belatedly and rather unsteadily. An awkwardly jointed tale within a tale, its combination of the weird—focused on the 'feyness' of the hero to which it owes its title—with more pregnant evocations of scenery and life north of the Arctic Circle made strong appeal to a public avid of the remote and the unusual, provided that the remote was not too remote and a substantial setting guaranteed the credibility of the unusual.

The success of *The Visionary* was repeated with †*The Barque 'Fremtiden'* (*Tremasteren 'Fremtiden'*, 1872) and †*The Pilot and his Wife* (*Lodsen og hans Hustru*, 1874). The latter, putting firm portraiture and the interaction of character on character in the forefront, anticipated the manner of Lie's greater triumphs, but these lay some years ahead, and a phase of frustrating uncertainty intervened. Lie had a shot at a lyric-dramatic poem about factitious people and sentiments in an Italianate setting such as the Romantic epigones loved (*Faustina Strozzi*, 1875); he toyed with stories of Christiania society (*Thomas Ross*, 1878, and *Adam Schrader*, 1879) and with modern comedy in *Grabow's Cat* (*Grabows Kat*, 1880). All were so unsuccessful in every way that Lie seriously bethought himself of going back to the law to which he had originally been bred.

Rutland (1880) and *Go Ahead!* (*Gaa Paa!*, 1882), two novels of the sea again, regained the ground lost, however, and with †*The Lifer* (*Livsslaven*), and †*The Family at Gilje* (*Familien paa Gilje*), both of 1883, Lie entered on his 'great period', which,

a Nobel prize for literature until it had been awarded to Ibsen. He died, long ailing, at Fleskum in the outskirts of Christiania on 5 July 1908.

He was properly generous in the tributes he paid to the co-operation of his wife, who had the better brain and a wider knowledge of literature than he and who encouraged the 'modern' side of his productions. She suggested the essential subject of *Lodsen og hans Hustru* (1874), in which this first had scope, and was not enthusiastic about his excursions into the supernatural realm; she also checked his tendency to prolixity, over-rigorously perhaps, since one could wish that he had been allowed more elbow-room for some of his finer works.

together with these two, comprised † *The Commandant's Daughters* (*Kommandørens Døttre*, 1886), *Life Together* (*Et Samliv*, 1887) and †*Niobe* (1893), as well as several others of only slightly lesser note.[1]

His supreme masterpiece, *Niobe*, published when he was sixty, proved to be Lie's last major work, though *Dyre Rein* (1896), a second, but weaker half-historical novel of the class of *The Family at Gilje*, almost equalled its great popularity; and *When the Safety Curtain Falls* (*Naar Jernteppet falder*, 1901)—the description, eleven years before the sinking of the 'Titanic', of a gigantic disaster narrowly averted in an Atlantic liner, with its effect on a haphazard group of passengers—more up-to-date, smarter in technique as well as *milieu*, won high praise from the discerning too.

(4) '*The Family at Gilje*', '*The Commandant's Daughters*', '*Life Together*', '*Niobe*'

Ibsen left the reading of books, he said, to his wife and son. Lie apparently followed much the same plan.[2] When he commenced author, he declared, he had read little beyond Shakespeare, Dickens, and some 'Red Indian stories', by which he meant Fenimore Cooper's and Captain Marryat's tales of adventure;[3] and the loose 'Anglo-Saxon' strain, though kept in check by Fru Thomasine, is always obvious in his technique; some of his lesser nautical figures belong to the family of Captain Cuttle. Sooner or later he got to know *The Sheriff's Daughters*, and for long his imagination was visited by its theme, the subjection of women as Camilla Collett[4] there had conceived it: two of his best and most characteristic novels form a direct link, *The Commandant's Daughters* through its title, *The Family at Gilje* through its ambience as well as its subject.

The Family at Gilje is put back some forty years, to the time that may be supposed for *The Sheriff's Daughters*, and the scene presents, though less harshly, another remote, unpeopled district, in which Captain Peter Jæger commands the local militia and manages his own middling farm. He has a devoted wife, a son (who does not figure in the story) and three daughters, of whom Inger-Johanna is the star, a radiant creature who, taken up by a fashionable aunt, becomes the toast of Christiania. There she is asked in marriage by her own god-father, a friend and coeval of Captain Jæger, who has done better for himself than the squireen of Gilje; she breaks off this advantageous engagement, however, and runs back home on realizing that her heart is given to a wayward undergraduate (of the same vintage as Georg Cold of *The Sheriff's Daughters*), whom her outward coldness has irredeemably pushed down the slope of debauchery. Nothing is left for her at Gilje but, as a maiden lady, to set up a small rural school. Meanwhile her elder sister and a clerk at her uncle's, having plighted their troth and, on grounds of social incompatibility, renounced it, she, Thinka, marries a middle-aged widower, a minor local official, and sinks into *embonpoint* and novel-reading, with the youngest of the girls, unmarried, to act as her housekeeper.

Lack of matrimonial opportunity is not a factor in *The Commandant's Daughters* as it was in Captain Jæger's (and Sheriff Ramm's) home. For Kommandør Witt is in charge of a training depot for naval cadets, so that plenty of eligible young gentlemen orbit round his girls, whose disastrous frustra-tions spring less from circumstance than from character. The adulation enjoyed by the Inger-Johanna of this story, Cecilie, goes to her head: her sharp tongue, imperious airs and apparent insouciance scare off Lieutenant Fasting, though each is in love with the other, and none is tempted to take his place. The mother's snobbishness ruins more straightforward Marta, when her marriage to Captain Børresen is vetoed on the ground that the vessel he commands is no more than a tanker. For, to force her parents' hand, she lets herself be gotten with child by her lover, but before this bombshell is burst in the Witt family circle Børresen's tanker catches fire at sea and he perishes. Marta has to be sent abroad, irretrievably disgraced. The story, though well supplied with the local colour Lie remembered from the time he lodged with the Kommandør of Fredriksværn, lacks the amplitude of *The Family at Gilje*; it speaks starkly for itself, and no attempt is made to surcharge it with pity or indignation.

As in the middle of *Rosmersholm* the ictus of Ibsen's sympathies is seen to shift from women to men when they are at odds, so Lie turned away from the tribulations and defeat of young people to concentrate on those of the middle-aged. By contrast with the latter, their children come, on the whole, to show up poorly—and this particularly, when they have been freed from the trammels which had galled their predecessors. Freedom, he came to see, was not enough—as Ibsen was stating, pretty categorically too, in *The Lady from the Sea*, at just this time.

This shift of sympathies comes out most strongly in *Niobe*; it is discernible, however, already in *Samliv* (*Life Together*), though the defects of the younger generation are played down in favour of another theme that yet again calls Ibsen to mind. The phrase in Nora Helmer's last speech, which is notoriously difficult to translate,* 'at samliv mellem os kunde bli'e et ægteskab', is picked up in the title of Lie's novel, where a shallower lady, whose outward circumstances are much the same as Nora's but who has passed through no fiery furnace, is exhibited as completely satisfied with them. Aletta Mørk, however, also slammed a door in her time—when she gave way to such petulance because her husband, a solicitor, went on discussing in her presence economic topics with his bosom friend Berven that from then on he never let her into those serious concerns which Selma Bratsberg (of *The League of Youth*) and Nora Helmer craved to share with their men. Only on their silver-wedding day does she learn that her husband had once been implicated in commercial speculations and, alone among his associates, saved from ruin by Berven's help. For twenty-five years they have been just 'living together'. The ensuing *éclaircissement* holds out some hope of an Indian summer—but rather a tepid one. Rebellious Susans were not much to Lie's taste, but he was near enough to the author of *A Doll's House* to make the picture of Aletta Mørk's 'successful marriage' a pretty dismal one: she has blunted her husband, and three of her children have been hopelessly spoilt.

* Archer, for once, misses the mark with 'That communion between us should be a marriage'; Farquharson Sharp's 'That our life together would be a real wedlock' is a little better; McFarlane does best with 'When we could make a real marriage of our lives together'.

Living Together was autumnal. *Niobe* is wintry. Lie, after
many years' absence, had spent the summer holiday of 1893 in
Norway and observed with concern the darker side of that
movement for emancipation to which he himself had contributed. Though saddened, he was not dismayed. Gains there
had been, but they might the better be secured if due account
were made of the cost, and this his new book was to do.[1]

His Niobe is no passive woe-begone young matron, a
classical figure in a fountain, all tears, but the wife, strong in
body, mind and determination, of a reasonably well-to-do
provincial doctor and the mother of six grown children whose
fortunes make up her own. In accordance with up-to-date
principles, calculated to prevent calamities like those which
befell the family at Gilje and the commandant's daughters,
the eldest have been left free from all parental interference
in the way of life to which their impulses lead them. Of the
two girls among them, the beauty, Minka, attaches herself to
a young railway engineer who, with spiritualism for his hobby,
professes to see a first-class medium in her, while the flibberti-
gibbet Berthea, without being exactly vicious, becomes the
talk of the town and eventually has to find a husband in
America. The eldest son, Endre, announces at the beginning
of the story that he intends to break off his university studies
and devote himself to the arts as a professional singer; nothing
comes of this or any other of his projects, and he returns home
periodically to sponge on the old folks. Their fatal worry,
however, is over Kjel, with his incurable itch for undertakings
beyond his capacities, which he ultimately has to supplement
with fraud. Ruin threatens. Dr Baarvig steels himself to throw
with apparent carelessness a couple of lighted matches into
the timber-yard of which Kjel has become the proprietor and
general manager. The insurance-money accruing from the
blaze only tides him over for six months, however, and father
and mother know it is only a matter of time before he will be
arrested for malversation of funds. There is a moving, tiny
scene, in which the ageing couple, lying in bed on 31 December,
hear the bells ringing in a New Year that can bring them
nothing but misery, the doctor mutters that a life with no chance
of doing good is not worth living and they give one another

one last, mute hug. Using his professional knowledge for covering up a second act of desperation, Dr Baarvig commits suicide on his daily round.

The three elder children remaining at home are quite blind to the tragedy. Hearing their talk, which makes it clear that, while Kjel has been reduced to a terror-stricken jelly, Endel is nothing but a windbag and that Minka is about to marry her engineer so that he may tour the country exhibiting her in *séances*, Fru Baarvig goes into the woodshed, takes an axe and, smiting a stick of dynamite left behind by one of the younger children with a practical turn of mind, sends herself and the three chatterers to Kingdom Come—a device which, ironically, Endre's grandiloquent vapourings have put into her head.

The exposure of the four young people is damning. But Lie, like Elster, always plays fair. As neither coincidence nor motiveless malignancy enters into his story, so in a variety of ways he mitigates an impression of wholesale denunciation or ineluctable doom. The family life of the Baarvigs is, day by day, a far from unhappy one, their relations with the little world around them normal. The unsatisfactory children have their qualities: Minka has beauty, the makings of something fine, Kjel enterprise of a sort, Endre's interpretation of Hamlet in the drawing-room moves even his disillusioned father. The parents, moreover, are not absolved from all blame. The doctor knew that Endre's sterile dilettantism should be nipped in the bud; his wife was sufficiently alive to Kjel's crookedness to warn a prominent business-man of their acquaintance against him. But Kjel was his father's, Endre his mother's favourite; and in a species of domestic log-rolling the parents fatally refrained from bringing their misgivings into the open. Over and above this, there is the faulty system—catastrophic, as it turned out—in which they deliberately had Minka, Berthea, Endre and Kjel brought up. Practically (as one might say), but naturally and unobtrusively, Lie is however at pains to show that a faulty system can be recognized as such and scrapped. Kept in the background in every sense, the Baarvigs have, besides the four mentioned, two other children; they, born late enough for the parents to have seen the mistakes of libertarian education have, with the assistance of a sensible tutor, been firmly but affectionately subjected to rule and discipline and grown into sturdy, reliable youngsters. When the crisis impends, their mother has sent them to finish their schooling away from home. The good stock survives.

While they do not blur or annul the essential tragedy, offsets such as these prevent *Niobe* from amounting to a schematic tractate on education or libertarianism. It remains the chronicle, rounded and sympathetic, of a nowise extraordinary middle-class family in a small town, such as, in nine cases out of ten, might have suffered some hard knocks, but would have steered clear of disaster. True, it concludes with a melodramatic crash akin to that in which Hardy saw fit to end that other great tragic novel of the time, *Tess of the D'Urbervilles*; but otherwise stark effects are avoided. It is Lie's gift to see the grandiose in the petty or humdrum, a noble ingredient in the grotesque.

As an example one may take a sequence of short scenes involving Schultheiss, the tutor, a wise, conscientious, wide-awake young man, but, alas, hunch-backed, with a shrill voice that ludicrously betrays him in moments of excitement. Schultheiss is passionately devoted to the beautiful Minka, without any illusions about requital and without much repining at his own predicament, but aghast before the downward path he sees her on. In a duel of words he has demolished the dangerous sophistries of his rival, who is doing much worse than violating Minka's body, but she remains untouched by his talk and merely pokes fun at his squeaking and uncouth antics. Unbearably tortured, he rushes away, to cry in his room. Fru Baarvig, who both knows the nature of his feelings for Minka and that only accepted love like his could, *per impossibile*, save her from shipwreck, hurries after him and, as he lies on his bed, comforts him as best she can by assuring him how tellingly he argued. And when, his confidence somewhat restored, she has left him, the poor man gets up to strut up and down before his looking-glass rehearsing his arguments in a more convincing and dignified style. Lie, on finding himself involved in theoretical discussions about Naturalism, could do little better than stutter about 'the natural'. What could be more natural than this?

(5) 'The Lifer' and naturalism

The four books on which Lie's reputation is most securely based are all middle-class 'interiors', as he himself would have called them. Some of the features that distinguished them were prefigured in the equally renowned, though comparatively clumsy *Pilot and his Wife*—notably the theme, a growing estrangement of a fundamentally devoted husband and wife through the former's latent jealousy and sullen taciturnity, happily resolved when all the cards are laid on the table in the earliest of the scenes of marital *éclaircissement* for which Norwegian literature became notorious. The book's title, however, points to two differentiae, linking them to others of Lie's stories: those of the sea and those about persons in humble station.

The Lifer[1] is the most impressive among those falling into the latter category. It tells the story of two Christiania slum-children, the bastard Nikolai and Silla, the daughter of his adoptive parents, from whose harshness Nikolai runs away as soon as he can, to live precariously by scrounging and casual labour on the quayside. He pulls himself together, however, goes into a forge and steadily works through his apprenticeship. Meeting Silla again, now a factory-girl, they become engaged, but their marriage is perpetually put off through the calls made on them by their respective mothers, one feckless, the other avaricious. A rare occasion presents itself for Silla, who has a healthy, innocent love of pleasure, hardly ever satisfied, to break away from home one evening and go to the annual fair with a party of other girls. There she is seen dancing with a smart young gentleman by Nikolai, who, sore and jealous, goes for her partner and deals him a blow that kills him. Silla throws herself off a bridge; Nikolai is given a life-sentence.[2]

On its publication in 1883 *The Lifer* was greeted as the first Norwegian novel of the naturalistic school, and not only by those who applied the adjective to any work which (as *Ghosts* had just done) outraged their sense of decency or savoured of pessimism. Christiania substituted for Paris, its *milieu* is much the same as that of the notorious *Knock-Out* (*L'Assommoir*), which Lie was bold enough to proclaim 'a mighty, epoch-making work'. And, equally, the determinism and pessimism for which *les naturalistes* were scouted could be imputed. The equivocal title itself suggests it: Nikolai is left a convict serving a life-sentence,[1] but he is also a victim of circumstance, the slave of life itself. Further, in the last analysis, what brings Nikolai and Silla down is their fidelity to their wretched mothers, virtue rather than vice.

Lie could, however, never subscribe to two of naturalism's pet doctrines, that beginnings in misery necessarily imply an end in misery and that man is essentially a ferocious, libidinous gorilla. *Go Ahead!*, for all its sad ending, illustrates the exact contrary. Man's moral instinct is, for him, as real and strong as the purely animal. Tragedies he may present, inducing the sombre reflexions tragedy must evoke, yet the reflexions are never those of despair. What is as remarkable in *The Lifer* as Nikolai's crime and the punishment it brings on him and his sweetheart is the effort of will which lifted him out of the downward rut and, but for a constellation of personal influences, would have given them the chance, a genuine chance, of a contented, useful life. For a chemically pure injection of *naturalisme* the Norwegian novel had to wait for Amalie Skram.

While Lie allowed little scope for *la bête humaine*,[2] he would ruminate from time to time on what he called 'the troll in man'. The two volumes of *Ogres* (*Trold*) were a product of his interest in the supernatural; although they were intended to have a deeper significance, they remained no more than a collection of ghost-stories, rooted in folk-lore, unsatisfactory to psychologist, connoisseur and general reader alike. His consciousness of something malignant in creation expresses itself better in the novel *Evil Powers*. Here he presents two men, fundamentally good men, whose lifelong friendship slowly and against his will is poisoned by the proliferating, always latent jealousy which one of them, an energetic entrepreneur, feels towards the other's superior refinement of mind and manners. The issue between them is enacted from first to last on the earthly plane. As little as he could swallow determinism did Lie possess a metaphysical mind. Even his darkest imaginings are nowhere tinctured by any suggestion of a malignant universe or of a President of the Immortals, happy to have created sentient beings and to torture them through their sentience.

(6) *Lie's quality and achievement*

Bjørnson once declared—it was during the time that the two old friends were estranged[1]—that Lie had turned out two or three good things (unspecified), but that his true genius had been deformed by his strong-minded wife: he had been destined 'to be our romantic, to write things of beauty in rich colours'. 'By Lake Enare', *The Visionary* and *Ogres* scarcely bear this out.

It is in the purely human drama, that Lie found his greatness —and it may be observed incidentally that his presentation of it is preponderantly scenic, not panoramic or summary. In the concatenation of the scenes there is nothing clever, hardly even exciting. Lie is no ingenious yarn-spinner, nor is his style remarkable, either for good or ill. He constructs no tableaux of any kind. The personages who play out their drama have nothing about them that would strike their neighbours in the *milieu* of Norwegian countryside, seaport or provincial town as out of the way. He made no effort to create 'characters'; no one as much individualized even as Mr Casaubon emerges from the pages of his greater works. The lessons that can be distilled from them can scarcely be thought revolutionary or even arresting. A string of negatives, this. How comes it then that the affinities with Lie that spring to mind are with George Eliot and Thomas Hardy or that that outstanding—and deeply read—creative artist, Sigrid Undset, should rank[2] him among the great novelists of the world's literature?

The answer to these questions must be sought in the moral realm, in the pervasive sense, such as is engendered by novelists in the 'Great Tradition', that utterly veridical delineations of men, women and the life they lead spring from a mind not merely aware of these fellow-creatures' motives, but conscious all the time how they are aligned to a broad scale of ethical values, wisely and humanely conceived.[3]

This sounds portentous. To infer, however, that Lie indulges in judicial reviews and sentences would be quite wide of the mark, or that the moral woof of his stories makes them consistently grim and solemn. Tragedy may lurk in all and swoops in some. But the hard-worked fisher-folk of *Go Ahead!* have grand sprees, described with gusto, the parties in Fru Mørk's and Fru Baarvig's drawing-rooms are not in the least Strindbergian. Like *The Pilot and his Wife*, *Go Ahead!* reaches a climax in one of Norway's famed domestic show-downs: but, when the husband's authoritarian doctrines of his rights begin to break down before the wife's good-humoured insistence of her own claims, '*Rejer laughed*'—a hearty laugh, and the *éclaircissement* is completed on a footing of cheerful banter. Lie's humour, to be sure, may sometimes be ironical, even tinged with the sardonic—as when in *The Lifer* he comments on Nikolai's mother's position in the economic structure of society as a professional wet-nurse, the only one she is fit for—but it is neither cruel nor forced, and there is quite a lot of it.

It was this humour, this ease and balance, the fairmindedness which he shared with the less genial Elster, the wide, deep knowledge of his country and its people—plus, perhaps, his ability unobtrusively to set his readers thinking—that made Lie unquestionably the most generally popular of the Big Four of the eighteen-eighties—Ibsen, Bjørnson, Kielland and himself. Whether or not Sigrid Undset's high estimate be accepted, he will have his permanent place as Norway's great 'Victorian' novelist. Apart from its intrinsic virtues, the goodly corpus of his work after the sporadic attempts of Camilla Collett, Bjørnson and Kristian Elster also gave the Norwegian novel a solid status comparable with that reached in most other European countries by a lengthy and multifarious process. Somewhat old-fashioned though he may have been, it is none the less well to remember that within the national context he was, as Mr McFarlane rightly claims for him,[1] an 'innovator, the first author to write of the Nordland for over 150 years, the man who wrote the first novels of the sea, the first novels of commercial life, the first love novels even, of modern Norway'.

KIELLAND AND AMALIE SKRAM

(1) *Two completely 'modern' authors*

ALEXANDER KIELLAND and Amalie Skram were born within three years of one another and began their writing[1] in the latter half of that decade which, in the literature of their country, inaugurated the great *Umwertung aller Werte*. They were the first Norwegian writers of eminence who, even before their formal débuts, had completely given themselves to 'Det Moderne'. The eyes of neither were lifted to Heaven, Parnassus or Utopia. On the rare occasions when they wrote about a bygone era, it was to give the pre-history of conditions in their own time. Their contemporaries saw them primarily as social writers, and, certain reservations made, they *were* social writers, with a fairly wide purview and intent on exhibiting the frustrations and distresses caused by accepted beliefs, conventions or conditions of life.

A deep difference, however, is to be noted between these two authors, who, as it happened, had no very great regard for one another. Kielland, whom one might think of as a Whig aristocrat, attacked his broadly and vividly limned subjects in a spirit of fiery indignation, both pointing and distancing it by an abundance of humour, wit and irony. Amalie Skram, sprung from the proletariat herself, was subdued to the dimmer material she worked with; the grey miseries she describes from her own experience break her heart; no lines of action for their alleviation are suggested; the social scene which, fully and faithfully enough, she constructs remains secondary to the personal tragedies enacted in them, felt with a deep sympathy, an agony quite alien to Kielland's detachment. *A priori* one might conclude that Amalie Skram would be the finer novelist of the two. Unhappily she had no art. All her books remain 'documents'; Kielland's best belong to great literature.

(2) *Kielland's 'Novelletter'*

When in 1871 Alexander Lange Kielland (1849–1906)* returned to his native Stavanger to settle down as a business-man
there, he gave himself to an intensive and protracted course
of reading, largely under the guidance of Georg Brandes,[1]
whose idols became his own: Taine, Strauss and, above all,
John Stuart Mill, for whom he made active propaganda among
his friends.[2] But the ambition himself to become one of 'The
Men of the Modern Break-Through', as their leader came to
rank him, only ripened slowly. The process was hastened by
Kielland's first sojourn in Paris, in 1878, where he experienced
a tonic liberation after the philistine narrowness of little Stavanger,[3] and also had the good luck to run into Bjørnson,
who gave him enthusiastic encouragement and found him
a publisher.

The first fruits were gathered in †*Novelettes* (*Novelletter*, 1879)
—with †*New Novelettes* (1880) and †*Two Novelettes from
Denmark* (1882) quickly to come from the same branch.[4] They
were at once hailed as the remarkable products they are. A
few may be somewhat trivial in content, but in every one of
them there is an absolute sureness of effect, as well as an elegant
ease of style which nowhere betrays the tyro and for which no
model whatever could be found in Norwegian literature. The
'provincial lion', as Edvard Brandes remembered him, stood
revealed as the cosmopolitan aristocrat—who in Bjørnson's
eyes outshone all others at the state-ball in the Palace of
Versailles where he first saw him—and, at the same time, a
consummate artist. Among the short-story writers of about
his time Kielland can sustain comparison with Hans Christian

---

* Alexander Lange Kielland was a member of the rich patrician family of that
name which had been settled in Stavanger for nearly a hundred years when he
was born there on 18 February 1849. Passing out of the local Grammar School,
he took a respectable degree in law at Christiania and was admitted an attorney,
but never practised. Instead, on his marriage to Beate Ramsland in 1872, he
acquired and for nine years managed a brickyard. Between the years 1878 and
1891, nearly half of which were spent abroad (Paris and Copenhagen), his literary
work was his chief occupation. Thereafter and until his death he was in public
employment, first as *Borgermester* (elective town-clerk, more or less) of Stavanger
and then as the state-appointed *Amtmand* at Molde. He died of heart and kidney
disease at Bergen on 6 April 1906.

Andersen (whom he knew), Theodor Storm (whom apparently he did not know), Maupassant and Chekhov (whom he could not then know). Moreover, he created virtually a new *genre* or sub-*genre*. This Gallio, however, cared for none of these things. He was the last man in the world of letters with ambitions to be known as a stylist or to figure in a history of aesthetics.

Broadly speaking, this sub-*genre* stands to the general run of more elaborate fiction as the *proverbe* stands to *comédie*. Kielland's *Novelletter* have the pith, wit and good nature of Alfred de Musset;[1] and, as a *proverbe* by title and sub-title holds itself out to do, they are designed to illustrate a moral.

A charming example is given by 'Peat-Bog' ('Torvmyr')— a piece that would have delighted Hans Christian Andersen— in which a 'respectable old raven', disturbed in his solitude, swoops down on a party of yokels busy with the reclamation of some waste land and frightens them out of their wits by screaming 'The Devil take me' ('fanden gale mig'), an objurgation he had been taught in captivity when young. The tale is a neat little reminder of the inconvenience which the proliferating lords of creation and the expansion of which they are so proud cause their humbler fellow-creatures and the far from noble example they set in their modes of expression. Others are more ordinary little satires, like 'Erotik og Idyl', contrasting young lovers' dreams, nicely warmed up by their friends, with the cold squalor ensuing on the quick appearance of six little pledges without any accompanying increase of means.* Indicative of a more specific and more persistent bias is 'Ballroom Atmosphere' ('Balstemning'), where at an embassy reception a nobleman hears from the lips of his beautiful, low-born *tête-à-tête* of the proletariat's despair and fury at the wasteful splendour all around them.

The most celebrated among the anecdotes and parables is 'A Skippers' Yarn' ('En Skipperhistorie').[2] After a huddle of ships have long lain comfortable in port, the captains exchang-

---

* As a youth Søren had wondered with what justification folk reproduced themselves. 'But time and practical life had fortunately cured him of these idle and mischievous cerebral exercises. Besides, he was too moral and well-bred to offend his unsuspecting beloved by contemplating so licentious a prospect as that she might have many children. It is just one of the beautiful things about young people that they leave such matters to Our Lord and the stork.'

ing amicable visits, with tobacco and toddy, they gradually go
off on their voyages, until at last only one is left. Its crew grow
impatient, and reluctantly the captain and mate agree to set
sail too, but just outside harbour, in not too safe a roadstead,
the captain casts anchor again. The 'yarn' is advertised as a
picture of Europe becalmed by the Holy Alliance. The laggard
ship is Norway; and the sting lies in the tail: captain, mate
and crew remain *ad infinitum* at the few cables' length to which
they have ventured.

(3) '*Garman & Worse*' and '*Skipper Worse*'

Even though nothing so remote as the Holy Alliance enters
into them, 'A Skippers' Yarn' flies, as it were, the back-cloth
to all of Kielland's full-length novels. It was his purpose—
purpose in the full sense—to set forth through them the lethargic
conservatism of his country, as he apprehended it, lying like
a pall of thick snow over the corruptions and cruelties it stifled
and concealed. This image is a *leit-motif*, as it furnishes the title,
of the novel *Sne*. Kielland also employed its opposite, that of
fire: 'I light up as it were a bonfire in the middle, on which I
am minded to burn one or other social evil, and, around,
there group themselves a flock of people on whom the light
of the bonfire falls stronger or weaker, but the illumination
comes always from the fire *alone*; for that reason my figures
remain one-sidedly lit up or, as people say, superficial.'[1]

The beginning was made with †*Garman & Worse* (*Garman og
Worse*, 1880). Like the *Novelletter* in their smaller way, *Garman
& Worse* sprang from its author's head fully formed, and a
superb form it showed: it may justly be acclaimed as the finest
Norwegian novel of its century after Lie's *Niobe*.[2] Two cousins,
or sets of cousins, establish the focal points of the story. One is
Madeleine, half-French, the doubtfully legitimate daughter of
the most dashing member of the patrician family of Garman,
Richard, who after a career in the diplomatic service has, to
everyone's surprise, returned to his native town[3] to settle as
keeper of a lighthouse near by. To nip an incipient love-affair
between her and a handsome young fisher-lad in the bud,
Richard Garman sends her to his brother's in town for the

process of 'finishing'. There she is courted and attracted by the sheriff's secretary, in many respects an eligible young man, but, deeply cast down on discovering his *liaison* with her uncle's daughter-in-law Fanny and anxious at all costs to get away from her house, Madeleine allows herself to be married off to a middle-aged clergyman, a widower with a toupee. Her three town cousins are Morten, the faithless Fanny's husband, already in business, and his juniors, Rachel and Gabriel. In accordance with family tradition the cadet is designed for one of the learned professions, but book-learning makes no appeal to him, and, on putting his father under a great obligation, he is granted his dearest wish, to enter the family business, that of ship-owners, ship-builders and general merchants.

The obligation referred to is presented in one of the bravura-pieces of Norwegian writing, the scene of a great conflagration in Garman & Worse's shipyard. A new wooden sailing-ship, uninsured, is on the stocks, to be launched with due ceremony on the morrow, when a drunken artisan, nurturing a grievance against his employers, sets fire to the sheds near the slipway. The yard is quickly ablaze, and the ship itself would have been destroyed if young Gabriel, who, instead of doing his homework, had not, as usual, been pottering about to observe the launching devices, and taken it upon himself to organize some of the workmen, so that successfully, if prematurely, the ship is got into the water before the fire spreads to it. Christian Fredrik Garman, the father, reacts as has been stated, but the shock of the impending catastrophe has brought on a stroke that soon proves fatal. His death in its turn gives her chance to Rachel, a purposeful, intelligent girl, who has nurtured the same ambition as Gabriel. Her father's will appoints as her guardian Jacob Worse, an energetic, liberal-minded member of the family whose connexion with the Garmans has become purely titular. He gladly grants her wish to leave the home against which she too has chafed and go to Paris, where on her own initiative she enters an American office to learn business methods. Apprised of this—and not without a hint from herself—Worse goes off to fetch her home, marries her forthwith and so re-establishes the firm of Garman & Worse.

The weight of the story attaches to Christian Fredrik Garman's family, but the fortunes of Richard Garman and his Madeleine are most subtly integrated by the scenes between the two elderly brothers, so different in experiences and outlook, but bound together by real understanding and comradely affection, and the framing of the whole through beginning and ending it with Richard's lighthouse, where Madeleine loved and lost. The family story is also the history of a firm, and these two strands are likewise knit together by the reuniting and prospective revivification of the business when a Worse marries a Garman. These are matters of composition, and it is because of its artistry that *Garman & Worse* stands out in Kielland's *œuvre*. The overriding intention, however, of all that *œuvre*—to provide specimens of utilitarian literature, *nyttepoesi*—is by no means overlaid.

For long its title was to have been 'The Malcontents' ('De Misfornøiede'), even if Kielland like Dr Johnson's friend had to confess that: 'Cheerfulness was always breaking in.'[1] The malcontents, reticent enough in voicing their frustrations, are, broadly speaking, the younger generation: Madeleine, who succumbs; but first and foremost Gabriel and Rachel, who, as is worth remembering, fight their way out of them. Discontent, however, goes beyond these three. Wise Jacob Worse, for instance, observes that Christian Fredrik Garman himself, the awe-inspiring head of the family and firm, was in his day a malcontent, a sufferer from the strife of the generations—which may explain his sympathy with the brother who broke away and made a life for himself. More prominent in the author's scheme are the scenes laid in the 'West End',[2] the ironically named slums where the firm of Garman & Worse—patriarchally benevolent as it is in many ways—houses its employees and where resentment perpetually smoulders, to flare up in the act of arson countered by young Gabriel's presence of mind.

Although not next in chronological order, it may be opportune to say something now about †*Skipper Worse* (1882), in subject-matter so closely related to *Garman & Worse* (though no knowledge of events thirty years later is assumed). It tells how the firm of Garman & Worse came into existence, when the stout sea-dog Worse, hearing that his employer Morten

Garman (Christian Fredrik's father) is in financial straits, puts all his savings on the table before him and the honourable old consul refuses to take them except from a duly accredited and acknowledged partner. The commercial side, however, is not much in evidence—though there is a brilliant chapter on the coming of the herring-fleet to Stavanger and the process by which it pumps the life-blood through the whole community from high to low. As far as *milieu* is concerned, the interest centres on the religious life of the small shop-keepers and artisans of the town who had come under the spell of Norway's Wesley, Hans Nielsen Hauge.[1] Kielland had made some study of the Haugian revival, and the successors of those who fought and suffered in its heroic years were all about. His delineations are full, fair and, in view of his usual handling of the religious, surprisingly sympathetic, as even churchmen were forced to acknowledge. 'Full-bloodedness', as he called it, always won his admiration, and he had a sincere respect for Haugianism, as the direct, forcible expression of individuals' genuine convictions (and also, one may add, because it was at odds with the Establishment). Of its dark side, nevertheless, the terror of sin, death and damnation which it instilled, the canting hypocrisy of its hangers-on, the joylessness which it inflicted on all who, with or against their will, came into its orbit, he was equally aware, and it determines the course of the story. In his retirement Worse is entrapped by one of the most repulsive of the Haugians, a widow, whose avarice enforces his marriage to her obedient elder daughter, passionately and reciprocally in love though she is with another. The simple-minded, hearty old man is reduced to wretched imbecility; and his wife's sister, when she sees no escape from another loveless marriage determined by her mother, throws herself into the harbour.

Skipper Worse lacks the variety, as it must lack the verve and geniality, of *Garman & Worse*, but a deeper plumbing of human tragedy gives it power of a kind at which Kielland did not aim elsewhere, and it has some splendid scenes—one, perhaps the finest Kielland wrote, when Skipper Worse comes in on a radiant morning of early summer from his epoch-making voyage to Rio de Janeiro and greets his owner, who rows out to meet him: 'We come late, Consul, but we come sound', the words of triumph on his lips years later as he sails into the next world.

(4) *Kielland's 'tendens'*

In all the novels not yet discussed *tendens* takes charge. One by one Kielland fastens on abuses, and the stories are constructed to bring out the evil they are and the blight they spread. The earliest of these stories, *Working Men* (*Ardeidsfolk*, 1881), doubly forms the spearhead of his attack. For it is the Establishment itself, in its narrower sense, the captain and mate of 'A Skippers' Yarn', at which the thrust is aimed, the all-powerful, all-pervasive civil service. It also gives the book its ironical title: in a speech its chief representative Statsraad (Cabinet Minister) Bennechen vaunts himself, his colleagues and underlings as 'the true working-men in the land'. The story exhibits their arrogance and the nasty immorality of their private lives, and also their torpor, incompetence, inter-departmental jealousy and recourse to the blind eye which leave honest, decent *administrés* either dead or embarked as penniless emigrants for America.

With *Else* (1881), the 'Christmas Story' of a young whore who perishes miserably, he shows up the codified pedantry, hypocrisy and tragi-comic futility of Vigilance Societies; with *Poison* (*Gift*, 1883)[1] the ineptitude, indeed the cruelties to mind and body, of the state-regulated school-system; in *Fortuna* (1884) the reckless, disastrous speculations with other people's money that the big business of the time, with its veiled conspiracies and accommodations, had brought in its train.[2]

More ubiquitous was the running fire which Kielland directed at the Church. Clergymen, with something to their detriment insinuated, figure in almost all his novels. Two of them are head-on attacks. In *Snow* (*Sne*, 1886) what, short of the episcopate, might be considered the aristocracy of the church is pilloried in two men of God, father and son, well placed, able and influential, but completely reactionary and unscrupulous. They engage on the holy-unholy task of breaking the spirit of the intelligent, free-thinking heiress to whom the son has become engaged. She stands firm, however, and fights her way out of

87

the cold, sterile snow that literally and metaphorically weighs on Daniel Jürges's rural parsonage and the country at large.

After the High Church, as it is called in Norway, it was the turn of the 'Low', which in course of time had taken over from the Haugians' pietistic revival all but its spiritual vitality. The central figure in *The Feast of St John* (*Sankt Hans Fest*, 1887) is Rev. Morten Kruse, a man of immense energy, a crude admonitory preacher and tireless organizer of 'good works', whose sole guiding principle is 'He who is not with us [i.e. with me] is against us'. His autocracy has spread a reign of terror through the town in which he holds a benefice and virtually paralysed all other leaders of opinion, as is exemplified by his annihilating—merely because he has not been consulted —a harmless summer-entertainment planned by a quartette of benevolently minded young fellow-citizens.

(5) *The Kielland 'affair' and its aftermath*

Kierkegaard had taught Kielland, as so many of his contemporaries, to look on the Church in the northern countries as nothing more than a branch of the civil service, principally concerned to preserve forms and keep the citizenry quiet and obedient. Essentially therefore *Snow* and even *The Feast of St John* were just one aspect of his general campaign against established institutions. But it was easy to construe his animadversions against the clergy as something more, and that, making Kielland the eye of a great political storm, was to have grave consequences.

After years of agitation and growing strength the Party of the Left had triumphed: they had, in 1884, successfully impeached the king's conservative ministers and established parliamentary government with their own leader at its head. They liked to consider themselves the Liberal party, but were, in fact, a distrustful coalition of the old, pious and fundamentally conservative country interest (the 'Peasants'), who had the voting strength, and the radicals, who provided most of the brains and programme. Some of the latter were—and more were suspected of being—'free-thinkers', an abomination therefore to all who took their religious and moral principles from the Church. Events of no great political importance in themselves conspired almost at once to strike the new régime at its vulnerable point. Late in 1885 came the confiscation of two allegedly indecent books, with the prosecution of the authors and the imprisonment of one of them, the like of which had never happened in the 'bad old days'.[1] It coincided with the 'Kielland affair', which had its origin in a proposal from Bjørnson and Lie that Kielland should be granted the public pension they enjoyed and which dragged its weary length through three parliamentary sessions,[2] to end in rejection each time, even when at last sponsored by the government. The cardinal issue was that formulated in the report of the first relevant committee—that Kielland's activities as a writer were 'deemed to stand in opposition to the prevailing moral and religious ideas in the country'. More remarkable than anything said in the parliamentary transactions were the silences. No one really spoke up for freedom of thought and speech; no one dared mention the fact that Bjørnson, the linchpin of the Left, had publicly renounced his Christian faith and still drew his pension;[3] from the Front Bench came only one speech, in which in the fewest possible words the prime minister said that he dissented from the rest of his Cabinet in opposing the government motion (!); the Opposition, the successors of those whom *Working Men* had helped to turn out of office, sat completely dumb, but *gaudens*, ready with its unanimous No and watching its adversaries commit *hara-kiri*. The Left was irremediably split; three parties contested the next general election, and the Right returned to power.

Kielland, too, kept silence throughout 'the affair'. No doubt it was a slap in the face that hurt. But he had fairly well gauged the political situation, and the result of the actual voting was no disillusionment. His pessimism about the society around him merely deepened: the Liberal triumph had achieved nothing that, to his mind, mattered; the new men thrown up in the turbulence were 'swinish', and the filth in which they delighted to wallow spattered everything. This view, obliterating all his old geniality and verve, conditions *Jacob* (1891), the story of a base country-lad who becomes a shop-boy (and starts stealing from the till on the first day), then a petty moneylender, then a shop-proprietor himself, systematically ruining all his competitors, and in the end a bank-director and piously spoken member of Parliament. 'He knew only one piece of biblical history; but he knew that from A to Z; and that was the story of Jacob, the scoundrel who swindled himself through life and ended as a patriarch in Heaven'; his eldest son, he was resolved, should be called after him.

Jacob was the last novel which its author, then aged 42 and with fifteen fairly active years before him, was to write. The reasons for this grievous cessation have been much debated.[1] Had the undoubted strain that imaginative writing inflicted on him become intolerable? (There are plain signs of fatigue in *Jacob* and even in *The Feast of St John.*) Was the scene before his eyes so black that to describe it could give him neither pleasure nor scope for his best gifts?[2] These were certainly powerful factors. But there was another. The author of *Jacob* saw the society around him as hoggish or abject; *in foro conscientiæ* he considered as mere trumpery the literature that was being written by his juniors in its obsession with themselves, their states of mind and their style, to the exclusion of all concern with their fellow-men; but, champion of Det Moderne as he had always been, he could not acknowledge that the rising generation was *wrong*. It must be he who was at fault: old-fashioned, superannuated, too far out of touch with them to exert any influence by his authorship. But the prime purpose that had governed it, to help his fellows to a better life, might still be attained along other ways; he, the inveterate enemy of the 'true working-men in the land', became one of them, a municipal and governmental administrator.

(6) *Kielland's art*

What Kielland had to say was important to him; how he said it much less so. We know little of the preparation of his books. The working-out of his theme, even if it involved exhausting labour, seems to have caused him as little real anxiety as the choice of stories and incidents in which to embody it. But he liked what he had written to be neat and fresh, like his turn-out; the stories left no loose ends hanging, the pictures were to be 'finished', the meaning of each sentence clear, without abruptness, ellipsis or dark allusions. His great bonfires of abuses vividly lighted up the faces and happenings in the foreground; what lay behind he left, except by implication, in the dark.

As the grandson of the richest man in Norway was a notorious dandy, so the chronicler of the Garmans was the great gentleman in his country's literature. Even if he is never obtruded in the first person singular, he comes out in a number of ways besides the well-bred elegance of his style. Indignation may have been the motive power behind his authorship, but he never jeers or storms at the rogues, tyrants and cowards in the pillory. He has a Chaucerian ability to cherish a fellow-feeling for the sinner while detesting the sin. When asked whether he had used any models in *Else*, he said, with ironical exaggeration, that the nearest to a model he had was himself—for Konsul With, the hypocritical lecher who sets Else on the road to ruin. Even for Rev. Morten Kruse he shows consideration. The man loved money; he had been cruelly despoiled in the great swindles described in *Fortuna*: he wanted to get back what he had lost and have his revenge on the society which had robbed and humiliated him. He may have been a scoundrel, but he was a wholehearted one.

Fortuna has a magnificent little scene when Kruse comes to Dr Carsten Løvdahl, the arch-swindler, who has deliberately adopted religious hypocrisy as a business principle, to learn that he is ruined and to ask what the next step is to be: Løvdahl paternally puts his hand on his shoulder and gives the answer: 'I will pray to Jesus, that he may help you.'[1] It is by comparatively mild touches that Kielland gains some of his finest effects and by unemphatic juxtapositions, as of the two funerals which take place simultaneously in *Garman & Worse*, the great convoy that follows Konsul Christian Fredrik Garman to the cemetery and the knot of bibulous labourers who drop into her grave the girl his son had seduced. In death as in life 'some people travel first class, some second, and some third'.[2]

Not only does *Skipper Worse* provide the prologue to *Garman & Worse*, but many other strands also—like that between *Fortuna* and *The Feast of St John* just alluded to—connect almost all Kielland's novels together. There is, however, nothing systematic about this; it was not his intention to compose one outsize 'genealogical' novel, as Galsworthy's *Forsyte Saga* came to be; nor was it to provide a sociology after the manner of Balzac's *Comédie Humaine*.[1]

The resemblance to Balzac, however, for all the difference of the two authors' temperaments, tone and style, is close; both realized and demonstrated how enormous a fraction of men's interests and time is occupied by their *business* and were insistent on the vast importance of sheer money in all human affairs; both knew thoroughly the channels through which it flows—Kielland perhaps the more widely and thoroughly of the two, but there is no discipleship to be established, any more than there is between Kielland and Thackeray, in spite of similarities in technique and tone. Nor, 'gripped' as he confessed himself by the novels of Zola,[2] did he undergo any nameworthy influence from him. Determinism, heredity, degeneracy and delirium have no place in his mind and art; nor was he out to exemplify any literary theory.[3]

What Kielland absorbed from the printed page came preponderantly from the philosophers and moralists. His early enthusiasm for Kierkegaard and Heine endured; though he came to deplore the style of the former, he revelled in the latter's pregnancy and wit; but it was always the objects rather than the manner of their satire that made the deeper impress. The only imaginative literature to leave a clear mark on his art was that of Charles Dickens. *Bleak House*, *Hard Times*, *Little Dorrit*, *Our Mutual Friend* had been bonfires such as those he wished to kindle himself; the progeny of Mrs Jellyby, Mr Creakle, the Barnacles and Veneerings people his scenes. The episode in *Working Men*, when at a wedding breakfast the understrappers of the Establishment uproariously ape the forms and sentiments of their superiors, would certainly not have been the same if its author had not read Dickens. The grotesque 'Noah's Ark', where Else lived with its eccentrics and failures, and, equally, Abraham Løvdahl's love-affair (in *Fortuna*) with the blind work-girl are entirely in his manner. But to Dickens's extremes of melodrama, rhetoric and sentiment it was within neither his intentions nor his power to run.

(7) *Amalie Skram's preoccupation with sexuality*

By contrast with Kielland's meteoric rise, Amalie Skram's*
was slow. Not until 1882, her thirty-seventh year, did she
publish a piece of imaginative writing; not till 1885 her first
novel. For fifteen years after that she continued fairly prolific,
with tales, novels and two plays.[1]

Amalie Skram's second play *Agnete* (1893) differs from Lie's
and Kielland's experiments with drama for being amenable
to the same critical standards as her fiction. It deals with an
idle, youngish *divorcée* who has been resorting to petty thefts,
false pretences and untruthful hard-luck stories to finance the
easy life to which she has been accustomed when she falls
deeply in love with an upright law don, long an admirer of hers.
He tells her straight out that her reputation forbids his marrying
her; she refuses a clandestine *liaison* (as she does a loveless
marriage offered by another) and finally goes off to earn an
honest livelihood as a housekeeper far away. For once, Amalie
Skram has presented two lovers who seem pretty well 'made
for one another', but the theme of the play—to recur over
and over again in her writings—is the formidable difficulty,
arising from temperament as well as convention, of adjusting
passion and marriage in the social conditions of her time. This
theme it is, not unskilfully varied in sub-plots and sustained by
plausible characters and dialogue, which holds *Agnete* together,
rather than any elaborate plot or even the vicissitudes of the

---

* Bertha Amalie Alver was born at Bergen on 22 August 1846, the daughter of
a shopkeeper in humble circumstances, but was well educated (and remarkably
beautiful). In 1864 she married Bernt Ulrik August Müller, a sea-captain of good
family, and accompanied him on many of his voyages all over the world until
he retired from the sea in 1876. From 1877 she dabbled in journalism and, after
separating from her husband in 1878 (divorce in 1880), mixed in liberal circles in
Christiania. In 1884 she married the Danish man of letters Erik Skram and
settled in Copenhagen, where she died on 15 March 1905 in poverty and neglect.
She had two sons by her first husband and a daughter by the second. Shortly
before her death she was awarded a small pension by the Danish government.
The contrast she felt between the friendliness of Denmark and her neglect in
Norway provoked her pamphlet *Landsforrædere* (*Traitors*, 1901) and the inscription
on her tomb: 'Danish citizen, Danish subject and Danish author'; but her most
important literary work belongs to Norway. Twice (1877/8 and 1894) she had
to receive treatment in lunatic asylums; her thinly veiled attacks on a Copenhagen alienist and the care of the insane in †*Professor Hieronimus* (1895) and
Paa Sct. Jørgen (1895) caused a great stir, not only in Denmark.

heroine. By the standards of the day it was a thoroughly untidy play about untidy people—the Bohemian *milieu* and scrappy construction resemble Strindberg's recent *Comrades*[1]—and, as one of the earliest of that kind, it met with scant applause at first. But on audiences that knew Chekhov it was to leave a deep impression.[2]

Half of Amalie Skram's novels are built on themes akin to that of *Agnete*. *Constance Ring* (1885), which makes the start, tells of a middle-class young woman's ill-starred marriages. The first is to a considerably older, insensitive man whom she has never loved and whose embraces revolt her, terminated, before the divorce she is contemplating, by his being accidentally drowned. The second union, with a younger, considerate and cultivated husband, is a more promising and more complicated affair. Constance comes to love him and is happy for a while, but the discovery of a former mistress—whom he still sees, but hardly does more than see—kills her love and her happiness stone dead; and a second discovery, that the seemingly inoffensive lover to whom she gives herself is likewise 'entangled', drives her, frantic with disgust at him and herself, to suicide.

Regarded as a novel, *Constance Ring* is an amateurish performance and, in varying degrees, this is true of all the author's work. For all her experiences and distresses, the heroine raises no interest and sympathy in herself; often enough the reader cannot make out what she and the story are 'at'; the tragic end is huddled up; and the style lacks all distinction. But its publication caused a great scandal,[3] even in the years when marital and extra-marital relations were under constant debate (*A Doll's House*, *Ghosts*, *A Gauntlet*, Kielland's *Poison*). The chief conservative newspaper of Norway stigmatized it as more indecent than *Nana*.[4] The outcry was chiefly provoked by the exhibition of a 'respectable' lady constantly preoccupied, decently veiled though they might be, with the carnal concomitants of marriage and 'love', and also by the suspicion that the well-known Fru Skram had given the public bits from her autobiography.

Hazardous though it may be to refer everything that an author presents to an actual experience in the flesh, it can scarcely be doubted that in *Constance Ring* and other stories

Amalie Skram was fighting—and trying to fight out—her own battle. The short novel *Betrayed* (*Forraadt*, 1892) throws a clearer light on this than *Constance Ring*. Aurora Ingstad at 17½ marries the considerably older sea-captain Riber and at once accompanies him on his ship. She is horrified by all associations with the marriage-bed and still more horrified at her husband's previous fornications, which she morbidly forces him to recount in detail. In return she 'gives him hell'. Riber, passionate, but also understanding, is so broken down by the sense of guilt and hopelessness which her recriminations and frigidity have engendered that he throws himself overboard. Something like the first half of this, one is constrained to believe, must have happened when, at about the same age as Aurora, the authoress married her first husband and sailed the seas with him.

It has been argued from *Constance Ring*, *Betrayed* and *Madame Inès* (*Fru Inès*, 1891)[1]—the story of a seemingly hot-blooded Spaniard who obtains no satisfaction when flirtation gives way to something more serious—that wherever the sexual element predominates in Amalie Skram's compositions they are 'tragedies of women who cannot love'.[2] This cannot be upheld. Constance Ring, Agnete and Petra Fridmann (to whom we shall shortly come), at least, are perfectly *capable* of love. What shatters them is the proximity of the highest erotic ecstasy to the 'swinishness' with which they brand all sexual relations falling short of this ecstasy, the fatal ease with which this proximity can be betrayed and the material difficulties of entering upon and preserving the 'marriage of true minds' which would sanctify the marriage of the body. Amalie Skram may not be the first clinician of female frigidity, but she did, to use Ibsen's phrase, 'move the frontier-posts' by putting into the forefront of a literary work the bewilderment, fear, desperate disillusionments and tragic heart-searchings of women who, imperfectly mated, are racked in mind and body from their failure to attain the 'miracle of miracles' (Nora Helmer's *vidunderligste*). Her revered predecessor Camilla Collett, in her pioneer novel of 'the woe of women', had stopped short at the altar. But, it may be noted, the twin focal points round which her junior's matrimonial tragedies revolve are the same as those of *The Sheriff's Daughters* —the imperative demands of all-transcending love and the lethal obstacles in the way of following its call.[1]

(8) *Amalie Skram as a pioneer of Naturalism*

The first of these points is, in any interpretation of the word, romantic. But the author who clung so desperately to this romantic principle is most commonly celebrated for something on the face of it quite alien—as the founder of Norwegian naturalistic fiction. Unless (as was done, for instance, in con-demnations of Ibsen's *Ghosts* and Kielland's *Else*) naturalism is summarily identified with indecency and indecency with any allusion to sexual relations, that claim is principally based on some works of hers not yet mentioned. Both in order of time and for the completeness with which it conforms to the naturalistic programme, the short story 'Ma Høier's Lodgers' ('Madam Høiers Leiefolk', 1882)[2] stands at their head. With unbroken objectivity and as much material detail as the limited compass allows, it presents the wife of a drunken, one-legged labourer, who is evicted from Mrs Høier's slum tenement, and, by giving her new-born twins spirits in order to lull them to sleep, brings a sentence of three years' imprisonment for infanticide upon herself—a sentence she accepts with gratitude, since it means at least a roof over her head.

Of greater substance are five novels: *Sjur Gabriel* (1887), *The 'Two Friends'* (*To Venner*, 1887), *S. G. Myre* (1890), *Off-spring* (*Afkom*, 1898)[3] and *Lucie* (1888), the last-named Amalie Skram's tepid contribution[4] to the literature of prostitution then proliferating in Norway. The remaining four were designed as a series,[5] under the collective title *The Hellemyr Folk* (*Hellemyrs-folket*). They make up the family saga of a wretchedly poor fisherman-crofter from Hellemyr, Sjur Gabriel, his wife and their descendants through three generations, who make their livings as seamen or as dock-labourers and ships' chandlers in the lower quarters of Bergen. Nothing spectacular or exciting comes within their ken. Respectability is the limit of their ambition; none of them attains to or even dreams of *grandeurs*. But there is abundance of *misères*, almost unalloyed;

their surroundings are sordid when they are not squalid; the practices of a lifeless pietism alternate with the workaday struggle for existence, beset by accidents, debt, horrible smells, death and disease; small wonder if some of them—but only *some*—give way to drunkenness, incontinence and crime. Amalie Skram said of herself that she 'wept her way through her books'; no fiction outdoes *The Hellemyr Folk* in calling up and sustaining an atmosphere of sheer grim misery.

'Zola's pupil from Bergen', it is facile to conclude. An unflinching realist Amalie Skram may truly be called, but she was a *naturaliste* with a difference.[1] She was never anyone's disciple. As a girl she was carried away by Byron (Byron!— but chiefly because in *Cain* he had said 'We, who know the truth, must speak it').[2] She venerated Camilla Collett, she came to venerate Tolstoy, but her art was that of an autodidact: her consistently flat style and total neglect of 'construction' show it. As for Zola, we may believe her when she said at the time of 'Ma Høier's Lodgers' that she had read very little of him, and at no time did she come nearer to him than there. She resembles him in the prominence she gives to accurately described *milieu* and its formative influence, in the inclusion of the proletariat within her purview and in her obsession with sexuality. In at least one very important respect, however— apart from temperament—the difference between them was radical. Any intention she may have had of making *The Hellemyr Folk* a quasi-biological object-lesson in heredity and degeneracy, like *Les Rougon-Macquart*, soon evaporated. *Sjur Gabriel* is about two irredeemable drunkards; but their descendants are not conspicuously a family of alcoholics. More than that, the last of the line to be introduced seem the soundest: young Severin in *Offspring*, a sturdy lad, and his sister Fie, who may have gone off the rails temporarily with an army officer, but settles down as the respectable wife of a skin-and-hide dealer. Sympathy was always there; there is a glint of hope at the end. The pessimistic, impassible, 'scientific' determinism of the Naturalistic school is in abeyance.[3]

A wretched microcosm, the world Amalie Skram knew as a girl, is faithfully presented in the saga of the Hellemyr Folk. A greater interest, however, even here lies in the purely personal realm, in the life-histories of Sivert, Sjur Gabriel's grandson, and his wife Petra. As he is the most fully portrayed of his family, so he may be designated the worst: he is the undetected murderer of his grandmother, he is a dishonest shopkeeper, defrauds his benefactor and dies in gaol on a charge of forgery; but his fallings away from honest resolution genuinely puzzle him; he thinks himself, on the whole, a decent fellow, and Amalie Skram's conscientious, compassionate record almost makes us come to think so too. With his wife we are back at the kind of problem broached in *Constance Ring*. An able, respectable working-class girl, Petra Fridmann is introduced as housekeeper to Consul Smith, whose wife is a bed-ridden invalid. Petra becomes his mistress. Her intercourse with him breeds passionate love in her, but it is unreciprocated. When Fru Smith dies, the consul takes a second wife from his own social circle and promotes the marriage between his ex-mistress and his sometime house-boy, Sivert. Petra's heart dies within her. She becomes an ugly, venomous shrew; the hell which her lovelessness makes of her home is shown as a much greater power for evil than indigence or hereditary alcoholism.

The figure of Petra Fridmann, if nothing else, demonstrates that no hard and fast line can be drawn between the author's social novels, on the one hand, and the psychological, erotic on the other. The naturalist Amalie Skram and the romantic Amalie Skram were one. That gives her work its singular and stimulating, if artistically unattractive, character. With her primarily erotic delineations she was more truly the pioneer, but it was the others which, on the whole, have won her the greater fame. Several, with less success, tried to follow in her footsteps; but only Arne Garborg can, as far as Norway is concerned, dispute the naturalist laurel with her.

6

GARBORG AND OTHER LANDSMAAL
AUTHORS OF HIS TIME

(1) *Garborg before 1892*

IN appearance, manner and the habit of mind revealed through
his finest works Arne Garborg (1851–1924)* strikes one as more
completely the countryman than any other great figure in
Norwegian literature. Nevertheless, during the first phase of
his authorship, a span of almost twenty years, he was more
exclusively involved in the literary life of the capital, under a
variety of aspects, than they.

Some inconsiderable juvenilia apart, his authorship began
in 1874 with a critique, long enough to make a volume, of
Emperor and Galilean, the latest work of Ibsen, whose *Brand*
and *Peer Gynt* had set his imagination on fire as only Nietzsche
was ever to do again. Careful and understanding as the
criticism may be, more than anything *Henrik Ibsens Keiser og
Galilær* is a document in Garborg's religious biography, a
final turning away from the simple and yet romantic beliefs
of his youth. His first serious incursion into belles-lettres came
in 1878, with *A Free-Thinker* (*Ein Fritenkjar*),[1] a pedestrian,
semi-autobiographical novel, whose only interesting portions,
however, answer to the same definition as the book on Ibsen.

* Aadne, the son of a small freeholder who had not yet attained to the dignity
of a surname, assumed that of his native farm, Garborg, and changed his first
name to Arne. He was born at Time, 15 miles from Stavanger, on 25 January
1851, and became a primary schoolteacher at the age of 15. He passed his matriculation examination in 1875, but did not complete his studies at Christiania
University. From 1879 to 1887 he held minor clerical posts under government.
In 1898 he was awarded a small State grant for his services to the arts, and a
national testimonial in 1921 brought in kr. 100,000 (£5,000). Otherwise, he
depended for a livelihood on his journalism and books. His first published piece
is of 1870; the last entry in his posthumously published diary (*Dagbok*, 6 vols.,
1924–7) was written a fortnight before his death, in the suburbs of Christiania,
on 14 January 1924. In 1887 he married Hulda Bergersen, like himself author,
journalist and Landsmaal enthusiast, also a prominent agitator for folk-dancing,
folk-songs, national costumes and a Landsmaal theatre.

Peasant Students (*Bondestudentar*, 1882), however, the first important piece of writing in Landsmaal since the death of Vinje, made its author a man of mark. It tells of a country lad, Daniel Braut, who has been good at his book and sent to the university at Christiania, where he reads Divinity. From sheepishness, poverty and lethargy, he fails to gain much, and his backers at home lose interest in their protégé; he is accordingly obliged to have recourse alternately to the patron of many other starveling undergraduates, the orthodox cleric known as 'Pater Omnipotens', and to a Grundtvigian chaplain. The former gets him a tutorship in a well-to-do farming family. In despair at worrying through to a degree by any other means, like another young contemporary of his he engaged himself to his employer's 'elderly, ugly daughter'.[1] The story ends with his entering on a brighter phase of existence by attending his first dancing class.

Peasant Students, the authenticity of which is not in question, gives a scathing picture, all the more distressing for the black shadows thrown forward in it, of university life in the author's time and country[2] as it affected those who came to it from farm or cottage. Of the advantages these young men are, according to their professors' high-flown phrases, to reap—at great sacrifice on the part of their friends and with no little cudgelling of their heavy and often undernourished brains—most in fact receive nothing beyond a diploma (provided they stay the course). Even theology is no more to them than an obstacle-race to an income, and Daniel Braut was not singular in changing his religious tenets according as the mild breezes of charity might fill his sails. From the moment they make their clumsy apology for a bow at Matriculation, the Peasant Students are segregated from those of their fellow-freshmen who have some cultural tradition behind and around them; their opportunities for co-operative self-education are so pitiably limited that only a few can partake in even this benefit. Yet to such clownish hermits is increasingly entrusted, in the decay of the old patrician and bureaucratic castes, the future of their country's civilization and morals.

Men-Folk (*Mannfolk*, 1886) went on further to investigate with the same unbroken impassibility the lives not only of undergraduates, but also of some seniors who, having weathered the rough waters depicted in *Peasant Students*, had reached a haven of sorts, not always very eremitical. Its central figure is another theological student of peasant stock, Laurits Kruse. His story mainly revolves about the amatory relations he entertains simultaneously with two women—the educated, vital Dagmar Dyring and a sensual servant-girl. The latter he gets with child, in consequence whereof she loses her place and is driven to the streets, Kruse doing nothing to help her in her confinement, the illness of their bastard or the trouble in which she involves herself with the police by kindly supplying them with a fictitious name for its father. All he proves capable of is renewed sexual intercourse with her on a favourable occasion and, within twenty-four hours, becoming engaged to Dagmar, after solemnly swearing that he has nothing in his past life with which to reproach himself.

Fiction cannot show a more despicable character than this candidate for Holy Orders, and the picture of the rising *intelligentsia* is even more devastatingly sombre here than in *Peasant Students*. In the Norway of the time one would scarcely look for the *raffinement* of the wasters exhibited in contemporary French fiction, but equally one fails to see one spark of the intellectual fire which Gissing's heroes so desperately strove to keep alight in London lodgings as miserable as those of Christiania undergraduates. And what serves as relief in *Men-Folk* does little to lighten the tone. It concerns Georg Jonathan, a somewhat older man, also embroiled in a *liaison*. Jonathan takes a curious pride in believing himself the illegitimate son of a passing Englishman, but this belief fortifies his energetic, pragmatic 'Anglo-Saxon' view of life; and, for all the cynicism of its motivation, he eventually makes an honest woman of his mistress, not through outward compulsion nor because he feels that their strong mutual affection involves him in any obligation, but because he has reached the conclusion that marriage, however imperfect an institution, is the common lot and had best be endured with a good grace. His friends, mostly whore-mongers, can hardly talk about anything but 'sex' when they meet, and, as in *Peasant Students* it was indicated that a young man will do anything for a pittance, so *Men-*

Folk teaches that he will do anything to get a woman at as cheap a price as possible.

Men-Folk constituted Garborg's contribution to the *Bohême-fejde* (Bohemia-feud) which caused such a far-ranging stir that something must be said about it here even if the literary value of its instigations was often poor. This is particularly true of its storm-centre, *From Christiania's Bohemia (Fra Kristiania-Bohêmen,* 1885),[1] by Arne Garborg's friend Hans Jæger.* It is the story of two satyrs, classifiable as intellectuals, one of whom, realizing that perpetual sexual intercourse is the one thing worth his living for and is impossible, shoots himself dead, while the other, a more philosophical type, concludes that he is a victim of determinism and that he can in some degree sublimate his lust by lecturing and writing about prostitution; he is left lying on his sofa, going on with the reading of Zola. It is a long, tedious and confused story, but, in one sense, not an immoral one: no one could be lured by it to Vika, the red-light quarter of Christiania which it describes. That milieu, however, makes it pornography all the same. Some of the scenes are grossly indecent and inflammatory. Living persons are introduced; there is a particularly scandalous passage about Bjørnson.[2] *From Christiania's Bohemia* was confiscated by the police within an hour of publication—the ban remained in force for sixty-five years—and, on a variety of charges, Jæger was sentenced to imprisonment and a fine.

Almost simultaneously with *From Christiania's Bohemia* appeared *Albertine* (1886), which tells of a decent working-girl's seduction by a police officer, who then has her registered as a public prostitute and ensures her utter degradation. It is a short, sober tale, quite void of general speculations or special pleading, by the painter Christian Krohg (1852–1925), whose great picture of the cardinal scene of his novel—Albertine being ushered into the police surgeon's room—now hangs in

---

* Hans Henrik Jæger (1854–1910) was one of the leaders, from the extreme Left, of undergraduate opinion in his early days and became a convinced anarchist. He wrote a small number of inconsiderable novels, plays and treatises besides *Fra Kristiania-Bohêmen*. After the condemnation of the latter, he went to pieces and died in extreme poverty. Now chiefly remembered for the portrait of an incipient alcoholic by Edvard Munch, in the Norwegian National Gallery, he is not to be confused with his exact contemporary, the worthy literary historian Henrik Jæger.

the Norwegian National Gallery. The public exhibition of this picture was long prohibited and the novel confiscated,[1] but Krohg was let off with a fine of kr. 100 (£5).[2]

Though scarcely presented as an object-lesson, the nemesis of the debauched brutishness prevalent in *From Christiania's Bohemia* and *Men-Folk* emerged in Garborg's *Tired Men* (*Trætte Mænd*, 1891), the central figure of which, Gram, is an older man than Braut or Kruse. At 40, his will and the poor flowers of his youthful idealism have completely wilted in the boring routine of a government department, mechanical visits to his mistress (a prostitute) and absinthe-drinking. He gets, however, the chance of pulling himself together for a new start in life by marriage to a healthy young woman, Fanny Holmsen, who earns her living in an office, belongs to approximately his own rank in society and is ready to take him.[3] But, haunted by imbecile doubts about her, he is unable to make up his mind, sinking further and further in alcoholism and despondency until she too despairs of him and marries someone else. The story ends with Gram, who has shown some vapid interest both in spiritualism and the religious velleities of the French *décadents*, making his way into a church, accompanied by George Jonathan's comment: 'The tired go to the priest.'[4]

The labouring poor do not come into them, but that rather trifling exception apart, *Peasant Students*, *Men-Folk* and *Tired Men* had proclaimed their author to be the most absolute *naturaliste* in the land. Some satire, to be sure, glinted here and there in his sordid chronicles, but they lacked all Kielland's verve and Amalie Skram's tragic compassion. His pessimism and determinism were complete: his social pictures were those of abject cattle, with squalid debauchery for the only high lights in *la bête humaine*'s existence, and the individuals in the herd were crushed by it, unless, like Georg Jonathan, they could armour their flanks with utter cynicism. A character in *Men-Folk* exclaimed: 'We are swine. But what the Devil are we to do?'[5]

The answer to this question which the end of *Tired Men* gives was one which could afford small satisfaction either to the author's old associates in the cause of Det Moderne or to those who had combated them in the name of the Ideal. The counter-question presented itself: Was Garborg, like Gram, about to creep into some tabernacle, or was he perchance donning the newest literary fashion, to show himself as the perfect Norwegian *décadent*?

In writing *Peasant Students* Garborg had not become a *naturaliste* by accident; prepared for it by developments in native literature, he knew what was emerging from the Cercle de Médan and the theories about literature held there.[1] And so now, a decade later, he was well aware of the variety of impulses arising in all parts of the world which the Austrian Bahr subsumed under his title *The Overcoming of Naturalism*.[2] One of them that had undoubtedly interested him was the flight into a completely passive aestheticism of the newer French novelists such as Huysmans, some of whom it was as easy to label 'Tired Men' as decadents. Garborg himself, at this time, was something of a tired man. He had passed through some of the hardest years of his hard life. He was suffering from the profound disillusionment experienced at this juncture not only by newcomers into the literary arena,[3] but also by some of their seniors—a double disillusionment, both at the extinction of liberalism when the Liberal party had come into power[4] and, the reverse of the same medal, at the apparent futility of the strenuous utilitarian literature characteristic of the eighteen-seventies and eighteen-eighties. Like Kielland he may have felt that he had come to a dead end. But it soon became apparent that the way out for him was neither the renunciation of literature nor 'decadence'.

A number of agencies, working upon him within a short space of time, came to dispel his hopelessness and, ultimately, the black pessimism to which his Christiania novels bear witness: Nietzsche, Tolstoy and the American sociologist Henry George. The impact he received from Nietzsche was of the nature of a therapeutic shock which permanently restored to him his moribund Will to Live; his specific doctrines, notably that of the Superman and his rights, however, he rejected. The hither-worldliness of Tolstoy's Christian teaching on the other hand left an indelible impress, while Henry George transformed his anarchistically tinged socialism by giving it a positive principle.[5]

More external factors were in play also: not only the success of his marriage, but also stimulating visits to Paris, where he fraternized with Jonas Lie, and to Germany, where the *avant-garde* saluted him as the fourth Evangelist from the North after Ibsen, Bjørnson and Strindberg. Last, but not least, after some twenty years' absence he revisited his native Jæren, the flat, desolate region south of Stavanger, and realized that his true life-giving roots lay there. Out of the inspiration of its wild landscape and weather, of his memories, both poignant and grateful, of what he had experienced there and of his renewed intercourse with its gnarled, meditative natives grew the group of works in which his powers as an imaginative creator and as a thinker attained to a power and a complexity that had had small scope in delineations of peasant students, debauchees and tired men. Simultaneously, his deep-lying concern with religious belief, which had long lain dormant, sprang to life again.

(2) *Garborg's great phase*

The transition to that second most characteristic phase of literary activity which ensured for Garborg his place amongst Norway's major writers was made by †*Peace* (*Fred*, 1892) in that Garborg could quite justifiably call it his 'naturalistic novel about Jæren'. A small farmer, Enok Hòve, is shown at the beginning of the story a continual prey to disquiet both about the carnality of his neighbours' lives and about his own inability to suffer a genuine religious conversion. The disquiet rises to spiritual agony, in a fit of which he feels, one night, distinctly in his hand the grasp of another with the mark of a nail upon it. For a time things go well with Enok, secure in the trust of his Saviour, but not with his family, which he continues to augment.[1] At first he separates himself socially and religiously from his neighbours, at the same time endeavouring in all things to lead the primitive Christian life prescribed in the Gospels: he does without paid help in house and farm, and receives into his home all the poor and needy who have recourse to him. Serenity is his reward and a self-assurance sufficient to permit his eventually resuming contact with his fellow-villagers, as a member of the official church, a school-manager and the like. This peace, however, proves fleeting. A couple of gipsies requite the kindness he has done them by stealing all his poor silver and debauching his son. He fears that his Saviour has forsaken him for having committed— since he can think of no other—the great nameless sin against the Holy Ghost. Temptations to suicide beset him. A dreadful thunderstorm, which rives a tree outside his cottage cherished by him as his 'lucky tree', nourishes visions of hell. The last blow comes with the news that his eldest boy, always sulking at the oppressive religiosity of home, has broken his promise to come back after a spell in town and, having begotten a child of sin, has fled to America. After he has confirmed these reports, Enok throws himself into a tarn by night, thus gaining the Peace the world cannot give, from which the novel takes its half-ironical title.

Peace has the same objectivity as Garborg's Christiania novels. In construction, however, it improves on them. Everything in it bears on Enok's spiritual wrestlings, but within its narrow frame the compassionate delineations both of a profoundly religious, questing spirit and of its environment, material and human, in the bleak Jæren community, combine to make it Garborg's masterpiece, a tragedy of rustic life fitly to be compared with Hardy's *Return of the Native*.

Peace was in two ways an act of *pietas*. First it was, if one may put it so, a sacrificial offering of its author's matured art to his native Jæren, which in rebellious, scornful anger he had quitted over twenty years ago. Secondly, it was to be a propitiation, through understanding, of the ghost of his father. Enok Hòve is modelled on him, the Jæren freeholder who, in the wake of mid-century revivalism, had undergone such anguish under a guilt for which he could see no pardon as to put an end to his own life. Against him, his religion and the harsh demands it had put on his family as well as himself, Arne had (before the tragedy) blindly revolted both in refusing to accept as eldest son the heritage (*odel*) of the ancestral land and cutting himself completely away from his home and its faith. Or so it seemed. *Peace*, however, did not lay its ghosts. Rather the reverse. Seven years later, in *The Lost Father*, we hear its supposed author beseeching one at least of the phantoms around him to vanish from his sight, and there is no doubt as to what phantom is meant; and for many years longer Garborg was constantly preoccupied with the search for a reconciliation with the faith he thought he had utterly abjured.

Peace, The Teacher (*Læraren*, 1896) and *The Lost Father* (*Den Burtkomne Faderen*, 1899) are linked together much as the Christiania novels were: all centre on members of the Hòve family.[1] The hero of *The Teacher* (*Læraren*, 1896),[2] a five-act prose drama, is Paulus Hòve, the son of Enok. He has been a theological student and returned home to farm his land. Like his father he becomes convinced of the inadequacy of even the most devout pietism practised by himself and some neighbours, whom as their Teacher he has gathered round him. Nothing can suffice short of complete surrender to the precepts of the Gospels, in accordance with which he sells his ancestral property (Hòve) and gives the proceeds to the poor, save for the amount needed to build himself a new cottage. He bitterly antagonizes those outside the circle of 'the brethren', who think his Christian communism both crazy and immoral. Particularly suspect are his affectionate relations with two of the Sisters, of one of whom his wife becomes so extravagantly jealous that she poisons herself. The play ends with his arrest for murdering her. The drama is convincing and powerful, more for the character of Paulus Hòve and for his teaching than for its dramatic execution, which is too lengthy and diffuse for the stage.

Chief among the characters introduced into *The Lost Father* is Paulus Hòve's brother Gunnar, who, broken by his life in the world outside, has come back, an elderly man, to Jæren and whose inner life, at least, may safely be identified with Garborg's. The book, supposed to be compiled from his diary-like jottings, describes his search for God and the peace that had eluded his father, through self-communings and talks with Paulus. It is a search for God, not for *a* God, since from the start Gunnar is sure that a God—even Jesus Christ, whose teachings remain fundamental both to Paulus and himself— always becomes a judge and as such instils fear and wretched-ness. Paulus teaches him, much in the spirit of Carlyle, that God is the All, every one of whose creatures' lives has a meaning for that creature, discoverable through hard work at the tasks obviously to hand, plain living, helpfulness to all in need of help and forgiveness.

Nothing of moment actually happens in *The Lost Father*, except that steps, slow and discontinuous like the *tempo* of the whole, are taken to bring the Hòve farm back into the family. The adventitious aids of the fiction writer have virtually all gone by the board, to make it essentially a contribution to religious thought, an item in the long controversies in which Garborg now involved himself;[1] and that is equally true of *The Returned Son* (*Heimkomin Son*, 1908), which reiterates Paulus's doctrines, reports much argument and just rounds off the Hòve saga when Enok's grandson takes possession of the family homestead. It also, as the title suggests, puts *quietus* to Garborg's long settling of accounts with the phantoms of his home-land.

Side by side with this cycle of prose works stand two long poems, themselves interconnected and also inspired now by Jæren, the land, its people and their lore, now by the speculations central to *The Lost Father*. Garborg wrote *Haugtussa*** (1895) as a relief from the grimness and naturalism of *Peace*. Its material is taken from peasant-life in Jæren, as he could just recollect it from the time before pietistic revivalism had invaded the neighbourhood. That life was both earthy and exuberant, hardly touched by Christian conceptions or morbid broodings over the soul, sin and damnation such as brought Enok Hòve to his end. It is seen through the eyes of the simple, sound country girl 'Veslemøy' ('Little Wench'), who, in consequence of a frightening experience in the wilds, has that form of second sight which enables her to see through and in the ordinary events that befall her the trolls and other spirits continually mingling in them. They tempt her to invoke them in order to secure a return for her unrequited love for Jon i Skarebrote, but, strengthened by the phantom of her dead sister, she resists them and dies too.

---

* English translators have shied away from this word. *Haug* is how or burial-mound, and in one passage *tussa* is equated with *huldra* = fairies. We may remember that Shakespeare had no difficulty in equating Holinshed's 'fairies' with the 'weird sisters' and 'witches' of *Macbeth*: any kind of supernatural being is indicated. For us 'goblins' are too apt to be 'goblins damn'd'; otherwise *How-Goblins* would be a reasonably satisfactory equivalent; perhaps therefore *How-Folk* being more neutral would seem appropriate enough.

How-Folk was the first long poem of merit to be written in Norway since Bjørnson's *Arnljot Gelline*, just a quarter of a century before, and in stature it comes up to its great predecessor. Like *Arnljot Gelline*, it is cyclic in structure, a collection of shorter poems, differing widely from one another in metre and tone, grouped round a single figure. Where the heroic nature of *Arnljot Gelline* sometimes approaches a style akin to the rhetorical, *How-Folk*, more primitivistic, tends to the gnomic. Some of its finest effects are produced by its delineations of the concrete—lyrical descriptions of Jæren, now smiling in the sun, now forbidding and storm-tossed, and of cottage-life in its everyday activities or in the uproarious jollities of Yule; but its characteristic quality lies in the interpenetration of that life with Veslemøy's supernatural visions—the phantasmagoric, in a word.

Phantasmagoria is even more in evidence in *In Hel's Abode* (*I Helheim*, 1901), where it rises to the apocalyptic: sin and damnation now come in with a vengeance. At the hand of her sister and guided by a Volva or prophetess, Veslemøy travels through the realms of Hel, the abode of the dead in northern mythology; she beholds scenes of fire and torment that call to mind pictures by the younger Pieter Brueghel, wanders, equally appalled, through wastes of black desolation, ultimately to reach Peter's Gate, through which, easily and without scrutiny, are admitted those whose lives have conformed to the Beatitudes. Apocalyptic as the poem may be called, yet in a sense—a sense vital to its message—it is not other-worldly. It is not the description of another actual realm outside the time and space we know. Seen through the eyes of a visionary, it is meant for a vast parable of the world as it *is* and as it is more or less willingly accepted by tormentors and tormented alike in their frenzied strivings for domination. Many, repelled by or indifferent to its imagery, censured it as a tedious, schematic projection of the doctrine more effectively voiced in some dozen lines by Paulus Hòve in *The Lost Father*.* The almost appalling power of some of the passages,

---

* 'True is the old belief that the Earth is Hell. Here burns the fire that never shall be quenched and where the worm dieth not. But the Fire is called Hate; and the name of the Worm is Thought. We ourselves are the souls that burn.

however, cannot be denied, nor the evangelistic fervour that welds the whole together. An influential critic—later to become a bishop of the Lutheran church—was not alone in saluting the author as the Norwegian Dante.[1]

(3) *Garborg and the Landsmaal*

In Hel's Abode marks virtually the end of Arne Garborg's imaginative writing. It had never formed more than a fraction of his output; the critical and publicistic activity which had accompanied it for some thirty years was to continue for another twenty.[2] Its chief subjects were the theological, already alluded to, the economic—the advocacy of Henry George's programme —and the linguistic.

Garborg was an accomplished writer of Riksmaal. All the imaginative works of his that have been discussed, however, were in Landsmaal, except *Tired Men*, which, supposed to be the diary of an educated townsman, he naturally wrote in the language such a one would use.[3] His genius advanced the work Vinje had so notably begun, confirming with verse and prose the pretensions of Landsmaal to rank as a literary language in the fullest sense and going on to make them good in the world outside Norway—Denmark and Germany chiefly —as Vinje cannot be said to have done. Apart from his literary gifts, Garborg resembled Vinje in two capital respects: he was, as Thesen emphasizes by the title of his books on him, a European—bringing with his wide reading and culture the intellectual concerns of the world at large to the knowledge of those who could most readily appreciate them through the Landsmaal; and he viewed the propagation of Landsmaal as a national and not merely a sectarian benefit. He denied the existence of a separate and distinct 'peasant culture', *a fortiori* that such a culture should enjoy preferential, let alone mono-

The blue flame shoots from us in evil deeds and out of our throats in oaths and evil words. And we ourselves are the Devils who torment. Wood we carry piece by piece to others' bale-fire. And we nip one another with fiery tongs, and burn one another with red-hot iron. And we spurt sparks into one another's faces and spit poison. But true it is also that the Earth is God's Kingdom. Few find it; for strait is the gate and narrow is the way...' (*Skrifter i Samling*, v, 1922, 352).

polistic, 'rights'.[1] What was thought and said in Landsmaal was an addition to the whole nation's intellectual stock.

Garborg fought for this cause in a variety of ways besides the indirect one of his fiction and poetry. He wrote a study of its prime mover, *Ivar Aasen* (1902). While still in his twenties, he was made chairman of its principal pressure-group, Det norske Samlaget; he became co-founder and editor of three Landsmaal magazines;[2] in them and elsewhere are published innumerable polemical articles;[3] and during the last phase of his authorship he conspicuously contributed to the national stock which it was his desire to enrich by translations from the great authors: Homer, Vālmīki, Shakespeare, Molière, Holberg and Goethe.[4]

(4) *The other Landsmaal writers contemporary with Garborg*

The Battle of the Tongues continued with unabated acrimony all the time.[5] The Landsmaal cause had to face a great mass of sheer conservatism, prejudice and vested interests, but also two understandable fears urged on grounds that went much deeper. The first was that the controversy itself and even a partial victory of Landsmaal over the Riksmaal would divide an already small nation into two halves, each furiously resentful of the other; the second, strongly voiced by Bjørnson for all his strong democratic bias, that the imposition of Landsmaal on any major scale would encourage the latent isolationism which long ago Welhaven had so bitingly satirized in his *Twilight in Norway*: it was not only that the age-old cultural links with and through Denmark would be weakened, but that the great Norwegian writers of even the last two or three generations also would become as incomprehensible to one brought up on Aasen's text-books as Chaucer is to the average English reader of today[6]—and, on the other hand, that the currency and fame of literature emanating from a Norway either divided or utterly self-contained would be equally impaired.

The Landsmaal movement nevertheless steadily gained ground. Its Achilles heel, that of all new languages and linguistic revivals, was on the purely literary side. (The weakness of its adversaries' pleas lay in their emphasis on this, a factor of little or no interest to the rank and file of the combatants.) Deduction and experience alike teach that the successful practitioner of any art enjoys an advantage in having the proven tools and skills of his craft ready to his hand, so that he has not to take away from the task of actual creation the time and energy requisite for fashioning them.[1] No wonder then that the Landsmaal received no support and little sympathy from the established authors of the day who had perfected themselves in the traditional language and, more than that, spread the renown of its literature throughout the world; nor could it have any obvious attraction for those ambitious of stepping into their shoes.

It was therefore no less than a second piece of luck for Landsmaal and its more enlightened advocates that, at the critical time following on Vinje's premature departure, another author and publicist of even more impressive stature should arise in Garborg, to expand to the fullest the capacities of the new language and energetically to champion its propagation. There was in his generation no lack of men of good will, eager enough to do what he achieved. They gave manful support to the societies and periodicals which furthered the cause,[2] they realized the desirability of furnishing it with belletristic adornments, they mustered the gifts God had given them for fashioning these adornments in prose and in verse, and their copious efforts were praised by their fellow-enthusiasts; but these efforts have hardly stood the test of time. If left to them, Landsmaal literature, throwing out an occasional spark, would have stood still in its rustic field during the five and twenty years that Garborg was scaling his heights: none of them could hold a candle to him for intellectual or artistic power.

This applies even to the man who in all respects stood nearest to him, his friend Ivar Mortensson (1857–1934),* whose *From Hidden Places* (*Or Duldo*, 1895), a prose 'dream-

* From Lille Elvdal in the Østerdal, the son of a farmer and rural M.P. At the beginning of his life he spelt his name Mortensen and at the end of it amplified his surname to Mortensson Egnund. Succeeding Garborg as editor of *Fedraheimen*, he supported himself mainly by journalism in his middle years, until, long qualified

poem', has the stylistic resemblances with *Thus Spake Zarathustra* found occasionally also in Garborg's prose and some of the aboriginal inspiration that comes into *In Hel's Abode*; his lyrical tragedy of the Viking Age *Outlawed* (*Varg i Veum*, 1901) shares with *The Teacher* the distinction of making Landsmaal a vehicle for serious drama.

Per Sivle (1857–1904)* was the most widely influential of the small group of three men devoted to the cause of Landsmaal who were born in the same year. As long as it was possible, he exerted himself in the political crises of the later eighteen-eighties to keep his party, the distracted Left, together, and afterwards he threw his weight behind the growing agitation for the complete severance of Norway from Sweden. This notable publicistic activity of his extended also to his verse, which, at its most characteristic, is simple, rousing stuff both in Riksmaal and in Landsmaal, very suitable for vociferation by male choirs. It had the merit of introducing something like poetry to unsophisticated minds incapable of coming to terms with Garborg's abstruse masterpieces; it has its interest too by virtue of the parallels ingeniously drawn between the feuds of his day and the exploits of his countrymen in their great Viking Age—to which Landsmaal literature had, in view of its roots in National Romanticism, been curiously slow to pay attention. Sivle's imaginative prose suffered from his poverty of invention and his failure to construct, which is particularly evident in what might have been the valuable experiment of the novel *Strike* (*Streik*, 1891), that of bringing the urban proletariat within the ambit of Landsmaal literature. His short *Bits* (*Stubbar*), however, which began to appear in 1887, testify to an exceptional gift for reproducing rustic talk; as this is mainly in the undoctored dialect of Voss (north-east of Bergen), where he was brought up, they already exemplify a

for them, he took Holy Orders in 1909. He was active in promoting the use of Landsmaal in church services and translated portions of the Scriptures into it; he also made a Landsmaal translation of the older *Edda* (*Edda-kvæde*, 1905).

* Peder or Per Sivle was born on his father's farm in Aurland (Sogn) on 6 April 1857 and was an early pupil at one of the Folk High Schools introduced from Denmark. His first book was *Poems* (*Digte*) of 1879. He received a state pension, a mark of the esteem in which he was then held, in 1892 but was chiefly dependent for his rather scanty livelihood on journalism. Sunk in drink, depression and indigence, he committed suicide on 21 October 1904.

splintering of the Landsmaal language which was to add to its handicaps.

Sivle had much to do with the formation of Jens Tvedt (1857–1936),* who, after a short period of uncertainty, took him as a model for language, style, subject-matter and approach. *Bad Luck* (*Vanheppa*, 1891) gave promise of something better than his mentor ever achieved, and the story of a young bumpkin, cowed by his horrible mother and sister and missing every chance to 'realize himself', can be ranked as a precursor of the 'stream-of-consciousness novel', almost everything being conveyed through the medium of his thick wits. Though tragedy occurs in it, it is not a tragic story, and justice is done to the humorous aspect of the hero's misadventures. The comic element, however, took the upper hand in the later stories about Per Dosi, and Tvedt made no attempt to go deeper into his material than he had done in *Bad Luck*.

Rasmus Løland (1861–1907),** of old yeoman stock, by a little the junior of the trio just discussed and a man of narrower interests and considerably less robustness, did sometimes try to probe a little below the surface. But even his best esteemed novel, *Aasmund Aarak* (1902), shows that it was a vain effort, and he was ultimately identified with a children's magazine which he edited and for which he wrote, following Sivle's example, numbers of appropriate tales.

The Swedish critic Ola Hansson praised Tvedt's *Bad Luck* as the healthiest novel of the day that he had read. The adjective is the best and most flattering one for characterizing all the Landsmaal fiction at this time outside Garborg's. Flat and monotonous in presentation, it has none of the vividness and only a grain of the poetry that had established Bjørnson's pioneer pictures of country life as classics. Even more than the most facile of these it was written to exhibit that life in its most reassuring aspects. Apart from a hearty murder or two,

* Jens Tvedt was born on 14 June 1857 in Aamvikedalen (Kvinneherred), the son of a colour-sergeant, and, like Sivle, attended a Folk High School. First a schoolmaster, he was appointed to a librarianship at Stavanger, where he died on 3 September 1936. *Madli und' Apalen* (1900) was his most applauded fiction, and the Landsmaal play *Kraaka* (*The Crow*, 1909) proved unexpectedly successful.

** Rasmus Løland was born at Sand in Ryfylke on 24 May 1861 and had no profession except that of letters. He died in Auker on 12 October 1907.

there is no crime, the occasional misdemeanour is put right sooner or later, there are no heart-searchings such as Enok Hòve succumbed to, rare even are the allusions to the disreputable rustic courtship customs, with their natural complications. When they approach the same milieu, the rather younger Riksmaal authors, it must be allowed, make much more of it.[1]

7

IBSEN AFTER 1882

(1) 'The Wild Duck'

THE aesthetic Podsnaps who waved Ibsen aside as a mere provincial were fond also of using the words 'sordid' and 'squalid' for slighting the setting of his plays and, with the setting, their content. In sober fact such adjectives are appropriate to *The Wild Duck* (*Vildanden*, 1884)[1] alone—and a special significance attaches to the circumstance, as will be seen later.[2] Four of its five acts are laid in the studio-cum-living-room of a cheap photographer, Hjalmar Ekdal, his drudge of a wife Gina, his decayed old father and the little girl Hedvig. Into it enters a not unfamiliar figure, a brother in the spirit to Lona Hessel and Fru Linde, with 'the demands of the Ideal' in his coat-pocket. The visitor is Gregers Werle, an old friend of Hjalmar's, whom he has not seen for fifteen years. He is as horrified by what he finds as the most fastidious of art-critics, but for very different reasons.

Hjalmar, the bright boy of his generation, has degenerated into a futile idler, phrase-monger and sponge. Old Ekdal, whom Gregers remembers as Lieutenant Ekdal, his father's partner in the timber business up north and a mighty Nimrod, has, after a term of imprisonment for illicit tree-felling, become a shambling old drunkard, who solaces himself by sporting expeditions in the lean-to attic which his son and he have fitted up for the purpose with withered Christmas trees and a little menagerie of hens, rabbits and the like. Gina, too, Gregers remembers, as the housekeeper in the parental home who became his father's mistress; and he convinces himself that Hedvig is not Hjalmar's child, as Hjalmar obviously believes, but his own half-sister.

This miasma must be cleared away. Hjalmar must be put on his feet, morally and (presumably) materially. Gregers being the man he is—in fact, the perfect Ibsenite—knows the way. If light and air are let in on the rotten foundations of his present existence, Hjalmar's noble nature (as he believes it to be) will sweep away all shams and pretences and, recognizing the devotion of his wife and her child, forgiving what there is to forgive, begin with them a new life of strenuous duty and pure love.

The tonic of Truth is duly administered. But its effect is not at all what Gregers expected. Hjalmar is neither appalled nor energized. He merely turns bad-tempered, resentful at the disturbance to his parasite's routine which he has made a pretty comfortable one. Worst of all he turns—in very brutal terms[1]—on innocent Hedvig and banishes her, heart-broken, from his sight. The idealist takes a hand again. A propitiatory sacrifice, he impresses on Hedvig, will convince her father (as she naturally believes him to be) of her love for him and restore his for her. She must sacrifice her dearest possession—the wild duck, which is the pride of the Ekdals' bogus hunting-ground and 'her very own'. She takes one of the old lieutenant's shooting-pistols and with unconscious insight discharges it into her own heart. This is what Truth and the Ideal can do.

The lurid light which *The Wild Duck* throws on these abstractions invites some further examination of them. One thing is clear: they are no longer absolutes, as they seemed to be in the plays just preceding. No microscopic analysis is required to bring out, in the realm of fact, the indeterminacy of the play's foundations—of the whole *donnée* which the retrospective technique elicits. How, for instance, was Ekdal senior caught up in crime and disgrace? Was it mere muddling (Dr Relling's 'The old Lieutenant was an ass all his days')? Guilt that all but involved his partner (the confidential clerk's view)? Victimization by that partner (Gregers's opinion)? Is Old Werle the underhand, licentious villain his son takes him for, or is he an ordinary man of the world handling the difficult problems of a discarded mistress and his ruined partner's destitution with much good sense, tact and generosity—in all, a man more sinned against than sinning, as his present housekeeper and wife-to-be asserts? Lastly, who is Hedvig's father? Gina, cornered, blurts out that a woman like her cannot tell. Hedvig has weak eyes, Old Werle is going blind: heredity or coincidence? The answer to all these questions is, in the common phrase, anybody's guess. As Pirandello, Ibsen's devoted admirer, was to demonstrate in play after play, Truth is no more than each of us thinks it to be.

Such unsatisfactory appearances might be saved. Underlying all this indeterminacy there may be some greater, comprehensive Truth in which the swarming subjective truths could be reconciled. A symbolic interpretation might bring it out. But this is treacherous ground to tread. On a view of Ibsen's imaginative writing as a whole, nothing suggests that for the author of *Emperor and Galilean* as well as of *An Enemy of the People* 'Alles Vergängliche ist nur ein Gleichnis' and, outside it, did he not observe that critics took to 'symbolizing' because they had no eye or respect for reality?[1]

Undoubtedly there are incitements to symbolistic interpretations, more numerous perhaps and more provocative in this play than in any other of the author's. They all bear on the Wild Duck of the title, the crippled water-fowl, never seen, that forms part of the Ekdals' tame menagerie, Hedvig's 'very own', come into her possession through Old Werle, who had winged her. She can be made to 'stand for' a number of things: an example of Old Werle's ominous benefactions; young Hedvig, the sport of cruel, tangled circumstance; the miasmic make-believe world in which Hjalmar plays about; Hjalmar himself—for, as Gregers sees it, after the trauma of his father's ruin he has plunged into mud and weeds, as, never to rise again, a wounded duck is said to do. All these ideas, it is well to note, are ultimately attributable to Gregers, the only symbolist of the party; but who at the end of the play would accept him as a guide to anything? And, even if some plausibility might attach to any one of them, it could not qualify for one comprehensive interpretation. The symbolic suggestions, like the constatations of fact, are, in a word, subjective. The author cannot be saddled with responsibility for them—and the same is to be said of all the comparable matters in the later plays that have provoked speculation. In his characteristically demure way Ibsen does an audacious piece of 'debunking' in his very next drama: the ghostly White Horses of Rosmersholm that are supposed to presage death and the old housekeeper thinks she sees through the window are only the shawl that Rebecca has been knitting and has thrown over her shoulders for her last journey.

The questionable frontiers between truth, illusion and delusion are deliberately approached from another angle in *The Wild Duck* with Dr Relling, one of the minor characters. A broken-down, shabby medico, leading a fairly disreputable life, he differs vastly from the smart, sententious *raisonneur* of so many semi-didactic plays of the time, but, even though it is no more than the personal opinion of an invented character, what he has to say is something that his creator meant to have taken seriously: he is plainly a man of insight, heart and robust good sense. The essential thing about him is that he represents the principle of 'the greatest happiness of the greatest number'—something one hardly expects to be much in evidence in Ibsen's plays; as a corollary to it he has formulated his doctrine and defence of the 'Life-Lie', the illusions with which human beings pad themselves against the whips and scorns of harsh reality; its counterpart is distrust and enmity towards every 'demand of the ideal', like Gregers's, that would tear away this protective cushion and put in its place unrealizable and therefore misery-engendering aspirations. Ideals are a luxury, quite beyond the reach of Ekdals struggling for subsistence and contentment amid squalor and sordidity; to such the vernacular for Ideals is plain 'Lies', differing from his own 'Life-Lies' as poison does from food. 'Life would be tolerable', Relling sums up, 'if only we could be rid of the confounded duns that keep on pestering us, in our poverty, with the claim of the ideal.' That life should be made *tolerable* for the poor in spirit and circumstance is the best that can be hoped for.

A lengthy discussion of *The Wild Duck* has been called for, not only because of its puzzles or the eminence now commonly accorded it, but also because it can be regarded as central in marking a turning-point in full career. Much of an older Ibsen is there and was to subsist: the firmness of characterization, affording, as he put it, 'grateful opportunities' to actors and actresses of quality; the equally firm setting in the lives and sur-roundings of outwardly unremarkable men and women of the contemporary middle class, higher or lower, and their unforced, if subtly nuanced speech; the constant appeal to judgement as well as emotion; the technical mastery that inexorably built up a situation fraught with catastrophe and, while doing so, compressed into the three hours' traffic of the stage an immensity of ancient history.

But, as Ibsen warned his publisher at the time of publication, it was something novel, something he saw as a new departure. Some of the unfamiliar features proved transient. The physical squalor of *The Wild Duck*, it has been remarked, was never reproduced; equally, its pervasive indeterminacy: we know 'where we are', what the relationships between the personages are as reliably in the later plays as in the earlier. What is Truth? ceases to be an insistent question.

Other new features remained. Foremost among them is the eclipse of the 'public sector' behind the concentration on personal relationships. After the play next to follow, *Rosmersholm*, the world outside a small charmed circle almost ceases to exist. No categorical imperatives issue from such a circle, and, if a general rule be distilled, it is only rarely and at great hazard. To the consternation of the true-blue Ibsenites—the most alert of whom had been put on their guard by *Ghosts*—*their* Ibsen was dead: no further recommendations, to be sure, were to be made of the Life-Lie nostrum, but he had blasphemed against Truth and the Ideal. A second phenomenon is the recurrence in all the later plays, despite their greater clarity, of 'symbolic suggestions', which, received though they must be with the utmost caution, inject into stories often harsh enough and enacted in completely realistic surroundings a whiff of mystery and poetry: the Lady from the Sea's mystic marriage, the vine-leaves Hedda Gabler sees in Løvborg's hair, Solness's heaven-aspiring towers, the rat-wife of *Little Eyolf* or the voices John Gabriel Borkman hears calling to him from subterranean fastnesses.

(2) '*Rosmersholm*'

After *The Wild Duck*, *Rosmersholm* (1886)[1] seems something of a palinode—since the savagery exhibited against ideals, idealists and their counterfeits is replaced by the sympathetic treatment, in its hero, of a man of real thought and principle—and also a step back, in bringing in again the 'public sector'. For the background to it is the constitutional struggle that brought Norway near to civil war in the early 'eighties, and that is clear enough to the initiated. But, solidly set as that background may be, through the figures that emerge from it, the unconsciously comic Tory headmaster and the louche journalist, it is sufficiently generalized to make any precise historical knowledge irrelevant; and none of the contestants could have considered *Rosmersholm* a 'contribution' to the party-strife of the moment.

In the nature of the case, however, party-strife throws light of a kind on the principles supposed to underlie it, on 'ideals' which had been so rudely buffeted between Gregers Werle and Dr Relling in *The Wild Duck*.

Johannes Rosmer is a man who can afford the luxury of ideals, the scion of an old, well-to-do family of country magnates, clerical and lay, looked to as leaders of opinion in their neighbourhood. He has led a withdrawn life of study and reflexion, gradually emancipating himself from the prejudices of his order. He cannot therefore accept the editorship of an ultra-conservative newspaper offered to him at the height of the political turmoil, and he is equally repelled by the vulgarity and mere opportunism of the rival sheet's editor when the latter scents a useful ally in an emancipated Rosmer of Rosmersholm. His own hopes point to a progressive enlightenment and humanity, which will fashion a new nobility, not of blood, wealth or even talent, but of character, mind and will, eventually to comprise the whole nation.[1] But such ideals are doomed to complete frustration. Tory and radical leader alike are in a position to blackmail him into silence. Rosmersholm, with its dignity and calm, cannot influence practical politics one tittle. The voice of the true Liberal will never be heard above the din of two million cats and dogs, as Ibsen described his countrymen.[2] So much for the public sector, when he took leave of it.

When a group of schoolboys asked Ibsen what *Rosmersholm* was about, he answered tersely 'of course about human beings and their fate'.[3] The drama, the tragedy of *Rosmersholm* is not about the disappointments of Liberalism in Norway; it is the first of those strange, deeply buried but authentic love-stories which Ibsen devised in his maturer years, the love-story of Johannes Rosmer and Rebekka West. Rebekka came into the Rosmersholm household, long before the action of the play begins, as companion to Beate its master's wife—a completely emancipated young woman, an *intrigante*,[1] who stayed on after he had become a widower, having begun to work on him as a likely tool for realizing the radical programme on which her heart was set. Then she had fallen in love with him, and he with her. Their love was undeclared, and as long as the austere aura of Rosmersholm remained untarnished no breath of scandal stirred. But when, worked on by Rebekka's fiery radicalism, Rosmer proposes to venture into the arena of politics, the vulnerability of his private life gave a handle to any who had a use for it. But beneath this commonplace situation, providing the link between Rosmer's inner and outer life, there were very sinister deeps he knew not of.

Briefly, realizing that Beate stood in the path of her marrying Rosmer and twisting him to her purposes, Rebekka had, through false insinuations of pregnancy, driven her to removing herself from it by throwing herself into the mill-race—had in effect murdered her. The process could have been pieced together by others. But the revelation does not come to Rosmer in such fashion. Rebekka herself makes a full confession of her passion and her crime and makes ready to go away from Rosmersholm, leaving Rosmer to work in his own way for the liberating mission to which she has roused him. The revelation does nothing to destroy his love for Rebekka, which is now made clear to her; but it leaves him with nothing else. He is not even convinced of the sincerity of her devotion, and he has come to see himself impotent to exert any influence whatever. She riposts that he has influenced *her*. Her revolutionary, ruthless zeal has yielded to the calm humanism of Rosmersholm, and her wild possessive passion for its master to a selfless love, which she will prove by ridding him of her in the way that Beate did. He can then live a completely free man. Rosmer realizes that for the man he is this solution is no solution. To live, he must have both Rebekka *and* complete faith in her. He sees no way but to accept her sacrifice—and join himself in it. Locked in their marital embrace, they throw themselves into the mill-stream.

The inner logic of the tragedy, worked out in a long *scène-à-deux* of a tension which Ibsen never excelled, is impeccable—in the eyes of some too impeccable, too cerebral. But it is well to remember that Ibsen had taken for his protagonist a man not unlike himself, an intellectual, who, racked by passion though he may be, must involve his brain in the urges of his heart. The drama of *Rosmersholm* may be about 'human beings and their fate', but the human beings are an uncommon man and an uncommon woman.

(3) '*The Lady from the Sea*', '*Hedda Gabler*' and '*Little Eyolf*'

After *Rosmersholm* Ibsen still had six more plays to write. Though not according to strict chronology, they fall into two groups, of which the first comprises *The Lady from the Sea* (*Fruen fra Havet*, 1888), *Hedda Gabler* (1890) and *Little Eyolf* (*Lille Eyolf*, 1894). Their kinship is admittedly not self-evident. The nature and strength of the appeal they make is far from the same: the first and third have come to rank as connoisseurs' pieces, while a revival of *Hedda Gabler* is always a popular 'draw'. They differ, too, very markedly from one another in tone and what may be called 'appearance'. Even though a sense of impending doom lies heavy on the last scenes of *The Lady from the Sea*, the play ends as a comedy and is meant as a comedy; except for one act in an airy Norwegian garden-room, it is played out of doors, with the comings and goings and noises of holiday-makers in the background; there is a good deal of humour, much of it sharp-edged, even saturnine, but sometimes genial enough. *Hedda Gabler*, all set in an elegant drawing-room, though lightened by the figure of the harmless, bumbling pedant Jørgen Tesman, who scarcely knows what is going on around him, has nothing suggestive of geniality about it: it is a tragedy, hard, and as stark in its effects as any high-life melodrama. Not starkness, but aridity is the key-note in *Little Eyolf*, the aridity of the Norwegian landscape in which it is set, clear and melancholy. Yet it is a comedy again, at least in the technical sense, as is announced at the end by hoisting the flag from half-mast (for the death of Little Eyolf) to the top. But, in its aridity, it lacks the last vestige of humour, and, for all the expressions of reconciliation and hope with which it is accompanied, that end is far from leaving the assurance one may readily accept in *The Lady from the Sea* that the *dramatis personae* will 'live happily ever after'.

Thematically, however, these three disparate plays belong together. One common element links them also to *Rosmersholm*. It is sterility. The turn of events in *Rosmersholm* had brought, with dreadful literalness, Rosmer and Rebekka to a deadlock in their personal relationship; but equally it had reduced both the fiery revolutionism of Rebekka and the reflective humanitarianism of Rosmer to impotence. In its most abstract aspect the action of *Rosmersholm* could be summarized as a sterilizing process. In the plays now under consideration the sterilization has taken place before they begin. *The Lady from the Sea* focuses on a woman, Ellida Wangel, whose morbid fancies, hallucinations and superstitious beliefs have turned her into a wraith, untouchable by the life around her; *Hedda Gabler* on another youngish woman, also visited by visions—though of a much more carnal kind— who has likewise turned her back on life, though she has ambitions of meddling in it; *Little Eyolf* on a wan scholar concentrated, to the exclusion of all else, on a work which, at best, will be still-born.

This *magnum opus* of Alfred Allmers is to be a philosophical treatise on Human Responsibility. That names the second of the themes common to *The Lady from the Sea*, *Hedda Gabler* and *Little Eyolf*, forming indeed their moral substratum and firmly fused with the first. The two comedies, after exhibiting the sterility of their protagonists, offer them a cure. Ellida, the Lady from the Sea, is assured that on her unfettered choice alone rests the possibility of breaking away from her phantasmal chains; she must make the choice, a responsible act; and, having made it, she sees that the novel 'freedom with responsibility', warmed by her husband's love, opens the prospect of a new active, purposive life before her. Alfred Allmers, in his turn, learns that responsibility, like charity, begins at home: theories and a self-centred existence devoted to their elaboration go by the board when he realizes the distress in his home and slum just outside it that energy and understanding can relieve. Cold responsibility and charity here again can be warmed by compassion; for, like Ellida's, his heart has not quite died within him. For Hedda Gabler, by contrast, there is no such cure. A shock is administered to her, as to Ellida and Allmers; but, to her, love is nothing but a 'slimy word'; compassion and responsibility are not even words. They cannot galvanize her withered soul to life. Everything she sees turning 'ludicrous and mean' under her hands, to an intolerable boredom from which a pistol-shot offers the only escape.

A full analysis of *The Lady from the Sea*[1] would read very much like a psychiatrist's case-book;[2] and all these three plays might be described as studies in shock-treatment.

We must believe in the reality of a worthy doctor's wife in a commonplace holiday resort who seems more like a mermaid than a creature of human clay; and, more and more extraordinary as her condition and its causes are revealed as being, the more complete becomes our suspension of disbelief, so that finally we are driven not only to accept the authenticity of her hallucinations and superstitious hauntings, but even to wonder whether, after all, she may not be, as she claims, the spouse in spirit of the fabulous Merman risen from the deep to seek an earthly bride. Nowhere can the dramatist's prime task, to make credible, in event and psychology, the predicament in which his heroes and heroines find themselves, have been more urgent and more difficult than here. The demolition of the phantasmal structure that holds Ellida prisoner is as masterly as its evocation. The spiritual bridegroom, hitherto kept far in the misty background, is brought on to the stage, demanding that Ellida shall follow him. By careful gradations he is shown to others than Ellida as no fabulous being, but almost a figure of fun, a half-cracked tourist on an English pleasure-cruise, a dangerous bully, an impostor—to Ellida herself at last, still a ghost perhaps, but one that an act of her own will can exorcise for ever.

Its comparative straightforwardness is one of the reasons for the general popularity of *Hedda Gabler*.[3] The plot indeed is elaborate, but its well-marked episodes, ingeniously intertwined as they may be, are free from mysteries that might throw doubt on its necessary development. The construction, if not exactly slick, is taut, as that of *The Lady from the Sea* could not be described: in fact, it is a trifle too taut as it rises to the last, tragic climax, which is certainly well prepared and leaves the requisite impression of inevitability, but is forced into improbable circumstances—the minor characters in the play having apparently forgotten all about the fatalities with which they have been afflicted only a few hours before. With 'le supplice d'une femme', her unsatisfactory marriage, crime, exposure to black-mail and suicide, *Hedda Gabler* comes nearest among Ibsen's dramas to the fashionable 'well-made play' of its time, and its being bracketed with Pinero's *Second Mrs Tanqueray* or Suder-mann's *Magda*, as it often was, was not unreasonable.

To be sure, it raised the usual crop of question-marks, an added recommendation to the more intelligent playgoers, as it remains to the distinguished *tragédiennes* who essay the title-role. For they all concern the personality of Hedda Gabler herself. The dramatic crux of the play is her burning of a manuscript entrusted to her, which embodies the life-work (to date) of Løvborg, a social philosopher and the professional rival of her far less distinguished husband, Jørgen Tesman. Was concern for the latter's advancement (in cash terms, at least), was fear of being found with incriminating evidence, was jealousy of the woman who had successfully been Egeria and mistress of Løvborg, her own old-time admirer, was a break-out of revenge-ful rage at her own impotence the overriding motive for the crime? Is she to be presented as a mask without a face—an English critic said he sat next to Hedda every time he dined out— or as a demon of destructiveness, or, being pregnant,[1] a hysteric in the proper sense of the term, or as pitiable a prisoner of her frustrations and delusions as Ellida Wangel, or as the aristocrat, General Gabler's daughter, drowning in the bourgeois tide of Tesman's old aunts and carpet-slippers? The most interesting point about these questions is that, whatever the answers returned, they do not affect the credibility of her doom. The form of the play, its technique, carries all before it. That cannot be said of any earlier play by Ibsen, or any later.

It would be said least truthfully of *Little Eyolf*,[2] the lack of theatrical tension making it for great stretches a flat, low-spirited play about a debile youngish man who dislikes the ardours of his wife, loses first his little boy and then his 'soul's mate', realizes that his authorship is leading nowhere and finally decides, in partnership with his chastened spouse, to start a new life by assuming responsibility for a ragged school. The one episode that raises the dramatic temperature comes too early in the play to maintain it. It is the irruption of a witchlike old woman (with a dog in a bag), whose calling it is to rid people's houses of rats and mice and similar nuisances by luring them out after the manner of the Pied Piper of Hamelin: she fascinates the crippled little boy Eyolf, who in various ways is an embarrassment to his parents and who, falling into the sea as the crone rows away with her pan-pipes, is drowned. The episode in its way is effective, 'creepy' and characteristic of the immixture in Ibsen's later plays of what are called romantic or poetic elements with otherwise realistic material—the death-presaging White Horses of Rosmersholm, the Wild Duck which plunged to the bottom of the fjord, Ellida Wangel's Merman and the Dionysian vine-leaves in Ejlert Løvborg's hair that Hedda Gabler talks about. They who see in these the rebirth of the romanticism that had engendered *Brand* and *Peer Gynt* might ponder the fact that, in one way or another, they are all pernicious.

(4) '*The Master Builder*', '*John Gabriel Borkman*', '*When We Dead Awaken*'

The Lady from the Sea and *Little Eyolf* had shown, even with a little pedantic emphasis, how on stepping-stones of our dead selves we may rise to higher things. The galvanic shock that may spur us on is not always effective, as *Hedda Gabler* proves; for the soul may be past revival. The other three of Ibsen's last plays differ from these, which were concerned with young or youngish people, in taking for their heroes men well on in middle life; but they too have an impulse to start a new life. Unlike Hedda Gabler's, their souls still have the vitality to respond to it; even if they have their life's work behind them, they are not altogether 'Dead Men', as Bernard Shaw labelled them.[1] Yet they perish. As Bjørnson would put it, they attempt something 'beyond our powers'. They play a game for which Death has loaded the dice.

The *leit-motif* of death is already sounded in the *coup de théâtre* which begins the action of *The Master Builder* (*Bygmester Solness*, 1892).[2] Solness has been expressing to his friend and doctor his terror of supersession; 'just you see, doctor, presently the younger generation will come knocking at my door...Then there's an end of Halvard Solness', and there knocks and enters Hilda Wangel, bird of prey, Valkyrie, angel of death. Ibsen was not the man to take fright at chimaeras; but he was in a position to have an acute personal understanding of one who might. Of late, various things had happened to instigate a process of mental stock-taking, painful in many ways as at his age of 64 it had to be, yet not necessarily terrifying: his removal—presumably the last removal he would ever make—to Norway, haunted by ghosts of his young days;[1] a recognition that love might still come his way, but that it must be abjured;[2] the loud call (which he had heard with his own ears) of Knut Hamsun for a new literature to supersede that of his own generation.

There were good reasons, which must have tickled Ibsen's sardonic sense of humour, why Hamsun's attack should not greatly upset him. As the royalties from quarter of a century's output kept rolling in and he reflected how long it had taken for that happy process to begin, he could mutter the Norwegian equivalent for *beati possidentes*. And, more important than this, the spokesman for the up-and-coming had chosen to disregard almost completely his own later work, in which he had in fact been meeting Hamsun's prime positive demand, concentration on individual psychology to the exclusion of social problems, solved by *clichés*. If the wind were blowing from that quarter, there was no need to trim his sails and anticipate shipwreck.

The projections of individual psychology on which the action of *The Master Builder, John Gabriel Borkman* and *When We Dead Awaken* rests have, none the less, one novel feature. They spring from the general stock-taking just described. Much self-dissection, self-contemplation and self-judgement enter into the delineations of Solness and Rubek (of *When We Dead Awaken*) certainly, and the overall wintriness of *John Gabriel Borkman* must often have cast its chill over the author's spirits as he neared his three-score-years-and-ten. In that degree therefore it is not altogether extravagant to call these latter-day productions lyrical—a word which acquired a new prestige in their decade.

The epithet by itself does not make Ibsen a veteran leader of the fashionable neo-Romanticism, let alone imply a return to the methods of *The Feast of Solhaug* or even *Brand*. Poetry, in the technical sense, was still barred. The structure of the new plays is obviously that of the old Ibsen; there may be fewer 'strong' situations than in *Hedda Gabler*, but the tautness of the latter's construction is even exceeded (and improved on) in *John Gabriel Borkman*, where the action takes place in *less* time than required for performance. Similarly, the general look of the scene is much what one had come to expect:[1] the interiors of middle-class houses, or, in *When We Dead Awaken*, the grounds and environs of a spa, the resort of men and women one customarily finds in such surroundings. Outwardly, too, even the chief of these are ordinary enough: a thriving, somewhat hardened building contractor, a bankrupt entrepreneur with a good-for-nothing son, and an elderly artist *en retraite* taking his young wife for a summer holiday.

In the environment and behind the façade Hamsun disliked, however, these were far from ordinary men. After all, as has been indicated, there was something of Ibsen in each of them, and they were marked not merely for death, but for tragedy, its seeds, as usual, sown by them far back in the past.

The 'case' of John Gabriel Borkman is the least abstruse of the three—the play about him[2] not being much complicated by introspection and gaining its magnificent tragic effect as a sustained *danse macabre*. Borkman was a financier on a national scale, who outstretched his lawful resources and came to grief through the perfidy, as he described it, of his chief associate: gaol and elimination from public life had been the outcome, and when the curtain goes up on the play, he has for years lived inactive, never leaving his room, as a pensioner of his wife or, more precisely, his wife's sister, Ella Rentheim, who furnishes the cash.

Two things distinguish Borkman from the ordinary stock-exchange crook. One is the nature of the 'betrayal' that brought him down: The 'super-scoundrel' Hinkel, his associate, had dishonoured the bargain for lending him support in return for his breaking completely with the woman whom that associate wished to marry, Ella Rentheim. (He failed in this, but not through any overt act of Borkman's.) The other was that in his ambitions money for its own sake or the pride of power fed by it were secondary to vast projects in industry, commerce and transport which could pour energy and wealth over the whole country and which he believed he alone could call into being.

Megalomania this may have been, and megalomaniac certainly is the belief sustaining his loneliness that the Napoleon maimed in his first battle will be recalled to command by a society convinced it cannot do without him. No deputation comes from the outside world, and equally fallacious is the hope that his redemption may be achieved through his son:[1] that young man prefers to spend his time in the gay circles of which Hinkel is a centre and eventually goes off with a cosmopolitan *demi-mondaine*. This second treachery stirs Borkman out of his inertia: all must now be done by himself alone and at once. Obsessed by all his old visions, though half conscious of their vanity, he staggers out into Norway's wintry night, which promptly puts an end to him.

Vision and collapse are equally what *The Master Builder* led up to. Solness's visions are of a different order from Borkman's. He wants to get *out* of the world of affairs, the pettifogging commissions and the bullying of subordinates that are wearying him, into an airy castle where another Solness, long overlaid, can come to life again in serenity and joy. The spur comes from a girl, Hilde Wangel, whom ten years back (when she was the sharp little *gamine* who had already appeared in *The Lady from the Sea*) he had kissed and promised some such castle or 'kingdom' and who now comes to have the promise redeemed.[2] Significantly, the whole episode has fallen out of his memory, but the time of its occurrence, when he was full of hope and energy, surges up irresistibly. So, never expressed, does passion. Hilde shall have her castle, and it is a new, revived Master Builder who shall build and lead her into it. The proof of his regeneration shall be his planting the triumphant wreath on the top of a tower he has just completed, a feat such as he has never dared to attempt for ten years. He takes the wreath, climbs to the top and falls.

In a second respect Solness differs from Borkman. Throughout, in his megalomania or monomania, visions and ambitions, both before and after the crash, the latter has never doubted that he was right. Solness, on the other hand, materially successful though he has been, comes to realize that the overlaying of everything else in him—from causes, indeed, not altogether within his control—by the daily grind of business, even if it brought him prosperity, has been a calamitous mistake: he has lost all vestiges of *livsglæde*, the joy of life, and he avidly reaches out to the chance of recapturing this that Hilde offers.

The claims of *livsglæde* had not been ignored by Ibsen even in his most austere moods. Mrs Alving of *Ghosts* already was visited with misgivings that the firm treatment she had meted out to her profligate husband had not been the right one and for that reason was willing to compensate the son with champagne and an incestuous union with his half-sister; and Relling's defence of the Life-Lie also, it may be remembered, was based on the principle of 'the greatest happiness of the greatest number'. The counterpart to Borkman's strenuous ambitions was to be given in the escapade of his son. Not much is said about that antithesis, and Ibsen holds the balance: he gives no indication of either approving or disapproving young Erhart's tearing away from his father's iron chariot-wheels.

In *When We Dead Awaken*,[1] however, the subject moves into the forefront again; and here it is fraught with the same intense personal emotion as *The Master Builder* and, plainly, a greater measure of spiritual autobiography.

At a health resort in Norway Rubek, a sculptor of international repute, meets again, after twenty years, a former model of his, Irene, who is an inmate of the local sanatorium. She had stood for him as the central figure in the statuary that had established his fame, 'The Day of Resurrection', and when she had served that purpose—and that purpose alone—he had brusquely dismissed her. For him, as he told her at the time, their association had been a mere professional 'episode'; but as, in the last of Ibsen's great *éclaircissements*, she now confesses to him, she had been passionately in love with him; and, after she had been turned off, as heart-broken as it is possible to be, she had turned her beauty to every kind of meretricious abuse.

Ella Rentheim had made John Gabriel Borkman an avowal parallel to Irene's confession, called him a criminal to his face, not for the frauds that had caused his downfall, but for having, with the fatal barter of her person, 'killed the love-life' in her. That had not greatly moved the ingrained entrepreneur. But Rubek the artist is appalled at realizing that his total surrender to his art, besides having kept him its joyless galley-slave, had made the physical and moral wreck that Irene now is of another human being, whose love and devotion could have given him the *livsglæde* he had missed. It is not (he thinks) too late: the way to freedom is still open, amends are possible—since his unsatisfied little wife Maja is that in hardly more than name and, moreover, well provided for by the lusty sportsman she has picked up at their holiday resort. Enraptured, he and Irene set out in the dawn on the upland path to light, love and joy, and there an avalanche sweeps them away before they know whether or not they were pursuing a *fata morgana*.

At the same time as it is final the end is characteristically enigmatical. Certainly the bear-hunter and Maja, who safely gets the freedom she has been longing for, come off best. But Ibsen, for all his pent-up emotions, was a stoic. Envy and remorse were not for him—and there were no 'crimes' to repent and atone for which common sense could allow.[1] He had given up much and knew what it was. But as 'The Day of Resurrection' would subsist in Rubek's imperishable stone, so his own life's work was a greater reality than any song the sirens sang. He had done his stock-taking, struck the final balance[2] and, there is no reason to doubt, saw that it was very good.

8

THE NORWEGIAN THEATRE: GUNNAR HEIBERG

(1) *The theatre: backwardness and anomaly*

THE swift rise to fame of Norwegian literature being in good measure due to its two great dramatists, almost all of whose plays were, at one time or another, found eminently stage-worthy, it is of interest to cast a look at the state of the Norwegian drama and of the Norwegian theatre during their lifetime. Since, as has been seen, the agitations of contemporary life—in politics, religion and morals—acted so strongly upon them, it would be natural to suppose that their art would in some degree be moulded also by the prevailing conditions of theatrical life with which in their formative years both were directly associated.

On comparing these conditions with those in other countries when they witnessed a sudden uprush of great drama, like the Spain of Lope de Vega, the England of Shakespeare or the France of Corneille and Molière, we shall find them unpropitious and in some ways curious.

In this domain Norway was perhaps the most backward country of the western world. Its theatrical history virtually begins as late as 1827 and, certain reservations made, its dramatic history goes but little further back. 1827 is the year of the establishment of what later received formally the name of Det Christiania Theater. The most remarkable feature of its organization was that, finance apart, it was a Danish theatre, with a Danish chief,[1] Danish players speaking in their native accents and a repertoire based on that of the Royal Theatre of Copenhagen; and so it persisted through more than three decades. From time to time patriots raised loud protests, but these were silenced by two hard facts: the love which the patrons of the Christiania Theater bore to their Danes, and the impossibility of replacing them. There were no Norwegian producers, no Norwegian actors or actresses, nor any Norwegian plays—or, to

133

be more precise, scarcely any plays that could be classed as more Norwegian than Danish.

For there had been, and still were, playwrights of Norwegian birth—most eminent among them Ludvig Holberg of Bergen (1684–1754), the 'Molière of the North'. But, founding father both of the Danish drama and of the Danish theatre as he may equally well be styled, Holberg's dramatic and theatrical activities were altogether confined to Copenhagen. This is the case also with a number of lesser lights a couple of generations after him, young Norwegians of a literary bent studying in the University there, who from time to time turned out a play designed for the Royal Theatre; true likewise of Carsten Hauch of Fredrikshald (1790–1872), a distinguished figure in the Danish world of literature and the theatre at the time we are now speaking of.[1]

It is an illuminating fact that none of the young Norwegians who wrote plays in Copenhagen at the end of the eighteenth century continued to do so when he returned to his native land and that the new University of Christiania failed to foster a breeding-ground for any like-minded juniors. Thalia and Melpomene clearly found the air of Norway inclement. The patriotic fervour, moreover, which fired the National Romantic movement was strongest among the 'student class', and those members of it who might have wooed the Christiania Theater looked on it not as a possible patron, but as an enemy, impregnably entrenched. The compiler of the first national bibliography[2] could only muster some twenty plays written by Norwegians in Norway between 1814 and 1850—a fair proportion of them one-act trifles.

(2) *The theatre: advance after 1850*

The impasse was broken not in Christiania, but in Bergen. A syndicate of enthusiasts opened a playhouse there in 1850 and defiantly gave it the name of Det Norske Theater. Their ambition was the twofold one of encouraging native drama and of rearing a troupe of professional actors to present it in the accents of their patrons. Ibsen, it will be recalled, was brought in as official house-poet to further the first aim, but, apart from the four plays he turned out, the crop of new plays by Norwegian authors was meagre to vanishing point. The second goal, however, was much more successfully achieved: Bergen became a notable nursery of native actors and actresses. Moreover, the example spread, and quickly. Already in 1852 a School of Drama was set up in the capital, laying particular stress on speech[1]—the everyday speech of cultivated Norwegian town-folk. Soon the pupils came to give public rehearsals and to form themselves into a company of professionals, with regular theatrical seasons at a theatre in the Møllergate. Thither, on becoming its director in 1857, Ibsen brought some of the Bergen company with him.

From lack of financial support in its community of less than 30,000 souls the Norske Theater (which had Bjørnson for its artistic director from 1857 to 1859) had to close down after thirteen struggling years. But it had shown what could be done. A reservoir of authentically Norwegian managers, producers and players had been created. There was an alternative to the Danish monopoly. Its days were numbered. For the people in the Møllergate were not only an alternative and an example, they were also competitors. True, they too went bankrupt (in 1862); but the managerial board of the Christiania Theater had both felt the draught and read the signs of the times, and in 1863 they dismissed practically all of their Danish personnel, replacing it by that trained in the Møllergate and at Bergen.

Ibsen was made aesthetic adviser to the Christiania Theater at this juncture. But he seems to have done next to nothing in this capacity. And, though shining with unaccustomed brilliance during the thirty months that Bjørnson was its director (1865–7), the old house went on very much as before, even if the voices heard on the stage were new. It could not be otherwise. Native playwrights were still far to seek. During the fifth season under the new dispensation, for instance, not a single new play by a Norwegian author was produced. Except that its comparatively limited resources prejudiced the presentation of dramas calling for elaborate spectacle and a great corps of performers,[2] the Christiania Theater continued to copy its repertoire from that of the Royal Theatre of Copenhagen, the texts, whether Danish 'originals' or translated into Danish, only occasionally and slightly altered.[3]

When in the late summer of 1863 its new régime began

operations it was again the only permanent theatre in the country. Subject to fairly rare and generally insignificant infringements, it enjoyed this monopoly absolutely for thirteen years, when the theatre at Bergen began, with much vigour, to function again, and in the capital itself for some twenty years longer. It was not until the eighteen-nineties that lesser houses of resort in Christiania which could be adapted to theatrical uses and had sporadically so been used began to give complete 'seasons'.

So advantaged, the Christiania Theater had to combine the functions of the Comédie Française and the boulevard theatres. It gave a home—and no unworthy one—to Holberg, Oehlenschläger, Shakespeare, Sheridan, Molière, Moreto, Schiller, but it also had to offer ordinary, run-of-the-mill entertainment: translations, for instance, of Scribe, Labiche, Sardou, Laube, Augier, Dumas *fils*, later of Feuillet, Moser, Schönthan, Sudermann or Pinero.[1] For both reasons its policy was conservative. Though a private concern, it had something of an official *cachet*, nor could it risk making its faithful subscribers uncomfortable.

It should therefore not come as too great a surprise to find that its approach to the playwrights who were to become the glory of Norway was gingerly. In *Love's Comedy* Ibsen had made fun of the honest Christiania bourgeois when he went awooing and mixed it up with high-falutin' stuff about poetry, renunciation and the 'call'; so the play had to wait ten years before (somewhat revised) it was thought fit to put on. The rowdy reception of *The League of Youth* gave misgivings ('ein garstig Lied, ein politisch Lied'). More often than not, though duly offered to it, a new Ibsen play had its first performance elsewhere than in the Christiania Theater. *Ghosts* was never given there. Bjørnson's relations were closer; but this fate also befell three of his outstanding dramas—*The King*, which called the institution of monarchy in question, *Beyond our Powers*, Part I, a stone of stumbling to the devout, and *Paul Lange and Tora Parsberg*, the dramatization of a scandal in high places, some of the participants in which might well have been in the stalls. In brief, the Norwegian theatre of their time did little for Ibsen or Bjørnson, after, materially, giving them their start in life, and they never afterwards[2] came to look upon themselves as purveyors to it, as

Shakespeare was for the Lord Chamberlain's men or Molière for his company. And, again, though they absorbed a thorough knowledge of its mechanics (in Bergen, mainly), with their bearings on dramatic effectiveness, it was the same that they might well have acquired on their youthful visits abroad.

In 1898 the Christiania Theater closed its doors. Though not glamorous and sometimes, from lack of competition, lethargic, it had honestly done an honest job. It had bred four or five players of distinction; the *décor* might sometimes be shabby, and the rapid turnover of plays[1] meant that some of them were under-rehearsed, but, with any detailed reservations they might make, foreign critics, like William Archer or the Dane Herman Bang, applied to its productions standards appropriate to any other metropolitan playhouse.

Its place was taken by the National Theatre (National Theater), opened in September 1899.[2] The State provided it with a magnificent site, and the municipality voted it a modest subsidy (oddly enough, for the upkeep of the band); otherwise, however, it was a private enterprise, governed by what we should call a trust, and so it has remained, even if from 1927 onwards it has received ever-increasing government grants. It took over, naturally enough, the best of the old theatre's staff, traditions and repertoire, but, with more elbow-room in every sense, it could be more enterprising.[3] It was not long before the banned plays were brought into the programme.

Very much of this striking *renouveau* is attributable to its first artistic director, Bjørn Bjørnson, the son of Bjørnstjerne, an actor to begin with and, like his father, a stage-producer of genius. He carried on and bequeathed to his successors the policy of mingling the grave with the gay, 'plugging' enormous hits like *The Merry Widow*[4] for all they were worth and devoting the profits to the production, on a scale impossible to the Christiania Theater, of 'unpopular' plays, whether they were unfamiliar foreign classics or esoteric tentatives by Norwegian newcomers.

The National Theatre did not enter into the monopoly that had been its predecessor's for most of its existence. A single playhouse could not meet the demands of a capital city by now counting quarter of a million inhabitants. The minor theatrical ventures increased in number, stability and reputation, so that in the twentieth century Christiania could usually offer a choice of at least three bills for an evening's entertainment. During the years before 1914 the most notable of these ventures (in Central-theatret at first) was that of two fine, courageous actor-managers and producers, John Fahlstrøm and his wife. Outside Christiania, there were Den Nationale Scene (now so called) at Bergen and, from 1911 and 1914 respectively, permanent stock companies at Trondheim and Stavanger, all lively, even if labouring under great material difficulties. In smaller centres the place of the old Danish strollers was taken by travelling companies, very often casually assembled, of Norwegian players. But the great hardships of long hauls and unsuitable premises left the theatrical life of the provinces necessarily poor.

These handicaps were particularly grievous to the partisans of the Landsmaal movement—strongest precisely in country districts—who rightly believed that the spoken word of drama could be a most effective means of furthering their cause. The pioneer Ivar Aasen had already pointed the way in the 'fifties with the play *The Heir* (*Ervingen*). The Christiania Theater[1] and the National Theatre, however, could not help, even if they would; a parody of Landsmaal from the mouths of players trained in the other language would have been the reverse of a recommendation. When, forty years after *The Heir*, the Landsmaal had advanced to something nearer parity of esteem with the Riksmaal, propaganda for its own theatre became really active. The leading spirit was Hulda Garborg, Arne Garborg's wife, a playwright herself, an amateur actress and a stage-producer, who, in 1895, got together the first of a number of amateur companies; for the most part, they toured the countryside, but they also performed in the capital. They were soon reinforced by suitable professionals, and finally, in 1913, a firm Landsmaal organization, Det Norske Teatret, was set up, with headquarters in a series of already extant auditoria in Christiania.

(3) *The tardiness of minor native drama*

If the Christiania Theater gave little stimulus to those whose twin statues now stand before its successor, it, less understandably, did scarcely more for lesser talents. It allured no swarm of second-rate or third-rate playwrights, such as clung around Marlowe and Shakespeare or Molière and Racine. For long the number of new Norwegian plays by others than Ibsen and Bjørnson remained minimal; and their quality rarely warrants consideration.

More frequently perhaps than in other countries, writers in Norway who have made their names in other fields—fiction, poetry or criticism—have tried their hands at drama. This phenomenon showed itself already in the late 'seventies, when Jonas Lie and Kielland made such attempts. It is exceedingly curious that, with the examples of *A Bankruptcy*, *The Editor* and *Pillars of Society* before them, men of their abilities, on applying them to play-writing, adopted standards so much lower than for any novel which they would have put their name to. *Grabow's Cat* by Lie and *His Majesty's Bailiff* by Kielland are amateurish rubbish, and their later efforts in the same *genre* hardly deserve a much politer description.

Quantitatively and qualitatively things improved in this respect during the eighteen-nineties. No heir, it is true, to Ibsen and Bjørnson announced his début during this decade.[1] But, whether their talents were great or small, poets, novelists and short-story writers—quite a number of them—took to writing plays worthy of comparison with the rest of their output: one can name Knut Hamsun, Peter Egge, Hans Aanrud and Sigbjørn Obstfelder, representatives of a generation whose work will fall for consideration in the next chapter.

(4) *Gunnar Heiberg*

From a general survey of nineteenth-century Norwegian literature another, similar feature emerges prominently: the greatness of the distance, in terms of value, between the giants and the lesser fry. A frequently reproduced cartoon of the middle 'eighties presents Norway's literary fleet, four stately ships ploughing the waves, with Ibsen, Bjørnson, Lie and Kielland for their figure-heads. Amalie Skram not having yet left harbour, all the rest would have been rowing-boats. It was not until a good deal later that a kind of trim and seaworthy middling craft became visible.

An exception, however, to several generalizations appeared just at this time in the person of Gunnar Heiberg(1857–1929).* He was metropolitan-born (as no Norwegian writer of any eminence had been so far), he belonged by origin to the half-Danish Establishment, he is a rare representative of the generation intermediate between that of the Big Four and *les jeunes* of the eighteen-nineties. No man of genius, he was an assiduous, serious craftsman, the first really professional man-of-letters of standing in his country and, at the same time, more completely a man of the theatre than ony other of its literary figures:[1] whether as stage-producer, critic or purveyor of plays, he gave over a span of some thirty years the best of his talents to the stage. Under one aspect, however, his career ran true to type: the Christiania Theater shied at him and refused to have anything to do with any of his plays but one[2]—*The Popular Assembly* (*Folkeraadet*, 1897, with incidental music by Delius), comparatively anodyne though it was, stirred up a rumpus in its conservative public all the same.

Gunnar Heiberg wrote thirteen plays. Some of them are inoffensive, straight drama, like *The Big Lottery Prize* (*Det Store Lod*, 1895) about a renegade radical who, in spite of a second tergiversation,is shot dead by a more constant brother-in-arms; others are just flummery, *Artists* (*Kunstnere*, 1893), for instance, or *Gert's Garden* (*Gerts Have*, 1894)—notable only for more colloquial dialogue than native drama had usually employed.[3] The plays for which he is remembered, however, were all shocking in one way or another. They fall roughly into two groups, the one 'erotic', the other which for want of a better term one may call 'publicistic'—higher journalism in dramatic guise.

A preliminary observation may be made about the publicistic plays, illustrative of Heiberg's midway position between two fairly well-defined generations. Executed in the manner of the

---

* Gunnar Edvard Rode Heiberg was born in Christiania on 11 November 1857, the son of a judge, related to the distinguished Danish Heibergs, and his Danish wife. His repulsive appearance thwarted his early ambition to become an actor. His earliest publication, a poem, appeared in *Nyt Norsk Tidsskrift* of 1878. He was the artistic director of the Bergen Theatre from 1884 to 1888 and thereafter, either in Christiania or abroad, supported himself by journalism, literary and political, and royalties; he was given a government grant at half the usual rates in 1891 and a full one in 1923. He entered into two unhappy marriages, with a more satisfactory *liaison* between, and died, in his native city, on 22 February 1929.

ordinary realistic drama of the day such as Bjørnson conformed
to, they revolve about persons and events of general public
interest and imply criticism of them, but they are not true
'plays with a purpose'; Heiberg's guiding principle he defined in
these terms: 'Art for art's sake, that is art for mankind. Art for
the sake of mankind, that is not art.'[1] And, significantly, the
'actualities' he presents are invariably actualities of the past,
even if it is the recent past.

This comes out in his first play of all, *Aunt Ulrikke* (*Tante
Ulrikke*). Written in 1879 and published in 1883, the supposed
time of action is 1873, the year of large-scale socialistic demonstrations in Christiania: one of the minor figures in it was copied
from Olaus Fjørtoft, an agitator who died in 1878. The model for
the equally recognizable central character, Aunt Ulrikke, was
still alive, and here lay the earliest of the stones of scandal which
were to strew the author's path. She was Heiberg's aunt by
marriage, Aasta Hansteen, whom under a much more tactful
disguise many had recognized in Lona Hessel, the lady who let
in light and air on to the Pillars of Society. A courageous *femme
forte* of good family, Aunt Ulrikke insists on addressing a public
meeting in the cause of socialism; her friends and relations
endeavour to 'play her down' as a harmless eccentric; her spirit,
however, fires that of her young niece, who defends her in
private and in public; the girl in consequence not only loses her
young man, but is turned out of the house by her father, who, in
view of a vacancy in the Cabinet, gives this earnest of sound
political principles.

Aunt Ulrikke conforms to Heiberg's ruling tenet: we may
admire Aunt Ulrikke's and her niece's pluck in espousing a
disreputable cause or disagree with the view attributed to St
Paul that women should not address the meeting, but the play is
not to be construed as a *plaidoyer* for socialism or for women's
rights. Essentially it moves on the private plane. So does *King
Midas* (*Kong Midas*, 1890), which followed next, though the tone
now has become definitely polemical; the polemics are turned
against the central character of the play, 'King Midas' himself,
and for him likewise there was a living model, none other than
the ruling dictator of the day in literature and much else,
Bjørnson himself.[2] The uproar was the more terrific.

Ramseth (represented as an editor by calling) is the Bjørnson whose 'chest-Norse' tones a dozen years back had adjured the youth of the nation unswervingly to 'be in truth'[1] and more recently had been conspicuous for his ferocious diatribes against what he called polygamy. A close friend of Ramseth's died assuring his young and extremely tender-hafted wife Anna that during their married life he had been completely faithful to her in thought and act. Ramseth disbelieves this both on general grounds, being a puritan, and because he has evidence that the dead man did once misconduct himself with the maid. Anna is contemplating a second marriage with an altogether eligible young gentleman, whom of course Ramseth believes to be a libertine too: for 'the poison of immorality... is in all, almost all young men these days—in thought, mind, word, look, speech, feeling and handshake'. Truth *must* out. Anna *must* have her eyes opened to the 'swinery' of men. They are, when, against every protest from others in Ramseth's circle, she is confronted with her former servant—and runs mad (very mad) in consequence. Ramseth is rather upset by this, but his principles do not appear to be shaken.

Ramseth believes that truth is pure gold; like the ancient king of Phrygia he finds that gold can kill. As Ibsen's *Wild Duck* (which Heiberg had been the first to produce) was the tragicomedy of truth's fanatic, so *King Midas* is its melodrama: well put together and exciting, but not admitting of a higher qualification. For the personages are not represented in sufficient depth to carry the conviction tragedy demands. They are stage-types, engineered into strong situations, except for Ramseth himself. He is certainly no Chadband or the Tartuffe of a rationalistic age; but, besides King Midas, may he not, deep down, be also King David, lusting after Anna-Bathsheba? Apart from Anna's not very strongly stressed suspicion of this, we get no inkling of the inner man. Only a carapace is shown. To fill out a complete personality, in fact, the audience had to put in what it knew about Bjørnson—there is an entertaining pointer in Ramseth's trying to bully a rustic member of Parliament into reading Herbert Spencer—beyond his notorious belief in his authority, as possessor of all righteous principles, to order all things and all men in all circumstances as these principles dictate.

Two more among Heiberg's outstanding dramas follow the

familiar sequence—an 'actuality', its distancing and pointing under the author's hands, and scandal due to the latter: *Lying in State* (*Paradesengen*, 1913), which, taking its cue from the disgusting practices of cinema-operators at the time that Ibsen died and Bjørnson was buried, gives a biting picture not only of the commercialism, but also of the general humbug, attendant on the death of the great;[1] and *I Will Defend my Country* (*Jeg vil værge mit Land*, 1912). The latter once more centres on one personage and, because that personage—even if greatly altered as far as his actions go—is substantially Heiberg himself, it has a complexity and life lacking in the portrayal of Ramseth. It has good theatrical situations, as a summary will indicate, but it is not vitiated by the crassnesses that are apt to taint the rest of the author's serious plays.

The time of the action is 1905, when, prior to the dissolution of their union, Norway and Sweden stood at the brink of war. Karsten Skogstad, a landowner of an ancient and distinguished Norwegian family, fervently desires complete freedom and independence for his country; and he breaks out from his rural retreat into the Parliament building itself to urge resistance to the Swede *à outrance*. But he is so bitterly disappointed by the manner in which his desire is, factually, fulfilled and so humiliated at the readiness with which what he believed to be a heroic nation falls in with a policy of concessions that, Norway having ceased for him to be a land in which he can live, he commits suicide.

As so far outlined, the drama is the unexceptionable tragedy of an ultra-idealistic patriot. What provoked the immense outcry was advertised in the title, the first line of the Norwegian patriotic song: 'I will defend my country.' First heard from the mouths of babes and sucklings—in this case, a party of pupils from an idiot school —it is taken up in the crowning scene of the play by the multitude gathered round the Storting, precisely at the moment when the news comes from within that they will *not* be called upon to defend their country. It is hardly to be wondered that, when with great courage the National Theatre eventually presented *I Will Defend my Country*, a former cabinet minister fulminated in the press: 'It is a disgrace...that Gunnar Heiberg is allowed on its national stage to jeer at the Norwegian people's memories of 1905 and at the men then in command...the loose-mouthed penny-a-liner.'[2]

As for Heiberg's traffickings with 'the erotic', attention need only be given to the two plays which sounded that blast most stridently: *The Balcony* (*Balkonen*, 1894) and *Love's Tragedy* (*Kjærlighetens Tragedie*, 1904).

The Balcony begins with a married lady's being surprised by her husband as she is bidding farewell to her lover after a night together in her bedroom, from which she just manages to get him out on to the balcony; thence he presently emerges, to explain his presence at so early an hour by his desire to buy the house. This fits in with the husband's plans, he vaunts the soundness of his property and, to prove it, takes a leap on to the balcony, which gives way and precipitates him to his death. The lady marries the lover, and, when he has started off on a journey (as she thinks), a third gentleman, a comparative stranger, but a Very Influential Person, effects an entry over the balcony and declares his passion in such vehement terms that she readily succumbs. Husband no. 2, having missed his train, returns to find the pair *in flagrante delicto*, declaims upon his sorrow and starts playing about with a revolver, but then thinks better of it and takes his departure—via the balcony, but apparently unscathed.

How seriously the author meant this scenario of a bedroom farce to be taken is hard to say; somewhat, at any rate: a man's breaking his neck, tiresome cuckold though he may be, cannot just be laughed off. Tone and dialogue, too, are definitely heavy; there is no wit, nor any suggestion that there is fun in adultery. But there were those who took *The Balcony* very seriously indeed, in one of two ways. The moralists were outraged by the naked— almost literally naked—exhibition of a double and quite un-repentant, lascivious adulteress in a Norwegian drama, and *The Balcony* was the occasion for their spokesman Christen Collin[1] to launch an immense diatribe against the immorality of the newer literature in general. On the other hand, the partisans of that literature bestowed their grave approval on Heiberg's play, partly of course for the author's courage in provoking the moralists, partly for proclaiming—one might say, at the top of his voice—that in love sexual congress is all that matters, and partly because of the 'symbolism' of the Balcony.

Love's Tragedy proved less exceptionable. In 1904, ten years after *The Balcony*, its author's notions of passion could not cause the same commotion. It realizes more fully than any other of his major plays his own ideal of art which is composed for art's sake, but incidentally clarifies the problems of mankind. Heiberg always venerated Ibsen for having—in the years after 1884 at any rate—consistently embodied that ideal; and from the title[1] on the play is full of echoes from the master. The central situation into which it develops is in itself that of *Little Eyolf*, that of a passionate, but unsatisfied wife with a decent, equable husband, who, unhappily for her, likes occasional bouts of solitude in the wilds. A character from *Rosmersholm* (Ulrik Brendel) reappears in the person of a vagabond poet and prophet, Hartvig Hadeln, to whom Karen recounts her woe and whom, after the treat of seeing her take a douche, she endeavours to seduce with the champagne Rita Allmers found equally ineffective for the purpose. Despairing of ever getting what her nature craves—unremitting carnal love—she knifes herself.

Heiberg wanted to be a Modern writer, not only in reaction against the solemn literature-with-a-purpose that held sway when he was coming to maturity, but also more positively. To be frivolous, as he rather disastrously attempted in *Gert's Garden*, was not enough: he wished to be ranged under the bright new banners of art for art's sake, psychology and symbolism. The first of these aims was achieved, even if conception and execution differed a good deal from the more usual acceptations of the principle. The art of the theatre is one of the arts, and Heiberg undeniably achieved theatre for theatre's sake. But, as regards his other ambitions, he failed. The symbol of the Balcony is as crass as it is obvious, and Heiberg did no better anywhere else. His psychology was equally ham-fisted.[2] In view of the heroes of *King Midas* and *I Will Defend my Country*, it would be unjust to dismiss the characters in his plays all as stereotyped 'parts', but they are always stagey in manner and in essence. *The Balcony* and *Love's Tragedy* were meant to be (and in fact were often taken to be) explorations of feminine psychology; they are, in effect, as are the tentatives of Heiberg's contemporary Georges de Porto-Riche, up-to-date versions of that mythical being of the boulevards, La Femme. Heiberg did not, as he fondly hoped, take his place near Ibsen, but, through and through a man of the theatre, with the author of *Amoureuse*, with Sudermann and Pinero.

THE NEW MEN OF THE 'NINETIES

(1) *The mutiny against the Old Guard*

The figures which virtually by themselves upheld Norwegian literature during the eighteen-eighties—Ibsen, Bjørnson, Lie, Amalie Skram, Kielland, Garborg—are apt to give the appearance of a solid phalanx: earnest, strenuous searchers for the true and the good, if not of the beautiful, fighters in the great 'break-through' to freedom and actuality inspired by Georg Brandes. Such an image, blurring great differences in their talents and interests, also distorts the fact that they did not in any way stand on a common 'platform'. They were in no position to do so. Ibsen's home was in Germany, Lie's in Paris. Amalie Skram decamped to Copenhagen, Bjørnson and Kielland spent lengthy spells abroad, the last-named and Garborg, though hailing from the same part of the country, saw one another only once and did not like what they saw. They could indeed be in strong disagreement with one another, over Bjørnson's unbending sexual puritanism, for instance.

Nevertheless, the image of their solidarity as well as solidity is not wholly factitious and it was already present in the mind of their contemporaries. To them it had aspects not now so obvious. For one thing, by the end of the decade, they were all middle-aged or elderly, and such common front as they seemed to make, libertarians though they were, could be construed as a form of tyranny of Age over Youth. A second consideration was their political involvement. As libertarians, they were not prone to toe any party line, yet the steady musketry they had directed against conservatism of every kind had powerfully contributed to the triumph of the Left; and they too had to pay the penalty of the universal disillusion that followed. Literature with a purpose —a purpose that had led to a desert rather than the millenium— was discredited.

Before 1890 this was not expressed in set terms, scarcely

implied even by any new direction in which Norwegian literature was setting: the 'Bohemia' hubbub, row between the young
and the old though it might be, had, first and foremost, social
objectives, and its literary expressions broke no new ground.[1]
After Gunnar Heiberg's virtual début with *Aunt Ulrikke*, in 1883,
not followed up for another seven years, and Amalie Skram's
Constance Ring, published in her thirty-ninth year in 1885, no new
writer of uncommon promise had come to the front. There was
no influential native critic to draw up a profit and loss account
or to point to possible new sources of gain abroad. For ten years
and more, Norway had been an exporter of literary *valuta*, and
what was going on in other markets had secured little attention.
Zola, of course, was well known, but regarded by friends and
foes alike mainly as the counterpart of the Old Guard at home;
Turgeniev had his admirers, but he was, after all, 65 years old
when he died in 1883.

To accuse Norway of any signal backwardness in this respect
would be unfair. Turgeniev's great successors in Russia were but
slowly coming to the rest of the world's notice during the
eighteen-eighties; the new poetry of France had only sporadic
admirers outside that country and Belgium. Except in Dutch
literature, where a clear break with the past came a little earlier,
the striking *renouveau* of literature in virtually all countries of the
western world was essentially an affair of the 'nineties, when
Dostoievsky, Nietzsche, Mallarmé, Maeterlinck, Kipling, Strindberg and D'Annunzio were seen as the brightest *novae* in the
literary firmament. In the mouths both of enthusiasts and
detractors, however, neo-romanticism, aestheticism, art-for-art's-
sake, symbolism, *fin-de-siècle*, decadence, often jumbled and very
variously conceived, were becoming the key words in discussions
among artists and literati. Concurrently, the interests of 'society'
and the interest *in* society disappeared behind concern with the
single individual and with fresh individual approaches to artistic
creation. There might be plenty of dreaming and melancholy,
but equally a great quest for the source of a new joy in life, so
long suffocated by 'problems' and pictures of misery, and over all
a spirit of adventure and experiment.

During the years of talk and subterranean grumblings,[2]
echoes, to reverberate more penetratingly a little later, reached

Norway mainly from two directions. One came from Sweden, the 'sister-country', with which literary relations had, on the whole, been scanty and one-sided; it was not Strindberg,[1] still in his realistic phase, who attracted most attention, but his juniors, Heidenstam and Ola Hansson, who were calling for colour, liveliness and deeper psychological soundings as an anti- dote to the low-spirited reportage characteristic of the new writing in their country at that time.

Two other matters of report, more familiarly, were coming from Denmark.[2] One was of the writing and ideals of an emergent group—lyricists, mystics and symbolists—eventually associated with the magazine *Taarnet*, who were to give a new look to Danish poetry. The other, once more, centred on Georg Brandes, who had lost much of his interest in 'problems under debate' and substituted for it a preoccupation with the personality of great authors (and others), and its revelation and fructifying effects in and through their works: at this time he was principally con- cerned with preaching the new gospel of Nietzsche. Fired by Brandes, Nietzsche, his 'aristocratic radicalism', the orphic style of *Zarathustra* and the doctrine of the Superman became subjects of hot discussion throughout the North.[3] The discussion was very powerful in stimulating speculation and imagination to break out of the narrow circle of social preoccupations and their 'bourgeois' context. Nevertheless it should be said at once that, even as the interaction of the young Danish and Norwegian poets remained on the plane of the many friendships between them and mutual encouragement, so also Nietzsche's direct influence on Norwegian writers was small, except as regards Knut Hamsun during a comparatively short phase.[4]

In 1890 the revolt came out into the open. Knut Hamsun, whose utterly unconventional novel *Hunger* appeared in full the same year, had an essay entitled 'From the unconscious Life of the Soul' printed in the new Norwegian magazine, *Samtiden*,[5] and he followed it up in a series of lectures given in Christiania and several other towns during the next autumn. They surveyed a fair range of literary products then in the public eye, the obser- vations on the Big Four naturally rousing the most interest. Hamsun lumped them together as creators of a literature appealing to the meanest intelligence and particularly suited for a nation of peasants with bourgeois velleities, its nature determined by the 'democratic, utilitarian urges that have governed our century'; its pictures of social life subordinated human nature to moral abstractions; the personages presented in its plays and stories were nothing but 'parts' or 'types'; anything touching the 'unconscious life of the soul' was conspicuous by its absence. Hamsun's eagerness to put all the Old Guard under one hat made much of his negative criticism preposterous. In order, for instance, to belittle Ibsen (who sat unmoved among the audience at Christiania) as a mere prosy reformer, he had to pass by *The Wild Duck* without a word, dismiss Rosmer of Rosmersholm as scarcely more than an aristocratic 'walking gentleman' and pronounce *The Lady from the Sea*, in which 'democratic urges' are very far to seek and a psychological 'case' is in the forefront, just 'God-Almighty bunkum' (*guddommelig dyft*). The inconsistency of his grievance against his seniors[1] was well hit off by a cartoon of the day[2] depicting him as a schoolmaster with a text-book on psychology in one hand and a birch in the other, fronting a class of little Ibsen *et al.*, who rub their protuberances while he shouts: 'When you write, you rapscallions, it is not to be so plain that every country bumpkin can understand it nor so obscure that I myself don't understand it.'

Hamsun's positive thesis, however, was clear, valid and seasonable: it was not that utilitarian literature should be abolished, but its hegemony, and a space left by its side for other kinds of writing, notably those concerned with the 'soul'.

(2) *The revival of poetry*

The neglect of soul is reflected in the virtual disappearance of poetry from the annals of Norwegian literature over nearly twenty years. It was natural therefore that the call for 'something new' should tempt young writers into the field of lyric, so long untilled. Three of them conspicuously responded, Nils Collett Vogt, Sigbjørn Obstfelder and Vilhelm Krag, all gathered in Christiania in the latter 'eighties. The first to do so was Vogt (1864–1937).* The oldest of them, he appears as in many

* Nils Collett Vogt, whose mother was a niece of Camilla Collett and an authoress, was born in Christiania, the son of a civil engineer, on 24 September 1864, had a grammar school education and matriculated as a law student, but

respects a transitional figure, as Gunnar Heiberg was—like him, a better-class native of the capital, brought up for a professional career in a correct, conservative *milieu*. The ferments and conflicts of ideas to which his young mind was exposed he delineated in two novels, *The Family Trial (Familiens Sorg*, 1889) and *Harriet Blich* (1903) and in the autobiographies of his old age.[1] Though he acknowledged Georg Brandes (still the Brandes of the 'seventies) as his great master, behind and beyond the master his inclination led him to the poets of an older time, and their living heirs, such as the Dane Drachmann. Life, he continued to believe, was a battle, and he conceived of it in the sober, strenuous spirit common both to Brandes's first disciples and the more thoughtful of their antagonists.

Even if some of the items in it could be construed as contributions to politics, the smell of the battlefield is hard to detect in Vogt's modest firstling, *Poems (Digte)*, of 1887. Not by temperament a propagandist, he had no intention of launching a manifesto, scarcely even of hoisting 'new signals', as the phrase then went. It caused, accordingly, little stir, and when it was noticed it was simply for being what it was, a collection of lyrics—carefully composed, though obviously 'sincere' and free from rhetoric and *cliché*, and equally free also of anything positively striking in vocabulary or verse-structure. When in later years Vogt made a selection of his verse, he saw fit to include only a single item from this volume, but, as the first strong chirp before sunrise and a fair example of the poet's special music, it deserves quotation in full:

Var jeg blot en gran i skogen

Det er blevet sent på høsten,
luften dirrer ikke mer,
luften står blot taus og ser
med sit isblå, kolde øie
på de unge ranke birke,
der lig gule altarblus
lyser op i skogens kirke.

qualified for no profession. He made a good marriage in 1894 with a Swedish lady, whose estate in Västmanland was the fixed point in the life of fairly extensive wandering in Europe, Italy for preference, he led for twenty years. He returned more permanently to Norway in 1912 and died at Lillehammer on 23 December 1937. Though he too was active as a journalist, he is not to be confused with his namesake and contemporary Nils Vogt of Bergen, for several years Norwegian correspondent to *The Times*.

Når så vinterstormen kommer
—hele skogen farer sammen,
og de gule altarlys
slukkes ud ved første gys,
blade flyger om som gnister,
luften blegner, sneen falder,—
er det kun de høie graner,
der lig store, sorte faner
suser gjennem skogens haller.

Og da driver jeg i skogen,
og jeg hører vinden sukke,
slide i de gamle toppe,
tude om det mørke fjeld,
som står lige mørkt deroppe.
Og jeg tænker ved mig selv:
Det er intet tællelys,
som det første gufs skal slukke.

Var jeg blot en gran i skogen,
der, når vinsterstormen kommer,
—luften blegner, sneen falder,—
suser gjennem skogens haller
lig en vidt udslagen fane,
til det grønnes næste sommer!
(*Digte*, 1887, pp. 46f.)

Seven years passed before Vogt published another volume of verse. By general agreement this, *From Spring to Autumn* (*Fra Vaar til Høst*, 1894), together with *Music and Spring* (*Musik og Vaar*, 1896) and *Hard-Won Bread* (*Det dyre Brød*, 1900), all enthusiastically received, mark the summit of his achievement as a poet. They are plainly from the pen that wrote the *Poems* of 1887. But they are distinguished not only by more colour and vivacity and a wider range both in sentiment and in scene (the sea, quiet or tumultuous, now occupied a prominent place), but also by a greater precision and pregnancy in the images evoked. *Hard-Won Bread*'s sombreness betrays also a deeper reflectiveness, a turning away from objects of sense to a concern for humanity's hard strife to win the bread it craves for body and soul. It was a natural choice in 1914 to commission him to write the words for the official Cantata to celebrate the centenary of national independence. But in the loss of spontaneity and charm he forfeited that position of leadership in his generation which *From Spring to Autumn* had seemed to promise.[1]

The place, it is now agreed, is Sigbjørn Obstfelder's.* His general reputation is that of an esoteric symbolist and mystic, with the usual corollary of recluse and decadent, and he was well aware of inner compulsions in these directions. Edvard Munch's portrait of him shows a face of almost manic apprehensiveness, and the horror of existence was always lurking to overwhelm him. He was, nevertheless, immensely resolute to hold the inward-driving forces at bay and far from unsuccessful in doing so. He had many friends; the totally different Gunnar Heiberg liked him; he brought himself to marry; he entered the lists when Christen Collin tilted away at the 'decadence' of the new literature; he thoroughly enjoyed the bustle of London and Paris. Better than any who pitied, censured or derided him, he knew that he needed balance, not only for his writing, but also for facing squarely the 'great horror', as mysterious and terrible to him as to Kurtz of Conrad's 'Heart of Darkness'; and he strove heroically to attain it.

It is from his poetry (including the posthumous 'prose poems') that the common image of Obstfelder is formed. His *Poems* (*Digte*) are consummate examples of the *fin-de-siècle* reaction in Norway and, though coming as early as 1893, already mark its apogee. As strange as their form—lines held together by unemphatic, undulating rhythms, a little assonance or alliteration and even less rhyme, sometimes expanding into sheer prose—was their ethos, if their heterogeneity warrants the term.

Three features characterize it: the intimate involvement of

* Sigbjørn Obstfelder was born in Stavanger on 21 November 1866, one of the sixteen children of a baker, whose father had immigrated from Holstein, and of his wife, of Norwegian stock. Educated at the local Grammar School, he entered the Technical School at Christiania, to become a structural engineer, and had a year's workshop practice at Milwaukee (1890–1). On his return to Norway, a breakdown consigned him for a time to a lunatic asylum, and he gave up all idea of a career other than in letters. He travelled a fair amount in Europe, married in 1898 and died on 29 July 1900 in the municipal hospital of Copenhagen, perhaps through over-exerting his weakly physique on a walking tour. The Czecho-German poet Rainer Maria Rilke re-created Obstfelder's image in his most celebrated prose work, *The Papers of Malte Laurids Brigge*.

the poet's sentiments with the images evoked that justified the appellation of symbolist poet; the exaltation, from time to time, to an ecstasy of delight in the sounds and sparkle of the living world (in his famous anthology piece, the 'Impromptu' on falling rain, for instance, 'Orkan' and the dithyrambic 'Hymne'); and, lastly, in the strongest contrast to such ecstasy, the extraordinarily low-toned quality of the love-poems.[1] The term itself for these may be thought inappropriate, illustrations as they are of the aphoristic lines:

> Love—that no one knows.
> Longing—that everyone knows.[2]

Crudely described, they are almost will-less, ineffectual gropings, both spiritual and bodily, fraught not with kisses, but sighs and sobs and a sense of isolation rather than proximity,[3] amid an atmosphere of mist and gloom that recall Georges Rodenbach's then famous evocations of Bruges-la-Morte.

The resemblance to Georges Rodenbach may be accidental, but that to another Belgian contemporary, Maurice Maeterlinck,[4] at that time approaching the acme of his renown, can scarcely be so. The very accents of *The Treasure of the Humble* and *Wisdom and Destiny* (not elsewhere, I think, heard in Norwegian) are reproduced in this curious praise of women: 'We speak best of them, perhaps, when we do not speak of them.'[5]

Such renunciation of speech was no paradox. Obstfelder was haunted by the 'unsayable' and, behind it, by what might almost be called the 'unthinkable', were it not for his devoted labours in and through *A Clergyman's Diary* (*En Præsts Dagbog*, posthumous, 1900) to establish some firm coherence for the spiritual intimations that, in oblique gleams, were all he could put to paper in his poems. The coherence which, religiously rooted, he hoped would banish the 'great horror' and give a new dimension to his poetry he never found. It is as a figure of promise rather than achievement that Obstfelder stands out as one of the most intriguing, as, in the true sense of the word, he is one of the most eccentric figures in the literature of his time.

The highest hopes were raised when, in 1890, an audience of

students heard read aloud to them the vivid poem 'Fandango'*
by one of their number, Vilhelm Krag (1871–1933),** and it was
printed in *Samtiden*.[1] Krag's volume of *Poems* (*Digte*), appearing
the following year, was seen after Vogt's firstling as a second
and more distinct landmark in the neo-Romantic resurgence.
Several of the few, short poems in his collection have the brio
and charm of 'Fandango', but not all. Fascinated, as Obstfelder was, by Edvard Munch's pictures (one of which in a later
volume, 'Night', he literally transcribed), Krag ventured also
on heavier lines and darker colours, at their best evocative of a
sombre, oppressive mood. With him, however, the impressionism, unlike Obstfelder's, remains peripheral. There may be a
good deal of superficial mystery, in the vulgar sense, but none
of Obstfelder's gropings to a mystical vision. Krag's brooding
has little to do with 'the soul'—his own or anyone else's—nor
does he engage in Vogt's 'battle of life'. He is the least symbolistic, most truly lyrical of the poets with whom he is usually
bracketed, as is attested by the frequency with which his lines
were made into songs.

The poems of 1892 were succeeded by collections in the two
years immediately following, *Night* (*Nat*, with the subtitle
Digte i Prosa, 1893),[2] and *Songs from the South* (*Sange fra Syden*,
1894), and by several others for a quarter of a century and more,

---

* 'Fandango' begins and ends as follows:

> Ikke janitscharmusik!
> Stille, I marschtunge rythmer!
> Stille, for fan, musikanter!
>
> Tscherkesserinderne, tscherkesserinderne,
>   lad dem blot komme!
> Ind skal de danse paa spæde smaa fødder
>   til dæmpet musik
>   fra fjerne guitarer . . .
>
> Musik, musik, janitscharmusik,
>   den store kinesiske tromme!

(*Skrifter*, IV, 1930, 7)

** Vilhelm Andreas Wexels Krag was born, the son of an officer in the Engineers,
at Christiansand on 24 December 1871, had a grammar school education in his
native town and matriculated at Christiania University, to mingle at once with
a crowd of coevals interested in letters and the arts. Prolific in all branches of
literature and in journalism, he had a wide public. For three years (1908–11) he
was director of the National Theatre. He died on his property at Ny-Hellesund
in Søgne on 7 July 1933.

but though they may have become surer in gaining the effects desired they do not reveal any growth in Krag's poetic personality. Settling amid one of the friendliest landscapes of Norway, in Søgne, near his native town of Christiansand, he made himself its laureate, celebrating in easy, well-turned, sometimes humorous lyrics (and in prose), its scenery and the rustic characters that peopled it.[1] Though, like Vogt, he lived to a respectable age, as a poet he was again essentially a figure of the 'nineties, one of promise rather than fulfilment.

The prime achievement of the three men just discussed was that of once more putting poetry 'on the map', and a kind of poetry very different from that which in Norway had held the field before. Cantata had given way to spontaneous song, the celebration of great men and events to private sensation and moods; rhetoric, regular strophes and metres had been banished and replaced by excited staccato or soft, flowing rhythms which often lapped over into a melodic prose. The new poetry was a gallant challenge and in that sense a successful one: never thereafter was poetry in Norway to be relegated to the inferior, ancillary position it had occupied between *Arnljot Gelline* and Vogt's début. Yet it scarcely lived up to its hopes and aspirations. An anthology of the best European verse between 1885 and 1900 would contain few items of Norwegian provenance, and the chief of them would have to be excerpts from Garborg, working away at *Haugtussa* quite independently of the aesthetic ferment among his juniors.

(3) *The symbolists in drama and fiction*

Quantitatively, too, the out-turn of formal verse during the eighteen-nineties was not very remarkable, even when the contributions of the Landsmaal writers[2] are taken into the sum.[3] And it is noteworthy how often, even in their early days, the pioneering trio turned to other forms of expression. Vogt's second book was a novel; Vilhelm Krag's 'fairy-tale drama' *In the Blue Hills West* (*Vester i Blaafjeld*) appeared in the same year as his *Songs from the South*, and the great popularity he won was to be sustained by his tales and plays of Sørland folk as much as by his poetry: the exploits of Major von Knarren

(*Major v. Knarren og hans Venner*, 1906) built up a kind of folk-lore figure, a Sørland Toby Belch, if not quite a Falstaff.

Of greater value, once more, than those of Vogt and Vilhelm Krag were Obstfelder's ventures into fiction and drama. By contrast with *In the Blue Hills West*—which is hardly more than a cluster of echoes from *Peer Gynt*, Rolfsen's *Svein Uræd* and the contemporary romantic plays of Drachmann—Obstfelder's *Red Drops* (*De røde Draaber*, 1897)[1] must be reckoned among the best experiments in the symbolist drama undertaken anywhere in the decade.

It is scarcely a surprise that the heart of this play should be a *Recherche de l'Absolu*, symbolized by the fluid—distilled but never applied—'which shall give men the power to live, to fashion their life according to their nature, the life of the individual, the life of the whole', so that the primordial harmony, peace and joy that have been lost may through alchemy be restored to all creation. The material setting centres on a chemical factory, not unlike that which, in *Fortuna*, Kielland had invented for his and Obstfelder's native Stavanger and as solid and credible. The same is true of the actual story—the oscillations of the brilliant but mystically minded young chemist, torn between the commercial business of his factory and the common claims of everyday life on the one side and his craving for the transcendental and the possibility of its materialization on the other. In his personal life this is mirrored by his attachments to the sensual society beauty Borghild and his cheery little laboratory assistant Lili, who stands for 'the life of the stars'. These cross-strands are well knit; there is nothing portentous or preposterous about the hero's moves from one plane to another. Lili dies (of consumption)—in ecstasy at having received from her lover the only kiss they have ever exchanged; and he, who has renounced his professional career and lost Borghild, goes back to them, persuaded that the joy of life promised by his red drops may also be reached in other ways. But his father, assuming the role of a Maeterlinckian sage, proclaims that he is making a second mistake: that the wisdom of old age shows him dreams to be the only Truth. As the hero contemplates the radiant light and the stars above, everything then falls away from him except the memory of Lili.

Obstfelder's three pieces of fiction have less to commend them. In fact, their sensibility turning into sentimentality, they were fair game for the mockers of symbolistic vapours and vapourings. The *Two Novelettes* (*To Novelletter*, 1895) amount to extended prose-poems. (In the first, an Icelandic working-girl dies of phthisis in the chaste embrace of a fellow-lodger, leaving him sad—and that is all.) The short novel *The Cross* (*Korset*, 1896), again, is an extended Novelette of the same sort, supposed to be the diary of a young woman who committed suicide by drowning. She has been driven to this extreme because her lover, who has not altogether unfounded suspicions of her 'purity', has tormented her, not by cross-examining and smacking her, but by failing to do so. One familiar with *Pelleas and Melisande* will recognize the scene where the lover sits covered by his mistress's hair—the hair from which the Cross of the title is fashioned.

(4) *The other new playwrights and authors of fiction*

At roughly the same time as Vogt, Vilhelm Krag and Obstfelder's 'break-through' into verse lie the beginnings of several other authors who comparatively rarely, if at all, ventured upon lyrical poetry, though they were equally anxious to join in the quest for 'something new' or, to put it somewhat lower, were animated by dissatisfaction and revolt against one or other aspect of the old order.

The most distinguished of these were Knut Hamsun and Hans Kinck, who call for consideration in a separate chapter, not alone by reason of their eminence, but equally because their literary careers stretched far into the twentieth century and the balance of their finest work was done then. The latter consideration applies also to Peter Egge, Gabriel Scott and Johan Bojer, who made their débuts between 1891 and 1894 and who also will be passed by for the present.

Dybfest, Finne, Thomas Krag, Andersen and Aanrud, however, have their 'centre of gravity' much more unmistakably in the eighteen-nineties, which, like Obstfelder, the first two were not destined to outlive. In Dybfest and Finne, indeed, the 'centre of gravity' might be placed even further back, closely linked as they were with Hans Jæger, the storm-centre of the 'Bohemia-row', obsessed with its defiance of conventional inhibitions and taboos in matters of sexual behaviour. (When Georg Brandes asked Dybfest what the work he was engaged on was about, the latter answered 'Rut',[1] to which the critic's retort was 'Oh, you Norwegians!') 'Soul' and poetry meant nothing to them.

Arne Dybfest (1869–92)* had a further connexion with Jæger through his interest in anarchism, which, he had the odd idea, was especially commendable for furthering the joy of life—the quest for which, muddily enough, underlay the revolt of 'Bohemia'. *Among Anarchists* (*Blandt Anarkister*, 1890) is journalism between the covers of a book, derived from contacts he had made in the United States and Paris, but his other interest takes pride of place in the little imaginative writing he was given time to produce. The novel *Ira* (1891) and the short story 'A Solitary' ('En Ensom'),[2] both about nymphomaniacs, dealt so faithfully with the joy of life as a function of the abdomen that the author was classed by friend and foe alike as the arch-decadent of his generation and the publisher of 'A Solitary' hastily withdrew it from circulation.

The same powerfully brewed mixture of desire and repulsion *vis-à-vis* the female sex is found in Gabriel Finne (1866–99).** His three-act play *Konny* (1895) presents another aspect of the great change that had overtaken attitudes towards women since Lona Hessel had held the centre of the stage at the end of *Pillars of Society*. Finne's heroine is made of much the same timber, only to have her engagement broken off when her *fiancé* declares his inability to live up to her ideals of himself and life in general. It is not unreasonable to see here the influence of Strindberg, since Finne was an ardent admirer of his (especially of *The Servant-Girl's Son*), and that appears elsewhere too. Finne

* Arne Dybfest, born on 30 June 1869, the son of a Trondheim skipper, worked as a journalist in the United States and at home and drowned himself in the sea near Bergen on 7 July 1892 to escape a police court prosecution.
** Edvard Gabriel Finne, born at Bergen on 10 February 1866 the son of a military officer, matriculated, like so many of his contemporaries, at the University of Christiania without proceeding much further with his formal studies. His novel *Doktor Wangs Børn* (1890), approved by both Kielland and Bjørnson, gives a picture of the clash between the generations to which he himself was exposed. He published four novels and three plays before dying, of pneumonia, at Christiania on 3 July 1899.

had learned from the author of *Comrades* the great theatrical effectiveness of sheer, violent rows, of which the second act of *Konny* affords as fine an example as could be wished. *The Owl* (*Uglen*, 1893),[1] though the ending is pacific, bears a strong resemblance—in the exhibition of mental disturbance raised to the pitch of hallucination—to the series of one-act plays Strindberg had just written, each a single dramatic situation shorn of everything but the direct impact of will upon will.

In the early work of Thomas Krag (1868–1913),* Vilhelm Krag's elder brother, the break with the literature of the 'eighties is much clearer than with Finne or Dybfest: the atmosphere of 'Bohemia', for one thing, has been completely dispelled. His output was very various.[2] Poetry was not so conspicuous in it as in his brother's, but the best of it can bear comparison with his; he was an essayist and a controversialist, entering into the perennial dispute about 'modern' literature and its bearings on morality or immorality,[3] but this was as late as 1901. His most interesting work, however, was done in the realms of drama and fiction.

Side by side with Obstfelder's *Red Drops*, Thomas Krag's tragedy *King Aagon* (*Kong Aagon*, 1894)[4] represents the most valiant effort in its time and place to create a new kind of drama. In spirit, inspiration and manner, however, it differs altogether from Obstfelder's.[5] Colour and plentiful, strong action, interspersed with poetry that should sound like poetry, were the objectives. *King Aagon* centres on the sober, elderly king of some undefined feudal realm who is cured of his physical blindness, awakened thereby to the sensuous beauty of the world he sees about him and resolved to enjoy its promises— including love—with a pride of life that amounts to megalomania. Up to this point and even beyond it—to Aagon's realization, conveyed through overhearing a conversation between the girl he lusts after and her lover, that in fact he is no more than a pitiable and rather silly old man—*King Aagon* is excellent for its freshness and variety, offset by a few ominous foreshadowings of

---

* Thomas Peter Krag was born in Kragerø on 28 July 1868. Ill-health prevented his making any mark at school or at the University of Christiania, where he only matriculated in his twenty-third year, and he soon devoted himself entirely to literature, with Copenhagen for his favourite headquarters. He died at Christiania on 13 March 1913.

retribution; but the author, unfortunately, could only flounder in the situation he had created for his last act. After Aagon has made a show of himself in the composite part of King Lear, Oedipus at Colonus and Grock, his kingdom is invaded by a stronger potentate whom he has challenged and, after the slaughter of all the other principal personages, he runs on his own sword.

King Aagon was looked upon as a 'symbolistic drama', and the vague medieval background[1]—not historical, in any sense— the picture-book character-drawing, the dull mutterings of indistinguishable peasants, the motif of blindness could be adduced to justify the ascription. It seems unlikely, however, that as a whole it was intended to impress one profound truth—that blindness is preferable to sight: for that would have been a poor apology for the exultant life-affirming literature that was to supersede the drabness, worryings and pessimism of the realists.

The two novels Thomas Krag wrote immediately after *King Aagon*—*The Brazen Serpent* (*Kobberslangen*, 1895) and *Ada Wilde* (1896)—were equally unconventional and more successful. The earlier deals with the broken marriage of an elderly country gentleman and his very young wife, whose adultery he discovers, to die of grief in consequence. The paramours marry, but the wife's son by her first husband, whom he strongly resembles, is a standing reproach to them. To remove him from their sight, they send him, scarcely more than a child, to sea in charge of a rough sailor, instructed to brutalize him and keep him away from home. His ship is wrecked in a storm, but he survives and returns to his native district. His stepfather is now dead, and his mother sees him but once, at a distance. Overwhelmed by remorse and apprehension, she never thereafter leaves her house and beguiles the time exchanging bawdy stories (not detailed) with her maid. During one of these colloquies she dies of a laughing fit. The son witnesses her funeral, loses his reason and is consigned to a madhouse.

The story is, in the main, told in the plain, straightforward manner and with the unquestioned morality of De Foe, its occasional angularities suggesting the telling of a series of legends that have gathered round the old manor house of an extinct family. The storm off the Azores, with its ominous prelude, its bursting and the shipwreck, is a splendid piece of realistic writing. It comprises more strange episodes than the summary of the plot indicates: the end of the boy's stepfather is mysterious: he just disappears, swallowed, it is believed, in a bog which has taken to spreading in an inexplicable manner; there is a wild nocturnal scene—only loosely connected with the story—of a churchyard, with a lunatic, a terrified clergyman and the scattered sacraments. For all the apparent matter-of-factness of the telling a sense of the eerie and ominous is felt brooding over all. One could leave the mysterious element at that, were it not for the enigmatic Introductory Chapter, intended to explain the title. In the desert, it sets forth, the People were plagued by snake-bites, but relieved when, at God's command, the Prophet erected for their worship a serpent made of brass,[1] as appropriate to their life. For 'brass is truth, and truth is beauty'—and that, apparently, is all we need to know.

Ada Wilde has less power and variety than *The Brazen Serpent*, and lacks its overtones of horror, mystery and (is it?) symbolism. It shows, however, many resemblances to the earlier book: life among isolated gentry, multiple adulteries, a very young wife who becomes a lonely old woman; the style again is both realistic and evocative. Thomas Krag was never to write anything quite so distinctive and original as *The Brazen Serpent*.

Like his brother Vilhelm, Thomas Krag became one of the notables in *hjemstavnsdiktning* or *hjembygdsdiktning*, literature about the home town or native district. This, in itself, was no novelty; it had its ancestry in the peasant tales of the mid-century, to which the younger Landsmaal writers, just before 1890, had given a greater authenticity and a more specific localization. But now (besides Garborg's new-found recourse to his native Jæren), Riksmaal authors by a little their juniors entered the field in numbers, and with long-enduring effect. This might be thought somewhat surprising in contributors to a 'movement' so thoroughly metropolitan in its origin, if it were not remembered that the movement was, all along the line, a reaction against the characteristically urban, bourgeois pre-occupations and projections of the old realists. The geographical shift of interest was accompanied by a historical one. The remote past, of course, the medieval, had been evoked in many romantic plays and poems, but, except by Lie in *The Family at Gilje* and Kielland in *Skipper Worse*, a more recent past had been neglected by Norwegian authors. The historicity of *The Brazen Serpent* and *Ada Wilde*, to be sure, has no great importance; it is, none the less, plain that these novels should be imagined as taking place a hundred years or so earlier than the time of writing, and their distancing in time as well as place contribute to the legendary atmosphere investing them. (There is nothing of this in *Skipper Worse* or *The Family at Gilje*.) The 'Danish time' before 1814—a subject to be handled only with the greatest circumspection[1]—had become possible matter for the exercise of the imagination.

Into this Danish time it was that Tryggve Andersen (1866–1920)* placed his best-renowned story, *In the Days of Cancelliraad Weydahl* (*I Cancelliraadens Dage*, 1897).[2] It is in effect the chronicle of a parish near Lake Mjøsa (where it was written) during the years of grinding hardship and scarcely permissible hopes at the beginning of the nineteenth century, when the old régime was crumbling in Norway's isolation through the British blockade and the enmity of Sweden. Against the indifference, incompetence and immorality of the constituted authorities a few men stood out for preserving some semblance of life and order, like Cancelliraad Weydahl, a heavy, conscientious, just and generous civil servant, also a true patriot and a model farmer. He too, however, is not immune from the prevailing moral laxity and, after carefully destroying documents that might incriminate others, dies before the hoped-for dawn, partly, it seems, from remorse at the infanticide of his young mistress and partly from the curse laid upon him by a malefactor whom he has convicted.

As regional literature in general, when it becomes distinguished enough (like Hardy's or Arnold Bennett's), ceases to be ranked as regional, so *In the Days of Cancelliraad Weydahl*

---

* Tryggve Andersen was born on 27 September 1866, in Ringsaker, the son of a lawyer-administrator, matriculated at Christiania in 1885 and gave promise of becoming an egyptologist of distinction until he was sent down for a breach of discipline. From 1892 to 1897 he held minor clerical posts and thereafter lived as a freelance writer, though his productivity was small. A man sick in mind and body most of the time, he died of tuberculosis at Gran on 10 April 1920.

rises above the trivial pawkiness, grotesque angularities and half-quaint humours of most *hjemstavnsdiktning*[1] to stand out as a minor classic. Its eminence is attributable not only to Andersen's impeccable, muscular style and to the careful construction of the successive episodes, but also to the authenticity of his delineations, personal and social, based on much historical research. Even in this novel the structure—like that of Selma Lagerlöf's more famous *Gösta Berling's Saga* (1891) with which it is often compared—is reared on that of the short story, to which almost all the rest of Andersen's small output was confined.[2]

In the art of the short story Tryggve Andersen's closest rivals among his coevals were Kinck and Hans Aanrud (1863– 1953).* Aanrud's chosen field was the peasantry of his native district, Ringsaker, from which he made occasional excursions into lowly urban life where he showed a certain unconventionality in exposing, good-naturedly enough, the corruptions of the proletariat without attributing them to the tyranny of social pressure. Temperamentally he was a tolerant lover of his kind in all its aspects and a conciliator; though he would have written much as he did whenever he might have been born, his work may be seen as a bridge between various opposites of his time, between puritans and hedonists, satirists and preachers, fantasts and realists, and between the Riksmaal writers like himself and the Landsmaal enthusiasts, with their concentration on the joys, sorrows and heart-searchings of farmers and farmhands.

In his short stories,[3] the kernel, more obviously than in Andersen's, is the expanded anecdote, given relief by short, unobtrusive descriptions of nature and of cottage-interiors and also by a mild sardonic spice that keeps at bay the sentimentality always lurking round the edges of the pastoral. An example of this quality is 'Simon Vanaasing', the tale of a crabbed individual, ill-reputed through allegations of maltreating his children, who meets his death after fighting his way

---

* He was the son of a small farmer in the western Gausdal, matriculated in 1883 as a law student, but did not prosecute his studies and for some forty years lived mainly from journalism. He directed the Bergen Theatre from 1899 to 1901 and acted as literary adviser to the National Theatre from 1911 to 1913, when he was granted a civil-list pension. After that his productivity virtually ceased.

through a blizzard with the medicine one of them needs; and who gets his 'reward' in a specially magnificent funeral organized by his conscience-stricken neighbours. Occasionally the sardonic spice is not called for, as in the beautifully handled 'Ane-Petter', in which a slightly 'wanting' young hind achieves his great ambition of driving the farm-wagon by himself when he is sent to collect a load of wood in the forest; disregarding the omens, he executes his commission, is then overtaken by the first winter storm and is found the next morning stark and stiff against a tree, the load in perfect order and his master's horse carefully protected against the snow and frost that killed himself.

Usually, however, the dangers of the idyll are avoided by humour of a straightforward kind: the silly old man rakes in his hay on the Sabbath, but his conscience pricks him into spreading it again; the two horse-copers interchange the most unexceptionable sentiments of brotherly pietism, busily over-reaching one another at the same time, etc.[1]

Aanrud was in fact that rare phenomenon in Norwegian literature, a genuine and almost invariably genial humorist as well as a good, pithy story-teller. This is evidenced in three successful farcical comedies: *The Stork* (*Storken*, 1895), *On the High Horse* (*Høit Tilhest*, 1901), *The Cock* (*Hanen*, 1906), all interconnected through the *dramatis personae*,[2] rascals and fly-by-nights from the lower quarters of Christiania, who swindle and deceive one another with the utmost bonhomie. The first two acts of *The Stork*, at any rate, when they are indefatigably busy 'passing the buck' to one another—the 'buck', as the title suggests, being children, born and unborn—may measure up to the great *comédie rosse* of its time, Gerhart Hauptmann's *Fur Coat*.[3]

KINCK AND HAMSUN

(1) *Their relationship to one another and their coevals*

HANS KINCK (1865–1926) and Knut Hamsun (1859–1952) are
far and away the most arresting figures among the Norwegian
authors who came to the front about 1890; and at the time both
were active they were habitually so linked. One may, then,
briefly indicate their relationship to one another and to the
others of that literary generation. Of the latter, in general, they
had a fairly low opinion, disliking especially any symptom of
what Hamsun called 'common or garden Baudelairean brain
fever'.[1] They shared, however, in the pervasive spirit of revolt
against the values and practices which they thought typical of
their predecessors and which Hamsun, indeed, had taken the
lead in repudiating; and they remained more consistently
faithful to the spirit of revolt than many of their coevals. They
too sought escape from the hidebound stuffiness of the towns in
the liberating expanses of the countryside and in the small settle-
ments, where they thought to find personalities which, less
subdued to a common pattern, would give scope for the study
of exceptional, erratic 'souls', while the nature surrounding
them would stimulate to ecstasy. In these two things, psychological finesse and ecstasy, *les jeunes* of 1890 had accused their
seniors of being especially wanting, and Kinck and Hamsun
went as far as any in supplying the alleged deficiencies.[2] Their
own literary affinities were with Nietzsche, Drachmann and
Dostoievsky, mentors of all who at that time clamoured for
the rejection of *tendens* literature and the supersession of realism
by impressionism.

When the work of each is considered as a whole the most
striking similarity between Hamsun and Kinck is the fact that,
though one was by breeding and even by disposition an
'academic' and the other an autodidact, both were, in the
original sense of the word, barbarians. That is shown not just

by their neglect of classical themes,[1] the unconventionality of their style and composition, or even their complete disregard of the Christian church and its civilizing mission, but, more importantly, by their disdain of all 'culture'—at any rate as it had developed for countless centuries—and their hatred or mere scorn of all who could be accounted its representatives. Kinck thought and hoped that an alternative might somehow be raised from the peasantry, whereas Hamsun, sharply distinguishing between the 'peasantry' and the 'people', believed there could be no such thing as 'peasant culture'[2] and was in reality indifferent to the creation of any kind of culture.

Kinck, so often blind to the goals towards which he was heading, professed himself an optimist, while Hamsun would have nothing to do with abstractions ending in -ist or -ism; from the writings of both of them, however, a profound pessimism is disengaged: the materialism that was their common abhorrence seemed to be winning all along the line. In Hamsun's imaginative writing, all this is implicit; only very rarely does he speak out his mind direct to the reader.[3] With Kinck, from quite early on, there is obvious *tendens* once more; his most impressive stories, certainly, were written for the sake of the lesson they were to convey.

The widest differences between the two men come out when they are considered as artists. Hamsun, working slowly and with great difficulty, always imposed his own perfect order on his matter, however eccentric it might be. Nothing is superfluous, and the diverse ingredients, if one may call them so— evocations of natural scenery, description of pregnant episodes, reflexion, talk—relieving one another, merge easily, almost imperceptibly. For achieving this, Hamsun developed his remarkable style, nothing *voulu*, never obviously varied to show how the focus of interest is shifting,[4] but, equally, never monotonous, even when the gaze is for long fixed on what would ordinarily seem most unpromising objects. At its most characteristic it has the quality of a cultivated man's talking to himself. The compulsive interest of his novels is, however, not a matter of arrangement and style alone. The man who is talking to himself is a man of great wisdom and sensitivity; he is, in the technical sense, the omniscient narrator and regards his scene from a long distance; but this omniscience and the wide perspectives he opens out disclose both a deep empathy and a constantly engaged judgement that appreciates the grandeur and pettiness of the world before him and the irony of their juxtaposition. These are binding forces too, and at the same time impart an extraordinary stereoscopic effect to all his projections.

Kinck aimed at doing everything Hamsun did, and more. A gayer, livelier man in daily life than one might guess from his printed words, he brought to his tasks a venturesome and exceptionally well-stocked mind, great industry and complete integrity. In his imaginative writing the 'ingredients', were much the same as Hamsun's. But he had none of his shaping genius, and necessity made him produce too much and too hurriedly. Even in the short story, which he practised the more frequently and which has found fervent admirers, and in lyric verse, he rarely achieved excellence.[1] In the eighteenth-century phrase, he 'wanted art'. At the time both men were alive, many saw him running a neck-and-neck race with Hamsun;[2] but in the end he has been adjudged *proxime accessit*.[3]

(2) *Kinck's dramas*

Fragmented as Kinck's* writings are, their parts always more impressive than the whole, revealing moreover little development either in their form or animating spirit, it may suffice to concentrate on only a few of them, in no chronological order, for giving an idea of their nature and intention.

The work of his to have won the most general acclaim is *The Horse-Coper* (*Driftekaren*, 1908),[4] a long poem in dramatic form.

---

* Hans Ernst Kinck was born on 11 October 1865, the son of the medical officer of health at Øksfjord in Finnmark and of his wife, a former maid-servant. His boyhood was spent in the country, in the inland Setesdal and a water-side village in Hardanger. After two years' secondary schooling in Christiania, he matriculated (1884) and took a first class in Arts (1890) at the university there. He hoped for, but did not achieve, an academic career and, after some temporary employment as a schoolmaster and librarian, from 1893 onwards lived by his pen, which, eked out by occasional travel-grants and a parliamentary pension (1912), supplied a barely adequate income. In 1896–7 he paid the first of several visits to Italy; otherwise he lived in suburban Christiania, where he died on 13 October 1926. In 1893 he married the authoress Minda Ramm, who predeceased him.

It centres entirely on the personality of a fifty-year-old itinerant horse-dealer called Vraal, who returns to his village under the spell of the only one among his many amours he can look on with some sentimental satisfaction, even if it did result in a bastard. His paramour, he finds however, is dead, and he lets her red-haired replica Bol slip through his fingers while with rhetoric and cunning he is endeavouring to make himself a power in village politics. His activities only make the prevailing dissensions worse and he disgraces himself by breaking into the church and becoming drunk on the sacramental wine; eventually he is driven out on his wanderings again, in the company of his chief associate, the broken-down huckster whom Bol has taken for her husband. The end, years later, shows him ministering at his scabrous individual's death-bed; there he is joined by Bol, who all along loved him for the beauties she discerned beneath his horse-coping and crapulence, so that a happy, regenerate old age now seems assured.

Kinck's *The Horse-Coper* is intentionally a pendant and corrective to Ibsen's *Peer Gynt*. Vraal, once more, is the not too savoury type of Norwegian rustic, the rootless man who is a mixture of grandiloquence and self-satisfied scoundrelism,[1] with this difference, however, that beneath his braggadocio lies an imagination not only profounder than Peer's, more contemplative and more akin to the visionary, nourished on poetry and the Sagas, but also truly redemptive. Its intimations enable him to work out his own salvation, whereas Peer, if he comes to salvation at all (and that is doubtful), does so through another's agency.

Wordsworth might have approved of Vraal, but it is more difficult to believe in him than in Peer. The inferiority of Kinck's to Ibsen's poem lies, however, not so much in this, or the dubiousness of the romantic thesis—the redemptive power of the imagination—which it embodies, as in its execution. After adverse criticisms of his style in the earlier verse-drama, *Agilulf the Wise*,[2] Kinck took pains to make it less rebarbative; but even if Vraal's rhetoric and visions attain to a power and jagged beauty beyond anything the author compassed elsewhere, it certainly remains too elliptical and harsh for the stage; the long central portion about parochial politics in the village of Klep is nothing more than a series of tiresome brawls; nor do any of the other scenes engender much genuinely dramatic tension.

Such cavils apply equally to the rest of Kinck's plays, whether like *The Horse-Coper* they are essentially timeless verse-phan-tasies[1] or, like *Between Processions* (*Mellem Togene*, 1898), realistic up-to-date plays or evocations of the Renaissance in Italy, such as *The Last Guest* (*Den sidste Gjest*, 1910), which even Arentino as its hero cannot save from tedium; and they are only very fitfully redeemed by *The Horse-Coper's* positive qualities.

(3) *Kinck's novels*

As a novelist, Kinck and his critics agree, he found himself in *Mrs Anny Porse* (*Fru Anny Porse*, 1900). It tells of a very young lady, daughter of a military landowner, who vainly endeavours to adjust her sensitive, ignorant and inexperienced self on the one hand to the relatively intellectual company of her husband (another landowner) and his family and, on the other, to the uncouth sociabilities of their neighbours. Her two babies dying, she gives up the struggle, alienates her husband and chooses to roam about, a kind of Maeterlinckian princess, accompanied by three village idiots, until they begin to make lewd advances to her. She then becomes certifiably insane.

Anny Porse's fate illustrates a theme persistent in Kinck's fiction: the isolation and blighting of the 'one' among the 'many'. In this and in other respects, as will have been seen, the novel bears a strong resemblance to Thomas Krag's earlier *Brazen Serpent* and *Ada Wilde*, notably in its environment, the Sørland country under its less friendly aspects. Like Krag, Kinck put the time of action in the past, into the 'fifties of last century, before steam had begun to revolutionize communi-cations, to account both for his heroine's neglected upbringing in the rough household of the squireen her father, who still takes to thrashing his labourers, and her breakdown later amid the Rabelaisian jollities of the Porses' neighbours, who can find few diversions except in drinking-parties, brawls, cards and adultery. In this, however, we should not be wrong in detecting signs—already prominent in the two novels about Herman Ek[2]

(1896 and 1898)—of the social criticism more unmistakably implicit in Kinck's later novels: while laying bare their roots, he was diagnosing also the ills of Norwegian society in his own day.

The descriptions of environment are well integrated with the personal tragedy in *Fru Anny Porse*. For *Emigrants* (*Emigranter*, 1904), where the 'purpose' has become quite obvious, his approach to his dual theme is, none the less, more tangential.

As his scene he chooses a village on an inlet of the western sea, and he deliberately meant this Knarrevaag to be taken as the essential Norway in miniature.[1] Boat-building has been its scanty population's main occupation, but when a newer, smarter craft than theirs is called for they refuse to meet the challenge and indeed persecute and ruin the bright lad who has independently taken it up. Instead, they decide to go in for the tourist industry, transform one of the houses into a hotel and generally titivate the village with an eye to English visitors; this ending in an immediate fiasco, they then lay themselves out to parade cottage industries and peasant costumes, trot out bits of folk-lore and arrange uplifting lectures and conferences for enticing serious-minded guests from the rest of Norway to a centre of 'folkly' culture. This scheme works quite well. A shadow, however, is cast by the determination of some dozen stout youths to clear out of this bogus mess and emigrate to America. Every obstacle is put in their way—not from distress at the loss of their presence or their energies, but from malignant jealousy at their staking everything on something really hazardous, bold and in a sense visionary. The young men, however, get away.[2]

In this village has settled a disillusioned widower, a retired doctor. Without ever making, or wanting to make, himself a member of the community, he observes it and speculates on it with the keenest interest—he is indeed as much a *voyeur* as a researcher—and has some part in accelerating the process going on before him. It is he, for instance, who puts English tourists into the villagers' heads and also, with an endlessly repeated joke about the letters W.C., helps to drive them away, whereupon his frail contact with his neighbours virtually ceases. He has his private troubles—there is a middle-aged lady who by becoming his mistress vainly hopes to become his second wife—

centring on his small daughter. She cannot strike roots in her new environment, nor can she be won by her father's solicitations for her affection; she wilts away and dies.

Kinck's approach in this novel was called tangential; for the little girl's sad story has no connexion with Knarrevaag's upheavals, and not much more with her father's *liaison*. The root cause of the child's decline, we are led to believe, is the memory of her father's quarrels with her dead mother; but they lie in the past and, even so, are only sketchily indicated.[1] The Emigrants after whom the book is named do not come into the picture before she has vanished from it. The two spheres, the personal and the 'public', touch, but they are not really connected.

Such constructional failure, making the confusions which Kinck delighted to depict worse confounded, must be held to mar his lengthier works. With *The Avalanche Broke* (*Sneskavlen Brast*, 1918–19), he made his most thorough effort to integrate into a satisfying whole his social diagnosis with a story of human interrelations, and up to a point he succeeded. It is a novel-trilogy of epic dimensions, taking in his fiction the place of *The Horse-Coper* in his drama. Exhibition of character may nowhere go as deep as in the presentation of Vraal, but it is more multifarious and has moments of inspired insight, even of subtlety. The sheer power of its outstanding episodes, notably in the first third ('Big Folk and Peasants'), when the tumultuous advent of the spring thaw is paralleled by an invasion of Peasants, who, liberated from their icy confinement, virtually sack the homes of the Big Folk (Storfolk) in their parish,[2] seeks its equal in Norwegian literature. The second part ('Young Mrs Sophie') is elaborately designed to describe the efforts of a cultivated, energetic young lady, 'committed' to her environment as the *voyeur* in Emigrants never was, for bringing together the two bitterly warring cultures, chiefly through communal fun and games. At this point, however, despite the promise of Part III's subtitle, 'Above the Avalanche', the story loses all its coherence and, with it, all interest. It sinks in the all-round defeat of Fru Sofie and her aides and the utter collapse of their bridge-building with this conclusion: 'One of the two cultures *must* perish—or both.'[3]

That Kinck, like Dostoievsky or Strindberg, should delight to dwell on chaos is well enough; his innumerable scenes of dispute and hurly-burly truly deafen, dazzle and appal. At the heart of his longer works, however, there is an incoherence which comes near to being calamitous. Such thread as a story may have been planned to supply is too tenuous to carry the weight of its episodes; nor have the central figures, with the solitary exception of Vraal, prominence or interest enough to act as their focus, in the way that, for instance, Dostoievsky's Idiot does; they are, in fact, bundles of notions, speeches and sentiments rather than personalities, with no suggestion that the incoherence is an illustration of a psychological principle (as it is with Hamsun). Incoherence equally marks Kinck's fairly obtrusive imagery. He is, for instance, very fond of the symbols of the adder and the bird, the adder which fascinates and the bird which the adder kills; but the adder, oddly enough, can stand also for the ever-defeated individual, since, in his expiring moments, he can still emit hisses, and the bird is now an eagle, now the song-bird on which the eagle preys.

(4) *Kinck's ideas*

Something should be said, briefly, about Kinck's overflowing ideas, mainly perhaps because he clearly meant his imaginative projections to be taken as parables and their lesson to be appreciated equally with their form.

For a self-styled optimist, deeply concerned with the state and future of his people, to have written *Emigrants* with this intention is as strange as that a literary recruit of the early 'nineties should indulge in parables at all. The final departure of the young men in this novel might have been presented as a victory for surviving vitality over *vis inertiae* in a specially backward parish. Instead, it is a miserable sneaking-away, leaving neither regrets nor hopes; no news comes that the lads of Knarrevaag were proving the latent vigour of the Norwegian stock in their new home. And Knarrevaag, we must remember, a community completely sunk in rotten, nerveless self-complacency, stands in Kinck's mind for all Norway in miniature.[1]

It is, indeed, unusual among the communities he describes

and, in the same degree, unrepresentative, in that it comprises no member of the 'Big Folk': for the retired doctor is in it, but not of it. Elsewhere, in *Anny Porse* or *The Avalanche Broke*, for instance, such figure prominently—but always at enmity with their lowlier neighbours, whose unremitting hatred reduces them to bitterness and an impotence their fundamental unsoundness forbids one to deplore. For a third 'class', to be sure, Kinck shows respect, the hill-farmers, remote and independent; but sooner or later the villages suck them in or invade them, and they are ruined. He remained, however, obstinately certain that salvation was to be found, specifically that the essential Norway lay in the 'folk', that a Knarrevaag represented the 'race'.[1]

From the pessimistic dead-end to which the contemplation of the contemporary scene around him actually led, he sought escape by two different routes, but they too led him either to confusion or to conclusions very different from those it may be presumed he hoped to establish. One was his study of the national past,[2] centring on the 'time of greatness', that of Haakon Haakonson, whose rise to power formed the subject of Ibsen's *Pretenders*. Seeds of its decay, however, were as plain to Kinck's sight as its greatness, and, if one examines his historical writings carefully, one sees that every age he writes about represents a degeneration (usually due to foreign influence); logically, therefore, the salvation of Knarrevaag-Norway could only be sought in a return to the aboriginal bone-age. That would be barbarism as perfect as one could wish it, but an objective that Kinck could scarcely have thought practicable for three million Europeans in the twentieth century.

The projections of the medieval North are stimulating, far-ranging, well-informed, sometimes brilliant. In even fuller measure this is true also of Kinck's writings about the Italy, new and old, where he found his second 'escape-route' and which he knew well as a traveller as well as a scholar. The colour, stir and gaiety that overjoyed him accorded well with his tempestuous, energetic style. He wrote not only journalistic articles[3] on current topics, and deeper studies on Italian subjects, but also tales and dramas with an Italian setting. These are often presented in double-harness: round Aretino he wrote

A Quill Driver (En Penneknægt, 1911) and the drama *The Last Guest (Den sidste Gjest, 1910)* and, on Machiavelli and his contemporaries, *People of the Renaissance (Renæssansemennesker, 1916)* together with the play *Towards Carnival (Mot Karneval, 1915)*.

What fascinated him, the ardent disciple of Jacob Burckhardt, and what he held up to admiration was the Renaissance with its magnificence and ruthlessness, its licence in the widest sense of the term and the free development of personality that it fostered. It was paradoxical in a man so intent, where his own country was concerned, with the 'folk' alone and the salvation of its soul. He was aware of this and strove to resolve the paradox by asserting that 400 years back Italy had liberated itself from monkery and had become a united people of which the Michelangelos, Machiavellis and Titians were natural emanations—a kind of argument he never dreamed of applying to a Nansen, a Bjørnson or a Grieg.

A learned and sagacious critic[1] has described Kinck as the arch-National-Romanticist. His passionate concern for his countrymen's weal and fullest independence, his quest for their 'buried treasure', his loving descriptions of their homeland may justify the appellation. But it would be equally easy to demonstrate that, after three generations, this baffled, uneasy spirit had—unintentionally, of course—proclaimed the bankruptcy of the cause that Wergeland had made his own.

(5) Hamsun's 'Hunger', 'Mysteries' and 'Pan'

In the succession of great Norwegian authors Knut Hamsun* ran true to type in one respect at least. He was a publicist,

* The name Knut Hamsun was originally due to a printer's error for Hamsund, the name of the holding, on Hamarøy in Nordland, to which his family had moved when he was four years old. Knut was the son of Per Pedersen, village tailor and crofter, and was born at Garmo in the upper Gudbrandsdal on 4 August 1859. He had little education beyond what he picked up for himself (which in course of time amounted to a great deal), and up to his thirtieth year he lived (in U.S.A. 1882–4 and 1886–8) miserably enough from a variety of odd jobs, journalism and itinerant lecturing among them. After 1890 he devoted himself entirely to writing, which brought him in enough for the acquisition of two properties—one at Hamarøy (1909–16) and the other the nobleman's estate at Nørholm, between Grimstad and Lillesand, which he ran energetically and enthusiastically as a

fertile and wide-ranging, as well as a writer of fiction, drama and poetry. Faithful as he remained to the ideal of 'art for art's sake', accepted by almost all who came to the front at the same time as he, he kept, however, the two sides of his activity in water-tight compartments. Although his total personality invites a study of profound interest, literary history can ignore many aspects of it.

With †*Hunger* (*Sult*, 1890),[1] in which he first made his assumed name famous, he produced at once a perfect specimen of the literature he was pleading for in the denunciation of his 'utilitarian' seniors, a piece of pure impressionism. Everything in it is just as it seems to the narrator, a man near to extinction from starvation, wandering homeless and friendless through Christiania town. He is never seen from outside, rarely forms part of a composition in which he is one of the figures. One hears occasionally of the pains in his body, but even his speculations on what is going on there take an insignificant place compared with the sights seen through his eyes and the welter of other thoughts that race or mull in his mind. The alternations induced by his condition between mental haze, sudden spurts of revolt or joy and the preternatural sharpening of the senses, projected in isolated scenes of extreme concrete vividness, provide for a variety and sense of completeness that make *Hunger* a *tour de force* unsurpassed in its kind by any of the French psychologists whose example he wished followed.

Hamsun never wrote nor tried to write another completely egocentric work like *Hunger*. The impressionistic manner, there carried to the extreme, came, however, to characterize all his most distinguished writing. It took on a new perspective through the impressions received by invented characters—a good deal of his superb natural descriptions comes in that way —and through the impressions of an uninvolved, neutral spectator of their doings.

Two long steps towards his perfected technique were made very quickly after *Hunger*: *Mysteries* (*Mysterier*, 1892) and *Pan* (1894).

gentleman-farmer. He was awarded the Nobel Prize for Literature in 1920. Long known for his German sympathies, he gave open support to Quisling's party, for which he was indicted and, though partially acquitted on grounds of mental failure (brilliantly belied by his *På Gjengrodde Stier*, 1949), heavily fined. He died at Nørholm on 19 February 1952.

† *Mysteries* is very properly so called, provided that all associations with mysticism are ruled out: Hamsun's was no metaphysical mind. It describes the doings and sayings of a young man, Johan Nagel, who spends some summer weeks in the hotel of a small sea-coast town, gets to know a number of the inhabitants, has two love-affairs and, failing to establish in them or elsewhere a firm relationship with any other human being, drowns himself in the harbour. Some of the events are mysterious in themselves. One hears of a theological student who was found dead before the story begins and who is thought to have killed himself from hopeless love for the girl Dagny with whom Nagel falls in love; before his effective suicide, Nagel has made an earlier attempt, but been frustrated because someone has substituted an innocuous substance for the poison he carried with him; was it the wretched cripple, Grøgaard, the butt of the town, whom Nagel tries to rehabilitate, and who eventually, we are told in a postscript, comes to a bad end, probably deserved? But such puzzles are left as reported, *obiter*. However intimately concerned in it, their clearing-up is no business of the story. More central, more pervasive, are the mysteries attaching to the personalities engaged, and they are equally unresolved. What kind of person is this half-buffoon Grøgaard, what was and is his true life? Does he merit, as a maltreated underdog, the sympathy and help Nagel gives him, or is he a sinister intriguer under the indignities heaped upon him? There is Nagel himself. He appears in the little community, where he is a complete stranger, accidentally, 'from nowhere'. We do not know what his real name may be or anything of his past life, except that it took him far afield and that a girl friend (who makes a brief and unexplained appearance) figured in it. He is a cultivated, mercurial man, alternating between fits of despair and exaltation, impulsive action and mere drifting, for the most part genial and generous towards his fellows; the virtuosity he displays in an amateur concert suggests the professional musician, but when the violin-case he has among his slender baggage is opened it is found to contain nothing but his soiled linen.

These unexplained, unresolved enigmas of course open the door to 'interpretations' of every sort. But as little as the factual puzzles constitute the basis of a detective story does Hamsun, either deliberately or unconsciously, build up Nagel and his vicissitudes into an elaborate symbolical structure. In positive terms one may say that the theme of *Mysteries* is the desperate search of a man, capable from temperament and choice of assuming a great variety of *personae*, for a firm anchorage to one of them, so that true life may take the place of the chameleon's existence, promise-crammed.

The words poison, suicide, puzzle, sinister, desperate which an analysis of *Mysteries* cannot well avoid, are, nevertheless, misleading. It is a sunny summer, with various local jollifications, that Nagel spends in the little town; his love for the unresponsive Dagny gives him ecstasies as well as frustration; his questing may be desperate, but it is not solemn. *Mysteries* in great portions is indeed a gay book. The ground-base to all is the vast complexity, even within a small circle, of all human relationships, the incalculability, in the strictest sense, of all behaviour since only the smallest fraction of the motives can be known. We all, Hamsun implies, have our own inner logic,[1] but each of us is an iceberg, exposing only a small portion to others' gaze and, what is more, always liable to tip over and present another, completely unknown aspect.[2]

†*Pan* (1894), perhaps the most magnificent of Hamsun's works, nevertheless in one way marks a return to the method of the lower-toned *Hunger*. Except for the brief epilogue reporting the death of its hero, Lieutenant Glahn, it is again presented in the first person singular, but here that is much more of a literary device (and, it must be allowed, not an altogether plausible one). While, naturally, the sensations which Glahn has somehow found time to put on paper must be a reflexion of Hamsun's, he is not Hamsun in the way one may take the hero of *Hunger* as being, but a projected *persona*, a character in fiction. Such partial distancing, however, does not impair the vividness, the immediacy, of the descriptions of scenery and of the episodes that fill the story. Nowhere in this quality was Hamsun to excel this account of the primordial hunter of beasts and women amid the colours, light and vastnesses of a Nordland summer and the ecstasies of which they were the fount and the setting. Like the quarries he pursues Glahn is a fragment—the title suggests a

personification—of primitive nature, in it and of it; what enhances the stereoscopic projection is the realization that, beast of prey that he is, he is also one against all, fundamentally an enemy, outside, warring as well as merged with his fellow-creatures, who ultimately lay him low too.

(6) *Hamsun's drama and poetry*

Between *Mysteries* and *Pan*, in 1893, Hamsun published two novels very different in kind from them: *Editor Lynge* (*Redaktør Lynge* and †*New Ground* (*Ny Jord*).[1] They have a Christiania setting, are told in a middle-of-the-road realistic manner and have nothing of mystery, fantasy, poetry or 'soul' about them. Such interest as they possess lies in the view Hamsun takes of society around him. It is a low one. The savagery with which he pillories the agents of publicity in their mere opportunist commercialism is only equalled by his contempt for their weak-kneed, debauched clients, the artists and writers, who puff themselves out with the claim that they are breaking new ground—and what ground, a putrid swamp! By contrast with them stand some solid, hard-working entrepreneurs, who really produce something. Linked with these two novels by similar *milieu* and the reintroduction of a character from them—a recurring phenomenon in Hamsun's *œuvre*, as with so many Norwegian authors—is his first play, †*At the Gates of the Kingdom* (*Ved Rigets Port*, 1895). It deals with the pressure put upon a research student of philosophy to modify his unconventional tenets with a view to the advancement in his career so urgently demanded by his poverty. In Kareno's racking struggle with his conscience and his manuscript he neglects his loving, but quite uncomprehending little wife; and in the end he is left deserted by her for a more assiduous lover and desperately working at the emasculation of his dissertation so that it may gain the approval of the academic Establishment[2] and the loaves and fishes in its gift.

At the Gates of the Kingdom moves on a high level of intellectual and 'human' interest. It is good 'theatre' too. The domestic crisis through which Kareno passes has some almost unbearably poignant moments, curiously heightened by his very imperfect awareness of it. But, in view of the strictures which Hamsun passed on the drama that was generally acclaimed, it is curious also in being somewhat conventional, and that in more than its outward guise. In moments of exceptional inspiration Gunnar Heiberg might have written it, and—of all things—it suggests at once a comparison with *Hedda Gabler*, Ibsen's own nearest approach to the fashionable drama of the time. The cards may be shuffled, but we are presented with another brilliant and original, defeated scholar, and again we have man of learning at the heart of a grave matrimonial crisis which almost passes over his head. And it is much to be doubted whether, gauged by *Hedda Gabler*, Hamsun succeeded in imparting to his play the psychological subtlety and authenticity in which, he held, drama had been so lamentably deficient.

Hamsun presumably recognized this: that the coarsening and simplifying which he stigmatized in a Shakespeare, a Holberg and an Ibsen are inevitable in the conditions of dramatic presentation. Certainly, after *The Gates of the Kingdom*, he avowed that he wrote plays only for the royalties they might bring in, and they never came near such artistic success as his first venture had attained. The two sequels to it, *The Play of Life* (*Livets Spil*, 1896) and *Evening Glow* (*Aftenrøde*, 1898), which show Kareno's progressive degeneration, and †*In the Grip of Life* (*Livet Ivold*, 1910) are a muddle of intentions and of talk, punctuated by high explosives.[1]

The hope of gain, however, can hardly have lured Hamsun to his two remaining dramatic ventures, the prose tragedy *Queen Tamara* (*Dronning Tamara*, 1903),[2] which the enemy of historicism wrote about a virtually unknown Caucasian princess of the thirteenth century, and *Monk Vendt* (*Munken Vendt*, 1902), likewise laid in the past and 'romantic' in its allures; he must have anticipated that theatre-audiences of every kind would assign them at once to the *genre ennuyeux*. Some of Hamsun's distinguishing qualities, certainly, are allowed to appear—ecstatic outbursts, the insistence on human incalculability, for instance—but for dramatic effectiveness such are handicaps rather than advantages. *Monk Vendt* (a nickname, attributable to a bald pate and a little knowledge of Latin) possesses, however, two points of adventitious interest: written in rhymed

KNUT HAMSUN

verse, sufficiently 'correct', but wooden in its rhythms and very
long-winded (there are eight acts of it), it marks Hamsun's
public début as a poet; and in the hero, something of a Peer
Gynt, as Kinck's Horse-Coper was to be, he presented in full
length the character of the vagabond, who in a variety of guises
was to reappear in all his later books.[1]

During the eight years following on *Pan* Hamsun had written
little that gave scope to his finest qualities. His best of this time
was the novel †*Victoria* (1898), a tragic little story, told with a
tenderness that avoids all sentimentality, of the poor village
boy—a poet to boot—who loves the squire's daughter. In 1903
and 1904, however, two volumes came out which gave a new
relief to his personality and his art. *In Fairy-Tale Land* (*I
Æventyrland*), called forth by the long journey he made right
through Russia to the Caucasus and the fringe of Persia, is one
of the most brilliant of travel-books. It is, as one might expect,
an entirely personal record—no history, no archaeology, no
statistics, no politics, a minimum of 'social' speculation, let
alone political prophecy. It rests content with conveying in a
superb unforced style, shot with the irony that from now on
becomes steadily pervasive in Hamsun's manner, the magnifi-
cences, squalors and personal predicaments that crowded in on
his senses from nature, strange races and fellow-travellers, and
the wonder, the joy rising to ecstasy with which they filled him.

The second book was his collection of verse, *The Wild Choir*
(*Det vilde Kor*, 1904).[2] Hamsun's approach to poetry sounds
unusual; it is, he declared,[3] 'the only form of literature which is
not at the same time pretentious and meaningless, but is
simply meaningless [*intetsigende*, nothing-saying]'. A less brusque
way of putting it would be to say that it is, or should be, purely
lyrical. So interpreted, Hamsun's practice conformed to his
theory; the contents of *The Wild Choir* are all what an earlier
generation would have called effusions. Some are short repro-
ductions of a fleeting sight of sentiment, in which the personal is
usually brought out at once by the use of the first person present:

> *Jeg* vanker indover det brune Fjeld . . .;
> *Jeg* blaser med Tuten *min egen* Basun . . .;
> Det synger i *mig* en Tone . . .;

and, simple and regular though their structure may be, from time to time a unique, elegiac beauty rises out of it. In others the ironic salt is added, as in

Om Hundrede Aar er Alting glemt

Jeg driver iaften og tænker og strider,
jeg synes jeg er som en kantret Baad,
og alt hvad jeg jamrer og alt hvad jeg lider
saa ser jeg mig ingen Raad.
     Men hvi skal jeg være saa haardt beklemt?
     Om Hundrede Aar er alting glemt.

Da hopper jeg heller og synger en Vise
og holder mit Liv for en skjøn Roman.
Jeg æder ved Gud som en fuldvoksen Rise
   og drikker som bare Fan.
     Men hvi skal jeg fare med al den Skjæmt?
     Om Hundrede Aar er alting glemt.

Saa stanser jeg virkelig heller Striden
og ganger tilsjøs med min pinte Sjæl.
Der finder nok Verden mig engang siden
saa bitterlig druknet ihjæl.
     Men hvi skal jeg ende saa altfor slemt?
     Om Hundrede Aar er alting glemt.

Aa nej, det er bedre at rusle og leve
og skrive en Bog til hver kommende Jul
og stige tilslut til en Versets Greve
og dø som en Romanens Mogul.
     Da er der nu dette som gjør mig forstemt:
     Om Hundrede Aar er alting glemt.[1]

As the irony approaches satire, Hamsun's poetry, despite his disclaimer, *does* occasionally 'say something'. His dislikes enter in: his antipathy to the proletariat and the Christian religion, to Arctic explorers and champions of 'welfare', to feminism and the ideal of universal peace. More unexpected is the positive factor, the admiration he expresses for Byron, for the Swiss painter Böcklin, for Drachmann ('the last singer in the land') and, in two magnificent poems, for Bjørnson.[2]

(7) *Hamsun's fiction after 1904*

Three heterogeneous elements characterize Hamsun's greatest
fiction. They are the figure of the wanderer; the evocation of
the remote, vast Nordland; and the indissolvable mixture of
sympathy and ironic detachment with which those who live
their lives in its wastes, homesteads and little towns is presented.
One or other of these elements often predominates (or may be
absent), but, usually, in varying proportions, they form his
unique amalgam.

The figure of the wanderer fascinated Hamsun all his life
through, all the more strongly perhaps when the experience of
the long, grim years when he was but a sojourner in two hemi-
spheres were well behind him. *In Fairy-Tale Land* had shown
him a zestful and adventurous traveller, but his middle and
later years very rarely took him far afield, divided as they were
between the cares of his estate and the strict, long office-hours
he kept over his manuscripts.

The wanderer takes on many guises, from the lay-about of
Hunger to the old man who called his last book *On Overgrown
Paths*. He may be little more than an unuprooted piece of sea-
weed floating backwards and forwards at the mercy of the tide
or he may be a mighty hunter before the Lord, like Lieutenant
Glahn. After the heroes of *Hunger*, *Mysteries*, *Pan* and *Monk
Vendt*, an odd variant appears in the titular hero of †*Benoni* and
its sequel †*Rosa* (both of 1908). A postman to begin with and
then, when he has been sacked from the public service, a
prosperous fish-dealer, he certainly leads a fairly peripatetic
life in both capacities. Primarily, however, he is a *parvenu*
adventurer, recklessly pursuing the main chance in business,
towards which Hamsun's attitude was typically ambivalent.
The sedentary shop-keeper was his pet aversion,[1] but from risk-
taking enterprise of all sorts, especially if it proved successful,
he could not withhold all admiration.

Benoni and *Rosa*, where the telling of a moderately complicated story with a good deal of bustle and superficial intrigue
seems to be the author's chief concern, formed an undis-
tinguished interlude in the composition of three linked novels
with which Hamsun's second great period of creation may be

said to begin: †*Under the Autumn Star* (*Under Høststjernen*, 1906), †*A Wanderer plays on muted Strings* (*En Vandrer spiller med Sordin*, 1909) and †*The Last Joy* (*Den sidste Glæde*, 1912). The wanderer here is not in the least an adventurer; in character, and what his mind makes of his experiences he is much more like what Hamsun himself would have been had he taken to the road, and that point is, in fact, doubly driven home by the use of the first person singular throughout and by giving the fictitious narrator Hamsun's proper name, Knut Pedersen. An honest, hard-working labourer, not in his first youth, he comes from a spell of road-making into the service of Captain Falkenberg, a country gentleman, and the first two parts of the trilogy (which in all covers some thirty years) centre on his life there. It is fairly colourful. His appearance and good manners recommend him to the ladies, and three of them are amorously attracted to him; in one case, that of his master's wife, the attraction is reciprocated, but nothing tangible comes of these affairs, and the wanderer leaves his job. Colour there may be, but it is matt. The air and light of autumn are over all. Intelligent and fine-feeling, Knut observes and speculates on the little world around him and, not least, on himself. More accurately, perhaps, he reflects on them: the opening of *Under the Autumn Star* makes clear that what he is recounting took place many years ago, indeed that his viewpoint is that reached at the end of the trilogy.

The minor key which is maintained throughout and gives the whole its distinctive soft beauty is announced by the title of the second part, *A Wanderer plays on muted Strings*; Knut returns after six years to his old employer, and his old love for Fru Falkenberg, now a desperately unhappy woman, revives—with the same negative outcome. In *Under the Autumn Star* he had learned to master his passion, now he is resigned to its futility. A fatal accident to Fru Falkenberg sets the full stop to it, and Knut goes off on his wanderings once more. *The Last Joy* is supposed to take place when Knut, become an elderly (and, against expectation, a well-to-do) man, all passion spent, has settled down in solitude as a 'universal uncle', unobtrusively watching over and helping those for whom he feels affection. The tints throughout have been those of the amazing Norwegian autumn, and now they are merging into winter. His last joy is not even beneficence or the sight of a new generation growing up, but the great peace of immersing himself in the impassive vastness of the earth about him and the stars above.

In the linked novels †*Children of the Age* (*Børn av Tiden*, 1913) and †*Segelfoss Town* (*Segelfoss By*, 1915) Hamsun covered his widest canvas to produce two indubitable masterpieces. The background is twofold: the immense expanse of Nordland land, water and sky, usually in their benign aspect, and, on the other hand, the lonely little community that becomes Segelfoss Town, with its comings and goings, troubles, aspirations and successes. Nowhere is the time of action precisely stated, but, somewhat foreshortened, it is the span of fifty years in which Hamsun had known Hamarøy; the *Children of the Age* and *Segelfoss Town* make up a chapter of social history as surely as does Zola's Rougon-Macquart series. But the means employed are as different as the ambience; there are no elaborately detailed inventories, no melodramatic abysses or sublimities, no 'close-ups' of passion or brawling, neither Machiavellian intrigues nor the stirrings of mass-emotion. Steadily, but with kindly irony, an Olympian looks down on the ant-hill below, fully aware of all that goes on in the homes and hearts of his creatures, even if he does not always see fit to tell of everything he knows.

In the forefront of his panorama, but still small to the Olympian eye, are three figures—a fourth is advancing to join them—who, successively dethroning one another, have, it may be said, the fortunes of the neighbourhood in their hands. The first is the hereditary 'lord of the manor' Lieutenant Willatz Holmsen, the stoic who unobtrusively holds patriarchal sway over his crofters and fishermen, helping their families in distress, paying their debts and having their promising children educated, even when he detests them, as a plain matter of inherited duty. He is succeeded by Holmengraa, the 'wanderer' of the story, the energetic adventurer who suddenly appears from the Cordilleras, bit by bit buys up Willatz Holmsen's bankrupt estate, uses it for building saw-mills, granaries, wharves, new houses for the work-people and the like, and then disappears again, leaving the field to Theodor paa Bua,

the shopkeeper of the now sizeable settlement, which runs
to a hotel (victualled by thefts from Holmengraa's stores), with
café, dance-hall and theatre, and a regular service by mail-
steamer.

Olympian though Hamsun's viewpoint may be, his detachment—the 'I' has disappeared from his narratives—is not
complete. Jove, while sincerely if uneffusively loving his
creatures, even the sinners and wastrels among them, also
judges them. In his tacit summing-up, he notes a degradation.
The entrepreneur Holmengraa, much cleverer, much better
versed in the ways of the Age that has caught up with Lieutenant
Willatz Holmsen, has none of his innate sense of values, no sense
of the dignity due to himself and all men. Yet he creates something, brings work and prosperity to a poor stagnant village.
His supplanter, Theodor paa Bua, merely buys and sells what
others have made, a monopolist battening on a community that
has gone awhoring after the idols of the market-place. This
steady undertow of deep pessimism stirs the web and woof of
Hamsun's irony and empathy, to give them, as it were, a third
dimension.

†*Growth of the Soil* (*Markens Grøde*, 1917) is 'O, Pioneers' in
the guise of a saga; commerce and speculation come into it, only
to vanish like the smoke of an autumn bonfire. Isak, a 'great
barge of a man'[1], comes to Sellanraa, an uninhabited tract of
land verging on moor, half a day's journey from the nearest
settlement, sets to, all by himself, to clear and break it up, erects
his cabin and (after all this has been done) obtains a legal title
to the holding. He takes to wife his hare-lipped servant girl
Inger, who labours by his side as valiantly as he. For long
unaided, they fell, plough, sow, reap and raise stock; they raise
also a small family and, bit by bit, the buildings and appur-
tenances of a complete, self-supporting, perpetually working
homestead. Their example spreads. By the time the story ends,
twenty-five years or so from the beginning, ten family farms have
struggled up in the unpeopled waste. This pioneers' saga, which
in itself has all the charms of a Robinson Crusoe story, with the
realistic but almost laconically presented details that Hamsun
knew from his own experiences, is diversified by incidents, both
in the domestic and in a slightly wider sphere—but they are

incidents, almost brushed off as irrelevancies, and always leading back to the steady plodding of the main theme. Inger, seeing that her third baby has a hare-lip too, at once wrings its neck and buries it, but a little act of piety betrays the deed, and she is away from Sellanraa for six years expiating it in prison. Isak—who suspected what had happened, but steadfastly adhered to his principle of 'least said, soonest mended'—utters no word of reproach or lamentation, and when, as naturally as a homing-pigeon, Inger returns to Sellanraa, they just go on as before—plus a sewing-machine. Copper is found on their holding, attracts speculators and is worked for a time, but turns out unprofitable. Isak gets a certain amount of cash for his mineral rights, but it all drips away through the pocket of his 'refined' elder boy, who sets up as a shopkeeper for the new community and has to decamp to the United States. But there are left his younger brother, a hefty chip of the old block, and the girl who will probably marry an enterprising neighbour. Soon Isak and Inger will retire to the small 'dower-house' with which he has rounded off his building programme, and the growth of the soil, laboured for and contemplated in peace and contentment, will go its unbroken way around them.

The horizon of Isak's saga is as far as he can see; it is broad enough, but not as wide as that conjured up in the Segelfoss books, and the distance from which it is seen is not so great. There is still some irony, however, to give perspective, very quiet, indeed affectionate: in the presentation of Inger, for instance, the devoted helpmeet, who goes off the rails from time to time, to pietism and adultery and her tragic crime, and who eventually acquires a great local reputation as an arbiter of fashion for which the sewing-room of Trondheim gaol has given her the necessary qualification. The author's detachment, however, is not so complete as when he surveyed Segelfoss. Jove, one may say, has been replaced by the Jehovah of *Genesis*, who 'saw everything that he had made, and, behold, it was very good'.

The Growth of the Soil betrays even a curious little piece of self-involvement on Hamsun's part. It escapes from the 'wanderer' of the tale, Geissler—like Benoni, a dismissed civil servant—who pops up from nowhere, kindly, understanding and helpful, whenever a crisis is upon Isak and then vanishes again, on no one knows what errand. Suddenly the man recalls a bridge and smells again the smell from it he knew as a child, and that bridge is firmly designated as that at Garmo, where Hamsun himself was born. Is Geissler, the man whom nothing can hold and who plays Providence whenever he appears, another variant of the wanderer that Hamsun would have liked to have been?

Most of those who have dealings with Geissler distrust him, now shabby and penniless, at other times, it seems, bursting with cash, always lavish with what he has. How warmly, if at all, do his ceaseless comings and goings, his plans and stamped papers, feather his own nest? How much of a fox is he? And, by extension, how much of a fox was Hamsun?

If Hamsun was a fox, he never played his game better than when he qualified for the Nobel Prize with *Growth of the Soil*. It not only exhibited his art at its most superb—in the world of 1920 the Swedish Academy could have found none with a stronger claim on that count. But it was also, one might say, custom-built to the conditions of the award, and in that measure, most famous of his books though it may be, it is untypical. The 'idealistic tendency' stipulated by the founder, scarcely discernible elsewhere, here is both pervasive and stated in words of naked appeal to all who, like the Swedes and Norwegians, had just faced economic isolation in the World War: 'Behold, a tiller of the ground, body and soul; a worker on the land without respite. A ghost risen out of the past to point to the future, a man from the earliest days of cultivation, a settler in the wilds, and withal a man of the day.'[1]

For another twenty years Hamsun's productivity continued unabated; but it is more than doubtful whether any of his later novels would have met that exacting condition for a Nobel Prize award which in its day had non-suited Ibsen. He concentrated again on the rootless man, sometimes in an openly humorous vein—the trilogy † *Tramps* (*Landstrykere*, 1927), †*August* (1930), †*But Life is Alive* (*Men Livet Lever*, 1933)—sometimes with kindly resignation, as in the last, † *The Ring Closed* (*Ringen sluttet*, 1936), sometimes with a biting, if restrained, irony; nothing that looks at all like a model of edification is provided.[2]

† *The Women at the Pump* (*Konerne ved Vandposten*, 1920), the next book to follow on *Growth of the Soil*, displays Hamsun's more characteristic art in its perfection. Such story as it may be said to have revolves round the most degenerate type of humanity that Hamsun was to exhibit in full, a hypocritical wittol and eunuch. (Nevertheless, the Olympian who once more holds the pen cannot disguise some admiration for the tenacity with which he wriggles his way along through the slime.) His environment, effectually quelling any who in any way try to rise above it, is as rotten as he—a Segelfoss at one step lower in degeneration. The originality, even attraction of what is, over all, a disgusting and depressing chronicle of moral squalor—not deficient, however, in opportunities for much sardonic humour—lies in the manner of its telling. Substantially all is conveyed through the tattle of the town's housewives as they draw their water at the pump. Literary impressionism carried to the extreme,[1] it has the effect of listening in to a tangle of conversations in a telephone exchange, with its abrupt switches from one line to another, its unanswered questions and answers to questions which can only be guessed at, its tantalizing gaps, the occasional exclamations of someone—is it the God in the machine?—breaking into the dialogues or monologues. But mosaic bit by mosaic bit, the day's gossip builds up a full picture of the gossipers' community and the lives of those of their neighbours which most intrigue them. The sardonic upshot, quite literally, speaks for itself. Even if the Women at the Pump are little more than gabbling automata, through them Hamsun created the supreme example of his special 'psychology', a stream-of-consciousness novel transposed from the reactions of the individual to those of a community. It exemplifies too the break-up, in a master's hands, of the century-old European novel-form, and for that reason may fitly be placed side by side with the *Ulysses* that James Joyce was writing just at the same time.

THE NEW CENTURY

(1) *Egge, Bojer and Scott*

As are its counterparts elsewhere, the received image of Norwegian literature in the *fin-de-siècle* decade is a distorted one. The features commonly dwelt on are positively summed up by broad generalities like poetry, symbolism, impressionism, individualism, psychology, a second 'renascence of wonder' or neo-Romanticism, art for art's sake and, negatively, by revulsion from the moral values, social preoccupations and naturalistic forms prevalent in the period just before. These features, in various combinations, certainly characterized the ideals and the work of Norwegian authors making their début in the years around 1890. But, while not denying that it had enduring and salutary effects, one is bound to concede that their 'movement' as such was a short-winded affair. It is not only that before the end of the century Dybfest, Finne and Obstfelder were dead and that others among their coevals—Vogt and the brothers Krag, to whom one may add Aanrud and Tryggve Andersen— had pretty well given the best of which they were capable: but there was a retreat all along the line from the extremer positions attained or aimed for. Hamsun had published two rather ordinary 'Christiania novels', and his *At the Gates of the Kingdom* was something very like an Ibsenist play; sociological speculations were colouring Kinck's fiction; though not quite worked out, the poetical vein showed no signs of proving very rich. Realism—to be sure, a more colourful and varied realism than that of the 'eighties—was reasserting itself among those who had scorned it and even *tendens* was rearing what they had abhorred as its ugly head.

For obtaining a truthful picture of Norwegian literature in the eighteen-nineties, one must not overlook, either, the massive contributions which the veterans were still making. Kielland had gone into voluntary retirement, but it was the decade of

Garborg's finest work in poetry and prose, of Lie's *Niobe*, of Bjørnson's *Paul Lange and Tora Parsberg* and Ibsen's last master-pieces; Amalie Skram had still to finish her Hellemyr cycle.

Side by side, furthermore, with the 'soft' clutch hatched out about 1890 and the energetically productive Old Guard, there was also a group of younger men who might properly be designated as 'tough'—and that not alone for the remarkable length of days allotted to most of them. They had been caught up in the general excitement and hopes of their fledgling years, but they never, or only for a short time, accepted the extremer articles of faith then promulgated. The field of poetry, it may be noted, the majority either shunned altogether or entered after they had won their spurs as prose-writers; essentially they were writers of fiction and playwrights.[1] From the ideals of the *renouveau* they retained much of its adventurousness, the will to see the spectacle of existence with unprejudiced eyes, to repro-duce it through individual experience, to judge it (if need be) by their own values, implying a disregard of time-honoured con-ventions, whether in the moral realm or in that of artistic expression. Art for art's sake, under their hands, issued in a new, fresh realism: we may recollect that in Britain the decade of Ernest Dowson was also that which witnessed the beginnings of Joseph Conrad, H. G. Wells, Arnold Bennett and Somerset Maugham.

The two outstanding figures in this second group of new writers, without doubt the most powerful and idiosyncratic among them, have already engaged our attention: Hans Kinck and Knut Hamsun. Next behind them come three others, who, like them, gave proof of their quality in the eighteen-nineties, and whose literary output belongs preponderantly to the new century: Peter Egge (1869–1959), Johan Bojer (1872–1959) and Gabriel Scott (1874–1958). Their clear heads and assiduity always ensured a workmanlike adaption of means to their ends (something one cannot say of Kinck!), but the comparatively small reading public on which they could rely drove them to over-production; they rarely found time to develop refinements of style or technique; they were often repetitive and sometimes took short cuts to obtain their effects. Their best, however, was very good. For his own 'Wessex', the Trøndelag, Egge wrote stories that may sustain comparison with *The Mayor of Caster-bridge*, while Bojer's *Last Viking* and Scott's *Ordeal* fall little short of *Growth of the Soil*, Hamsun's diploma picture for the Nobel Prize.

The fiction of Peter Egge* ranges fairly wide both in space and time. Those works in which his imaginative engagement is closest have for their central figures the ordinary laborious, true-hearted folk of his native district, town and country. After a somewhat unpromising start his personal ambitions and problems gave an increasing depth and complexity to studies of exceptional characters, strugglers amid hard surroundings for a sustaining inward creed (one might compare *Jude the Obscure*). Some find it in a Carlylean acceptance of the work that lies nearest to their hand; others, the more interesting and individual, are driven to seek liberation and solace, as Egge himself was, in art.[1] The frustrations which they have to suffer and often succumb to give a resigned and melancholy, even tragic and pessimistic, tone to most of his fiction.

Gammelholm (1899), *The Heart* (*Hjærtet*, 1907), *In the Inner Fjords* (*Inde i Fjordene*, 1920), *Jægtvig and his God* (*Jægtvig og hans Gud*, 1923) and *Hansine Solstad* (1925) are generally looked on as the most conspicuous milestones on Egge's long career. Comparatively late though it came, †*Hansine Solstad*, now regarded as a classic, may be taken to exemplify his art at its most characteristic—for the authentic, but not overladen descriptions of the heroine's *milieu* in country and town, for the slow, inexorable unrolling of her fortunes and for the projection of strength and character in an outwardly 'unremarkable' woman from the working class. In a sense, she is worsted in the long struggle of her life, but never bowed or corrupted; nor, for all his love and admiration, does Egge sentimentalize over her.

---

* Peter Andreas Egge was born at Trondheim on 1 April 1869, the son of a moderately prosperous livery-stable keeper, had little formal education and for some years picked up a living as sailor, journalistic factotum, photographer's assistant, mason's mate and clerk. He published his first novel, *Almuen*, in 1891 and thereafter lived by his pen. He liked to travel as often as he could afford through the length and breadth of most European countries, though his imagination does not seem to have been much affected by their sights or their culture. He was granted a writer's state pension in 1916 and died in Oslo on 15 July 1959.

At her confirmation, asked which of the Commandments she would put highest, she answers firmly: 'Thou shalt not bear false witness against thy neighbour', and thereby sounds by inversion one of the two *leitmotive* of her life's story. For, when she is in service as a young parlourmaid, a guest tips her with a gold coin that is identified as a theft; all efforts to trace the donor fail; the belief that she was the thief drives her out of the neighbourhood to Trondheim and dogs her ever after. The second *motif* is her determination to wipe out the stigma on her family in the bankruptcy of her husband, a prosperous fish-merchant. Her beloved son, with whom she hopes to achieve her two great aims, proves a weakling, however, and does nothing towards nailing the lie about her thieving or rehabilitating his father's name. Hansine, lonely and always suspect, dies as an old woman in one of the almshouses round Trondheim cathedral. Just before her end she is visited by an elderly lady, the daughter of her one-time employer, bringing with her a registered letter to her father that had arrived on the day after his death and been bundled unopened among his papers at that moment of confusion: the writer of it certified that the fatal gold coin had been his present. Except when she fiercely defends it during her courtship by the young man who becomes her husband, the heroine's 'purity' does not come into question, but there is a good deal about her that recalls *Tess of the D'Urbervilles*—which equally hinges on the accident of an undelivered letter. Egge, however, neither arraigns the Immortals, nor does he make it his business to dilate on man's inhumanity to man. The peasant's pragmatic fatalism, not a reformer's or metaphysician's indignation, is basic to his view of life.

In addition to his abundant fiction Egge wrote a number of plays; indeed, he may be thought the best Norwegian playwright of his generation. Dialogue, the necessary economy of the dramatic form and a good sense of 'theatre' saved him from the heaviness and monotony that constituted the chief dangers to his narratives. His drama does not probe so deeply into human nature as the best of his novels; but it exhibits a somewhat surprising variety. Egge in fact gained some of his most notable successes in comedy, both of the light, superficial variety, such as *Wilhelmine's Bureau* (*Wilhelmines Byraa*, 1915) and of the kind of low comedy for which Aanrud had shown the way. If it were not for the too comfortable happy ending, Egge's *Jacob and Christopher* (*Jakob og Kristoffer*, 1900), laid in somewhat less sordid surroundings, would, with its skilful plotting and splendid acting-parts, challenge *The Stork* for first place among the 'thieves' comedies' of the time.

In the serious vein which for some years (1910–20) he sedulously worked, Egge showed equal powers, notably in the village-drama *The Fiddle* (*Felen*, 1912). Though it skirts both melodrama and farce—the confusion between two chests, one with macabre contents, is that of Stevenson and Osbourne's *Wrong Box*—it preserves the ring of tragedy in the rustic musician's persecution by his puritan neighbours and his perilous devotion to the precious violin which his charlatan of a son tries to filch from him. *The Fool* (*Narren*, 1917) is almost as powerful. With a good deal of sexual promiscuity and an urban setting, it is more conventional, but remains a fine, convincing and admirably planned study of a weakling going from the strong, good woman who truly loves him to a wanton who will see that he has every comfort in a fool's paradise.

Bred among the crofter-fishermen of the Trøndelag, in a milieu contiguous to that of Egge, and undergoing similar youthful experiences, Johan Bojer* has all along the line much in common with him: first and foremost his sympathy and admiration for those living the hard lives he had known so intimately. Bojer, however, was the better story-teller, and his more vital personality lent a power and sweep as well to single episodes as to the total impact of his novels which his colleague's lower tones could not compass and to which his wider fame may be due. On the other hand, though he strove for psychological depth[1] and was fascinated by the interplay between deliberate and instinctive motives for action, his insight into character was

---

* Johan Bojer was born on 6 March 1872 in Orkedalsøren, near Trondheim, the illegitimate son of a village shopkeeper and, as a lad, tried his hand at much the same occupations that Egge did, ultimately training to become a non-commissioned officer in the army. From 1895 on he devoted himself entirely to writing, on which he had made a beginning the year before with a play, *En Moder*. For long periods he lived abroad, chiefly in France, where he established a reputation that spread to other countries, as Egge's and Scott's scarcely did. He died at Hvalstad on 3 July 1959.

superficial by comparison with that shown in *The Heart* or *Hansine Solstad*. The texture of his writing is coarser, his outlines are thicker and rougher. While an English reader of Egge's fiction is often reminded of Thomas Hardy's, he cannot find it altogether inappropriate that Hall Caine was invited to write the introduction to *The Power of the Lie*, the English translation of Bojer's *Troens Magt*.

Quicker to develop than Egge, Bojer, already at 24, published a mature, characteristic novel, *A Procession* (*Et Folketog*, 1896).[1] Amid full and variegated pictures of a typical Norwegian constituency, half agricultural, half maritime, it centres on the disastrous career of the chairman of a District Council: on an admirable programme for alleviating the little man's problems and hardships, he gets elected to Parliament, to find himself not only checkmated by the party-machine, but simultaneously driven into irretrievable debt by the expenses of a politician's life. The presentation is straightforwardly realistic, unaffected by the tendencies towards the fantastic which the contemporary fiction of Thomas Krag, Hamsun and Kinck was exhibiting. It is also, discreetly and with little overt irony, shot through by a fair amount of *tendens* that has none of Kielland's openly radical satire, points indeed in a conservative direction, without, however, forfeiting the liveliness and freshness of approach by which the new writers set such store.

Bojer was always at heart a moralist, but in his best novels he kept anything like 'special pleading' well in check. The earliest of these, † *The Power of Faith* (*Troens Magt*, 1903) strongly resembles *A Procession* in many ways. Though Lake Mjøsa takes the place of the sea, the setting, human and topographical, is much the same; it too culminates in a public jollification; and one of the two men about whose feud the plot is constructed is brother to the hero of the older book and, like him, ends miserably. *The Power of Faith* also resembles Egge's *Hansine Solstad*, since it too turns on an unjust accusation and its dire consequences. The essential difference between the two authors comes out very clearly from the parallels between their stories. Egge's is a tender study of his stoical heroine, the slander against whom has no loud-voiced, let alone vindictive, mouthpiece and which, though a lowering cloud over the whole of her long life, is hardly the cause of all her misfortunes. *The Power of Faith*, on the other hand, in an action confined to eighteen months or so, focuses on a hotly contested legal process with its dramatic elements of police and public trial. The chief character Norby is not the victim of the slander but the slanderer, an active, middle-aged, prosperous farmer, who wins his case through perjury and then, as far as one can tell, lives happy ever after.

Bojer has been described as a moralist, but the morality of Norby's triumph may seem in the highest degree dubious, the more so as his adversary Wanger is left penniless, broken, a convict. Bojer's intention, however, is anything but crudely ironical. He mitigates, with an insight as great as his technical skill, the shock of his tale. For all the good faith on which he prides himself, the wretched Wanger, through muddling that amounts to dishonesty, deserves to be ruined; sooner or later life would have broken him; and, innocent though he was of the forgery for which he was indicted, he had in fact, as was proved at his trial, fabricated one of the documents produced for his defence. His enemy, on the other hand, honestly believes him to be a noxious creature, whose radical activities— calamitous at that—menace the patriarchal relations between rich and poor of which he himself is an unexceptionable exponent. There is more to be admired in *The Power of Faith* than such structural dexterity. The title given to the English translation, *The Power of a Lie*, is apt enough; so would have been a more biblical one, 'The Grain of Mustard Seed', since the tragic issue has, plausibly enough, quite trivial and adventitious an origin. Bojer's own biblical title, nevertheless, has a deeper significance. What he exhibits is not a miscarriage of justice, but the progressive degeneration of mind in two self-righteous men, whose fanaticism for their shaky causes, infecting others besides themselves, finally leads them genuinely to believe as truth the falsehoods fabricated in their support.

Intrigues, involutions, the weighing of guilt by scruple and drachm have gone the way of *tendens* in † *The Last Viking* (1921). It vies with Lie's *Go Ahead!* as the finest Norwegian novel of life at sea as experienced by the crofter-fishermen who set out under sail for the Lofoten banks through the winter storms. By the time that Bojer wrote, many of the details of this life had passed away, and a perspective is imposed on his picture by a fore-shadowing of the all-pervading revolution wrought by the advent of steam. With the death of Kristaver Myran, master of 'Kobben', on one of his voyages, it is recognized that the last Viking Age has come to an end.

More than anything the story of Kristaver and his crew calls to mind one of the half-naïve panoramic 'murals' in which modern Norway delights. Within the panorama *The Last Viking* is a series of episodes—uproarious, heroic, touching—and each in its own way is projected with a power that makes much of Kipling's *Captains Courageous* look cheap: they range from the brooding anxiety of the women waiting at home and the administration of the last sacrament to a dying sailor in all that his mates have at hand—ship's biscuit and a dram—to the wild party for giving the youngest his footing as a *Lofotkar* ('Lofoten-chap') or the heroic battle of the sailing ships against the trawlers when these shut them off from their accustomed fishing-grounds.[1]

Younger than Egge or Bojer and taking longer to establish himself, Gabriel Scott* nevertheless retained certain charac-teristics of the time when all three had come to man's estate which they discarded. The first publications of Gabriel Scott were two volumes of *fin-de-siècle* poetry, *Poems* (*Digte*, 1894) and *Day* (*Dag*, 1895), and, though this formal verse is of little account, he remained, in imagination and style, much more the poet than they. Bojer strove for a metaphysical view of his world; Scott had it inborn, and all through his long career continued to give pictures, both historical and psychological, of his invented characters' religious life which evidently mirrored his own. Two or three of his outstanding works may bear comparison with Egge's and Bojer's by strictly equal criteria, but there is, more commonly, an aura of phantasy about his writings which, for ill as well as good, can impart a

---

* Gabriel the (legitimate) son of Rev. S. Holst Jensen, assumed the surname Scott. He was born on 8 March 1874 at Leith, where his father was in charge of the Norwegian mission to seamen. The family soon after returning to Norway, he trained as an engineer at Skien technical school, but encouraged by Hamsun, devoted himself entirely to imaginative writing from his twenty-first year to his death at Asker on 9 July 1958. He was granted a civil-list pension in 1951.

softness not attributable to them. Some of his most applauded books were written for children.[1]

† *The Source (Kilden,* 1918) affords the best example of Scott's gentler manner and, at the same time, an index of the almost mystical *Weltenschauung* to which his absorption in the more benign aspects of his beloved Sørland had brought him. Very simply it tells the life-story of Markus, a poor fisherman on the Agder coast, as he plies his trade, extends and adorns the little patch of ground on which he has put up his cabin and supplies his neighbours with such necessaries of life as are at his disposal. In all, his contemplative mind is supported by a steady, un-dogmatic trust in a pervasive God, the Source of a supreme contentment that gives the book its title.

In a minor key *The Source* plays some of the motifs of *The Growth of the Soil.* The parallels are much more obvious in † *The Ordeal (Jernbyrden,* 1915),[2] which preceded it by two years.

Where *The Source* is uneventful, quietistic, *The Ordeal* is strenuous, often harsh, with the rumble of happenings in the world outside breaking into a short, violent storm over its hero's head. Like Isak of Sellanraa, he, Jan Vibe, is a settler come from afar to carve out a large and prosperous holding for himself. With the same immense physical strength and energy as Isak, he is not, however, essentially a solitary: he concerns himself with his fellows, helping them not alone with example (e.g. by introducing potatoes into the district) and advice, but actively alleviating their distresses in three terrible winters of famine. The climax of the story, an example of his altruism, is reached in the magnificent chapters describing the heroic attempt of Vibe and another man to save two girls from execution, after torture with red-hot irons, when they fight their way to the foot of the scaffold with the offer to marry them, in the mistaken belief that this was a recognized legal process for obtaining their reprieve. The Ordeal is twofold, since by making his bid Vibe had to renounce the girl to whom in his heart he was pledged.

This culminating episode is based on an actual event of the eighteenth century, and, though Vibe is an invented character, others known to historical record come into the tale. It is supposed to be told by the parish clerk of Høvaag (where Scott's father was the incumbent) and, avoiding the hazards of painful pastiche, *The Ordeal*, like its sequel *Enok Ruben*,[1] is stylistically superb, interpenetrating an epic strength and vividness with (not too much) pawky peasant-speech and the faintly archaizing suggestion of old, unhappy things and battles long ago.

(2) *The women authors*

Hamsun, Kinck, Egge, Scott and Bojer had all made their début by 1894; it took a dozen years before any newcomer appeared in the literary arena destined to make a name comparable with theirs. Not that, as has been seen, it was empty. The annual lists of new publications by Norwegian belletrists were swelling to proportions undreamed of twenty years before. By the beginning of the twentieth century, it may be said, an assiduous reader could for the first time be fully occupied if he confined himself to native novels, short stories, poetry, plays, essays and reviews. Most conspicuously, perhaps, the Norwegian novel, for so long a somewhat sporadic growth, had established itself as a vigorous, varied art-form, cultivated by a substantial number of talents, great and small, in continuous production.

Midway between the great and the small we find a number of women-writers, who, *pace* Camilla Collett and Amalie Skram, had not hitherto made any large contribution to the national literature.[2] One of them has already been mentioned, Hulda Garborg, Arne Garborg's wife. She was exceptional not only for her extra-literary labours, but also for using Landsmaal and being a playwright. The others were all writers of fiction in Riksmaal and (like Hulda Garborg) well educated and familiar with cultivated circles, more concerned than their male colleagues with depicting social life in the narrower sense. The chief, during the early years of the new century, were Ragnhild Jølsen (1875–1908), Nini Roll Anker (1873–1942), Barbra Ring (1870–1955) and Regine Normann (1867–1939). They may be ranged in two pairs: Ragnhild Jølsen and Regine Normann, for one, whose literary affiliations lie with the neo-Romantics of the eighteen-nineties like Thomas Krag, and, on the other hand, Nini Roll Anker and Barbra Ring, who though smarter, more up-to-date, more professional, link on to the older realistic tradition of family stories of which Jonas Lie had been the great master. In each of the two groups one was, at any rate as a literary personality, much the more impressive, whose best work is likely to survive among the minor classics of the time.[1]

Ragnhild Jølsen's* first novel, *Ve's Mother* (*Ve's Mor*, 1903), tells of a young, gently nurtured woman, married to a man much older than herself while involved in a passionate love-affair with a splendid gentleman brigand—something like Hamsun's Lieutenant Glahn—who intermittently comes into the neighbourhood for sport. Torn between her two men, she goes out of her mind three times in the course of the story. Two children are born to her, the second hydrocephalous, but not quite imbecile—presumably the son of her lover; and, left a widow, she regains her mental equilibrium by looking after him and, at long last, learning to love him.[2]

Ve's Mother is set in a large old lonely manor-farm, plainly the same as that in which the author was born, brought up and later returned to live. That is also the centre of her later novels, in which, however, the interest is not so exclusively focused on a personal drama: the family, its collective fortunes, its position in the neighbourhood and, above all, its eerie legends and the sense they give of continuity with the past, assume a greater prominence. The Jølsens were an old family that was coming down in the world, and the tone of *Rikka Gan* (1904) and *Fernanda Mona* (1905), the next to follow on *Ve's Mother*, is elegiac where it is not tragic. The theme again is 'the woe of women', but there is no arraignment of society after the manner of Camilla Collett's *Sheriff's Daughters*. In some degree Ragnhild Jølsen's last books broke from this charmed circle. The locality remains the same; but in *The Hollas Chronicle* (*Hollases Krønike*, 1906) its centre shifts from the manor-house to the village smithy, four hundred years or so back, whose grotesque, vital owner gives the chronicle of his practices and malpractices an immediacy and humour absent from the earlier books; and the author's last book *Farm Histories* (*Brukshistorier*, 1907), on the other hand, virtually brings the chronicle down to date, describing conditions

---

* Ragnhild Jølsen, the daughter of a landed proprietor, was born at Enebakk in Romerike on 28 March 1875, received a good schooling in Christiania and died unmarried in her birthplace on 28 January 1908.

in which she actually lived with an objectivity stripped of all romantic, evocative overtones.

Such overtones and other particulars which the account of *Ve's Mother* may have indicated clearly have much in common with Thomas Krag's unconventional *Ada Wilde*. Equally plain is the resemblance between Ragnhild Jølsen and Charlotte Brontë. If *Ve's Mother* might be described as her *Jane Eyre*, with *Farm Histories* she had advanced to her *Shirley*; whether she was carrying a *Villette* at the time of her death no one can tell. The strength and growth of her talent do not rule out the possibility that *deo volente* Sigrid Undset might, fifteen years or so later, have had a worthy rival of her own sex.

The romantic strain, coloured by legends more properly belonging to folk-lore than Ragnhild Jølsen's, is at least as evident in the weaker—even if more varied and numerous—stories of Regine Normann (1867–1939).* In *Krabvaag*, 'pictures from a little fishing village' (1905), with which she made her belated start, she at once struck two veins, which turned out to be her richest and which, at the same time, differentiated her from Ragnhild Jølsen: the Nordland scene with its humbler inhabitants, and the religious life of the latter. In *At the Time* (*Dengang*, 1912) and *Eilert Hundevart* (1913), where conditions a hundred years before her own time are depicted with an authenticity comparable with Tryggve Andersen's and in which a more concentrated narrative replaces the sketch-book technique of *Krabvaag*, she worked these veins to the full of her capacities.[1]

Although Nini Roll Anker (1873–1942)** had by then been productive for twenty years, the work of hers which seems most likely to endure belongs to the post-war era. This is the trilogy of *The House in Søgate* (*Huset i Søgaten*, 1923), *In the Sheriff's Residence* (*I Amtmandsgården*, 1925) and *Under the sloping Roof* (*Under Skråtaket*, 1927), which makes up one of the long middle-class

* Regine Serine Normann was born in Vesterålen, the daughter of a country schoolmaster, on 27 July 1867 and died in Trondenes on 14 August 1939. She was twice married (the second time to Tryggve Andersen) and twice divorced.

** Nicoline Magdalene (calling herself Nini) Roll was born on 3 May 1873 at Molde, and died at Asker, outside Oslo, on 20 May 1942. Her two successive husbands were called Anker, the second being the well-known shipbuilder. Her earliest (1898) and some of her later books appeared under the pseudonym Jo Nein.

family sagas so abundant everywhere at that time (Galsworthy, Jo van Ammers Küller). Laid in Trondheim towards the middle of last century, there is something nostalgic in its tone; but there is no aura of the romantic, let alone of the mysterious or of the 'folkly' about the author's stories. The daughter of a judge, the wife first of a landed proprietor and then of a successful business-man, she was better placed than any other Norwegian author in the first and second rank to fill a gap in the literature of her country by giving, as she did from the beginning, faithful descriptions of the 'top people', the personalities bred among them, their daily lives, the troubles and frictions to which they were exposed. To her—and especially after 1914—the most significant of these frictions was between the 'get-rich-quick' mentality that was then taking more blatant forms and the resistance offered to it by the longer-standing pillars of society. Among the latter she gave pride of place to the old Establishment, the same that for its alleged inefficiency and lack of understanding and principle had so continuously been under fire in plays and novels such as *Tora Trondal, Working Men, An Enemy of the People* and Hans Kinck's contemporary writings. As in her stories the milieu has, after its long excursions into the countryside, shifted back to the town, the feuds between peasantry and the 'great folk' of the village have disappeared; and the fundamental cleavage in society now was, in her view, that between the profiteers and the administrators, with the latter in the *beau rôle* for once.

Nini Roll Anker's second *leit-motif* shows her as the late heir of Camilla Collett: her delineations of young women's struggles for emancipation in the era in which they were supposed to have achieved it. Here, particularly in *The Weak Sex (Det svake Kjøn*, 1915), an element comes in that was passed over by the more notable of her predecessors—though it was prominent enough in the more or less edifying writings of their obscurer sisters—and that was the religious. The heroines struggle not only against the restrictions of family life and the *convenances* that stifle the development of their emotional life, but also for the right of private judgement in matters of belief and morals in the deeper sense. The cross-currents set up hereby within the conservatism of the society admired by the author—and very often by her heroines as well—give Fru Anker's fiction a tension and an abiding human interest that lifts it well above the ordinary *feuilleton-literature* of her time.

A lively, forceful personality and for long years a most prolific authoress, Barbra Ring* became increasingly eager to make her stories right up-to-date by bringing in topics of the day with the new jargon appropriate to them. Interesting though it may be to have this variety of contemporary reportage, even her most ambitious books, such as the novels *Before the Cold sets in (For Kulden kommer*, 1915), *Under Sail (Under Seil*, 1916) and *Eldjarstad* (1931), have a superficiality which will presumably deny her any lasting consideration.[1]

After Mesdames Jølsen, Roll Anker, Ring and Normann one comes by a natural transition to the young woman writer destined to write the greatest novel in the literature of her country. Honesty must admit, however, that her début was far from promising. Nothing in Sigrid Undset's** *Fru Martha Oulie* (1907) or *Jenny* (1911), sad little stories, flatly told, about the 'insect woes', as Arnold Bennett calls them, of young ladies who have to make their own way in the world, one a schoolmistress and the other a painter, gives an inkling that a rival has appeared to Nini Roll Anker or Ragnhild Jølsen, let alone Knut Hamsun. Her time of greatness lies outside the limits of this study.

(3) *The next generation*

The same is true of a number of Sigrid Undset's contemporaries who made their public appearance at about the same time as she. For that reason they can only be discussed here quite summarily, to indicate 'for the record' that after a long lull the notable phalanx of active veterans—Hamsun, Heiberg, Kinck, Egge, Bojer, Scott—was gaining recruits worthy of stand by their side.

* Barbra Mathilde Ring was born on 4 July 1870 in Drammen, the daughter of a lawyer of that name who later became a high court judge. She was twice married and died in Oslo on 6 May 1955. Much of her most applauded writing was simple, healthy stuff, plays as well as stories, specially addressed to children and adolescents.

** Sigrid Undset was born at Kalundborg, Denmark, the daughter of a distinguished Norwegian archaeologist, on 20 May 1882. *Viga-Ljot og Viglis* (1909) was her first incursion into the Middle Ages, the feeble precursor of her masterpieces, *Kristin Lavransdatter* (1920–2) and *Olav Audunssøn* (1925–7), which won her the Nobel Prize for Literature in 1928. She died in Oslo on 10 June 1949.

The heightened national self-consciousness due to the final severance from the Swedish Crown is sometimes seen as responsible for the remarkable inrush of fresh literary talent that followed hard upon it, though it is a curious fact[1] that the actual crisis of 1905 left no notable mark on belles-lettres except Heiberg's caustic *I Will Defend my Country*. The inrush falls into two streams. On the one hand there are the novelists, the heirs of those just named: besides Sigrid Undset, Olav Duun (1876–1939), Kristofer Uppdal (1878–1961) and Johan Falkberget (born 1879); on the other hand, a generation of lyrical poets who came to fulfil the disappointed expectations of the 1890 *renouveau*: Olav Aukrust (1883–1929), Olav Bull (1883–1933), Herman Wildenvey (1886–1959), Tore Ørjasæter (born 1886) and Arnulf Øverland (born 1889).*

There were many resemblances between Duun, Falkberget and Uppdal. They came (like Bøjer and Egge) from the Trøndelag, were humbly born and self-educated; their fiction was almost wholly concerned with the labouring poor, and their reputation rests mainly on three vast concatenations of novels, to which they gave collective titles: Duun's *People of Juvik* (*Juvikfolke*, six volumes, 1918–23), Falkberget's *Christianus Sextus* (three volumes, later distributed among six, 1927–35) and Uppdal's *Dance through the Realm of Shadows* (*Dansen gjenom Skuggeheimen*, ten volumes, 1911–24).[2]

They also presented themselves to the public at about the same time, in the years 1905–7.** It will be seen that Duun and Falkberget's big works took their time in coming. None the less, what preceded them gave some foretaste of their maturer

* A few plays were to come from these; but 'professed dramatists', it will be observed, do not figure in the lists. The best plays in the two decades after 1900 were those of Bjørnson and Egge and two highly diverting light comedies by authors who only intermittently wrote for the stage: *The Happy Election* (*Det Lykkelige Valg*, 1913) by the critic and essayist Nils Kjær (1870–1913), and *The Kid* (*Ungen*, 1911), a worthy successor to Aanrud's *Stork* and Egge's *Jakob og Kristoffer*, by the minor novelist Oskar Braaten (1881–1939). Hans Wiers-Jenssen's powerful costume-play *Anne Pedersdotter* was successfully produced at the National Theatre on 18 February 1908 and gained international fame through Mr John Masefield's English version (*The Witch*) and as a film. The chief professional playwright of the next generation, Helge Krog, made his début in 1918 with *The Great 'We'* (*Det store Vi*), an effective exposure of the newspaper-press.

** Ole Julius Duun was the son of a farmer in Namdal, where, at Fosnes, he was born on 21 November 1876 and died on 13 September 1939, at Botne. His first achievements, notably Duun's *Awry* (*Paa Tvert*, 1909) and, for Falkberget, *Eli Sjur's Daughter* (*Eli Sjursdatter*, 1913) and *Lisbet on Jarnfjeld* (*Lisbet paa Jarnfjeld*, 1915). Both already had set their characteristic scene, Duun where the Trøndelag merges into Nordland, Falkberget in the old mining-town of Røros and its environs; Duun in his own particular Landsmaal, Falkberget in Riksmaal, were elaborating the rugged style consonant with such bleak surroundings and their uncouth denizens; for both the history of individuals, however strongly marked, is also the history of the community with which by the instinctive ties of ancestry, kin and comradeship they are united.[1]

To Uppdal* a little more attention may fitly be given here. For already by 1915 half of his great cycle was completed, and *The Overman* (*Stigeren*) of 1919, it is generally agreed, displayed his powers at their best. They are usually thought inferior to those of the colleagues with whom he is bracketed, by reason, mainly, of stylistic deficiencies, in the broadest sense. There is not merely his idiosyncratic language (based on Landsmaal) for the reader to wrestle with; the collective title of his most celebrated work, *The Dance through the Realm of Shadows*,[2] itself gives an indication of something more fundamental. As vast in its range as in its bulk, the work leaves the impression of an enormous and badly projected cinematographic film of the old sort, jarringly at variance on the one hand with the earthy, solid substratum of observed fact that lends the episodes most of their interest and, on the other hand, with the scarcely veiled purpose of the author to mould them into a twentieth-century prose epic; for long stretches his presentation manages to be at the same time angular and monotonous. He suffers under the same handicap as Hans Kinck, which with him too counterweighs signal merits. In his long career Uppdal not only showed himself more versatile than Duun and Falkberget—publishing

book was *Løglege Skruvar og anna Folk* (1907). Johan Petter Falkberg or Falkberget was born near Røros on 30 September 1879, the son of a miner. After some locally distributed trivia he published *Svarta Fjelde* in 1906.

* Kristofer Oliver Uppdal was born, the son of a crofter, at Beitland in Nord-Trøndelag on 9 February 1878 and died on 26 December 1961 at Olbu in Sør-Trøndelag. Though he had two spells at Folk High Schools, he chose to become an unskilled labourer and, with some intermissions, followed that calling for some dozen years. Thereafter he lived by his writing, which earned him a government pension in 1939.

aphorisms, much lyrical poetry and, finally, a verse 'trilogy' running to twelve hundred pages, *The Cult* (*Kulten*, 1947);[1] as is shown particularly by the last-named, which comprehends the metaphysical and religious findings of its seventy years, he also possessed a more labile, philosophical and widely ranging mind and perhaps drew on a richer fund of experiences.

All those experiences, garnered in great part during the early years when Uppdal was by turns poet, navvy, miner, lover, journalist and trade-union delegate, flow in a mighty torrent into *The Dance through the Realm of Shadows*. Central is *ralleren*, the navvy—now hard-working and socially responsible, now a rogue and a skrimshanker. Every aspect of his existence and several aspects likewise of his urban counterpart, the factory-hand, make up not only a vast canvas of a society seen from its lowest viewpoint, but also, focused as it is on a succession of strongly marked representatives of each type, partially justify the term 'epical'. For all his shortcomings, comparisons with the work of more widely known contemporaries, like Martin Andersen Nexø or Maxim Gorky,[2] do its author no discredit.

Five new poets, now to be mentioned, all a little younger than the new prose-writers, became with Falkberget, Duun, Uppdal and Sigrid Undset the outstanding figures of Norwegian literature in the nineteen-twenties, combining to prove that the long-hoped-for renascence of poetry had become an established fact. With one exception, however, they too had by then been before the public for a number of years, and all had given substantial foretastes of their own special—and extremely various—talents.

Though in his maturity, commonly held to date from the collection *Secrets* (*Hemmeligheter*, 1919), he struck deeper notes— some of his nature-poems come within hailing distance of mysticism—Herman Wildenvey* was seen during the first dozen years of his authorship as a belated, if the most brilliant exponent of the eighteen-nineties' *l'art pour l'art* principle in its least pretentious form. Vilhelm Krag had been ecstatic and

* Herman Theodore Portaas, who assumed the name of Wildenvey, was born on a small farm near Drammen on 20 August 1886 and died at Stavern on 27 September 1959. Most of his formal education was received at a Lutheran seminary in Minnesota, where he read English and American poetry in preference to theology. Before leaving for America, he had published some verse under his own name (*Campanula*, 1902, recast as *Den glemte Have*, 1920); as Herman Wildenvey he

gay: Wildenvey at once achieved elegance, the elegance of a man-of-the-world entertainer. This was an almost unknown quality in Norwegian poetry and not universally appreciated: Bjørnson, who just had time to read Wildenvey's *Bonfires* (*Nyinger*, 1907), dismissed the aesthete and hedonist with the sour remark: 'he is presumably not so great a swine as he makes himself out to be'.[1] All the poems in this collection—both the irresponsible love-poems that stank in Bjørnson's nostrils and the others—are bright as the picnic fires from which it takes its title, warm without becoming sultry, crackling here and there with the good-natured satire that was to become more conspicuous in the poet's later writing. Whatever grave and reverend signiors may have felt, *Bonfires* was immediately acclaimed, and Wildenvey became the most generally popular poet of his generation. Not just his insouciant attitude ensured this, but equally his unlaboured, conversational style, with gentle rhythms that avoided all suggestions of the 'prosodic'.[2]

With Olaf Bull (1883–1933)* the formal appeal is, again, the strongest, but the response came to it rather from the connoisseurs than from the great public that Wildenvey captivated. He was much more the conscious craftsman, using a variety of carefully weighed metrical forms, subjecting his work to meticulous scrutiny and revisions (whereas Wildenvey immediately found and then stuck to what he recognized as 'the definitive version'). His earlier poetry especially has much of the novel frivolity that distinguishes Wildenvey, but, as with his senior Nils Collett Vogt, whom he highly admired, it was in course of time sicklied o'er with the pale cast of thought, not particularly arresting in itself, as far as it can be judged through the obscure, symbolizing imagery that was intended to convey it.

The copious literary output of Arnulf Øverland, born the son

made his début with the collection of poems *Nyinger* (1907). He continued fairly productive until the time of his death. Besides lyric poetry, he wrote his memoirs, beginning with *Streiftog i Hjembygden* (1924), a free verse-adaptation of *As You Like It* (1912) and, rather less successfully, original plays and short stories.

* Olaf Jacob Martin Luther Bull, the son of Jacob Breda Bull, was born on 10 November 1883 in Christiania, where he died on 20 June 1933 and which, a conspicuous member of its 'Bohemian' circles, he often celebrated in verses gay and grave. He travelled much, however, and felt himself completely at home in Paris, where he was familiar with *symboliste* poets and their followers. His first *Digte* appeared in 1908.

of a ship's stoker at Christiansund in 1889, has continued to the present day. Mainly a publicist, in the broadest sense, whose powerful voice and sharp satire first attracted attention in the polemics called forth by the First World War,[1] his earliest publications, however, were poems—*The Lonely Feast* (*Den ensomme Fest*, 1911), *The Hundred Violins* (*De hundrede violiner*, 1912), *Advent* (1915)—and all his long life through volume after volume of verse has come from his pen. Its quality is sustained, and its range is wide, from pure lyric to political denunciation and satire. As one might expect, the aesthete is far to seek in it; but like Wildenvey's and Olaf Bull's poetry, Øverland's is conspicuous for its formal excellence,[2] an excellence very different from theirs, forthright, hard, even laconic, in (for the most part) short sentences, lines and stanzas, ordinary words and comprehensible images. As Wildenvey had been, he was fired in his youth by the outward simplicity and directness of Hamsun's *Wild Choir*, but his nearest affinity among native poets, in the matter of poetic style, is perhaps with Ibsen.

The two other important poets of their generation, Ørjasæter and Aukrust, stand apart from the three just discussed, and that not merely for writing in the Landsmaal and developing it in a manner as idiosyncratic as Uppdal's. No less than Wildenvey and Olaf Bull, they had their own ideals of style, to be sure, and sedulously laboured at it, from time to time producing effects of surprising force and beauty, but they did so primarily, one might say, to provide a fit vehicle for their personal philosophies and the handling of problems which were of intimate concern to them; little attempt was made to win readers by lucidity, let alone charm or elegance.

The more concrete problems agitating Tore Ørjasæter* are (as in the novels of Uppdal and Duun) those engendered by the economic and social changes in the rural communities amid which he grew up, as the industrial revolution advanced both to threaten and allure them, and by the ensuing conflict of ambitions and loyalties within these communities themselves.

* Born, the son of an elementary schoolmaster, at Skjåk in the north-western Gudbrandsdal on 8 March 1886, Tore Ørjasæter devoted himself from the first to imaginative writing—lyric, 'lyrical-epical', prose, drama poetical and expressionistic as well as realistic—for which he was awarded a state pension in 1929; at the time of writing he is still alive.

The very title of his first collection of poems, *Ættararv* (*Heritage of the Race*, 1908) points to them. Speculations of a more metaphysical nature, tending to the mystical, bulk however more prominently when the whole long range of Ørjasæter's writing is brought into account. Naturally, they must in great measure be spiritual autobiography, but they are often suggested obliquely, as in 'dream-plays' like *Anne paa Torp* (1930) or *Christophoros* (1948) to which Strindberg's had given the impulse. Both in his early and the later work, more conventionally lyric effusions mingle with the esoteric—love-poems and celebrations of Ørjasæter's homeland, between rich plain and menacing mountain, that rank among the finest in Landsmaal literature.

Although by a little the senior in this group, Olav Aukrust (1883–1929)* chronologically can only just be included in it, having by 1920 but one book to his credit, *The Cairn of Heaven* (*Himmelvarden*, 1916). It had been preceded by a single poem, 'Norrønsang', printed in *Syn og Segn* for March 1915. The strong patriotic-moralistic strain pervading this early verse, fortified by a passionate love of his home-country's wild nature and by his absorption in the oldest literary monuments of the Northern (*norrøn*) peoples, suggests that it was the seismic spiritual turmoil induced by the spectacle of war that, comparatively late, turned Aukrust to poetry. More enduring was the religious strain, deeper and more completely integrated in him than in Ørjasæter—a unique amalgam not only of biblical and pagan elements after the fashion that his master Mortensson Egnund[1] had developed from Grundtvig's principles, but also of ancient manicheism and up-to-date psychological theories, such as those of William James and Bergson. The direction and value of the visions bred in this welter it has proved far from easy to make out, but there can be no doubt of the poet's innermost commitment to them, of his faith in their liberating power or of the massive strength applied to bringing home their message.

* Olav Aukrust, peasant-born, came from the neighbouring parish to Ørjasæter's, being born at Lom on 21 January 1883. Trained as a schoolmaster, he became head of the Grundtvig-inspired Folk High School at Dovre from 1914 to 1917. He died on 3 November 1929. His extraordinary elongated physiognomy may be seen among the figure-carvings of Trondheim cathedral.

CODA

LATE in the eighteen-fifties, when Lorentz Dietrichson, later to achieve distinction as an art-historian, experimented at Uppsala with lectures on the literature of his native Norway, he found that it was totally unknown in the 'sister-country'. Certain of his compatriots, as has been mentioned, had over the genera-tions settled in Denmark and made a name there, but essentially as Danish authors, and it was only at this time that the Copen-hagen critics began to take an interest in what was being written in Norway itself. Outside Scandinavia there was the same ignorance and lack of curiosity as in Sweden. For this the linguistic barrier—inoperative where the Danes were con-cerned—cannot be held wholly responsible. Hans Christian Andersen was building up for himself an immense international public, and Fredrika Bremer and her novels were well known far beyond the boundaries of her native Sweden. With her, literary quality was not the sole title to renown; and a similar caveat should be entered in respect of a seeming exception to the sweeping generality just made about Norway: Asbjørnsen and Moe's *Norwegian Folk Tales*, which, at the time we are speaking of, were just in process of winning recognition abroad, being native to the debatable territory between folk-lore and literature. It must be admitted that the only serious sufferer from this neglect was Henrik Wergeland, who laboured under the perennial handicap of writing poetry.

After two generations had elapsed, Norway, it is safe to say, running a neck-and-neck race with Russia, had come up from the back to reach the front rank among the literary powers. It had added a last lustre to Romantic poetry in its decline. The authors instrumental in achieving this had advanced further than any other in conquering the province of drama for triumphant realism. When its objectives and prestige were challenged, a Hamsun had appeared to take over the baton from Ibsen and Bjørnson.

In manpower, the country could, from the nature of things, not be rich. The strength of its literature had lain in its leaders, on two of whom in the first twenty years the awarders had bestowed the Nobel Prize for Literature, while having to pass by one greater and a fourth had refused to be considered for it; and the strength of the leaders lay in their artistic integrity, independence and vigour, their individuality, the strength of their very diverse personalities.

This may seem the merest platitude, but it leads on to other general reflexions of perhaps a more interesting character. The new Magi from the north, abundantly criticized and attacked as they might be at home, there too were acknowledged and respected as leaders, and as leaders in two senses.

In the first place, they were pioneers. Ibsen and Bjørnson, it has been seen, began to write plays—plays, moreover, that very soon were distinguished by quite exceptional effectiveness—when the arts of the theatre had scarcely been transplanted to Norwegian soil at all. Simultaneously, Bjørnson's *Synnøve Solbakken* at one blow brought the peasant-story, hitherto hardly viable there, to its richest flowering; similarly, if rather more tardily, Lie, quickly reinforced by the early-ripe genius of his junior Kielland, created the Norwegian novel out of next to nothing; and, when these two had blazed the trail that many reputable if less distinguished talents were to follow, Hamsun came along to hew out strange by-paths and lure others to do the same.

Gunnar Heggen, the most intelligent character in Sigrid Undset's novel *Jenny*, delivers himself of a great diatribe against the adulation of artists in Norway for the mere fact that they had '*brøt*', 'broken' or 'broken away'. What he deplores he acknowledges at the same time as a fundamental trait in the national character, the suspicion and slighting of routine and tradition, of anything in the arts savouring of the academic. There is no doubt that the great writers who won world fame 'broke' and that, at home at least, they gained additional kudos from the fact. Nor is it surprising that in a land of great uncultivated expanses the true pioneer should hold high esteem and that the solitary adventurer, whether he be the Nansen of history or a Lieutenant Glahn of fiction, should be a perennially fascinating figure. Individualism, individuality, strength of personality are at a premium.

In the narrow field of literary history, a relevant point may be made. The great men founded no 'schools' in their native land. There are no lesser Ibsens; one can scarcely speak of a minor Lie or—at any rate among his juniors—of a minor Kielland, even if the art of the novel may show more continuity than that of other genres; almost self-evidently there could not be a minor Hamsun: Kinck would certainly have repudiated such an ascription. Hence that long-lasting deficiency of 'middling talents' that may be taken for the gravamen of Gunnar Heggen's charge.

Norwegian authors have been leaders also in a second sense— one that has perhaps already been too often alluded to: in their *tendens*. From the time of the pugnacious Wergeland, whose mantle descended almost visibly on to that tribune of the people, his adulator Bjørnson, the imaginative writers took a more active concern, perhaps, than those in any other country with public questions. Some directly, most of them indirectly too, gave their opinions upon them. They were expected to do so and, even when their views were not published in set terms, their writings were scanned for any 'message' in the moral, if not in the sociological and political realm, that might be distilled. It was considered their business to be leaders of opinion. Even when Knut Hamsun turned against literature with a purpose, the bill of divorcement between art and utility which he loudly proclaimed was something of a public act, indeed intended as such. It may seem anomalous, but it is indicative of the national love of independence, opposition and iconoclasm that, though the opinions disseminated were invariably hostile to those commonly received, they were, with the same regularity, rewarded from public funds.

One signal manifestation of this iconoclasm has to be mentioned again, an illustration of the kind of barbarism imputable to Hamsun and Kinck. Among those who 'broke' a very high place must be given to Ivar Aasen and Vinje for inventing the Landsmaal and making it a vehicle for literary expression. For long there seemed to be justification for the Landsmaal's more responsible opponents of its propagation and extremer aims; they saw therein not only the waste of energy which revolutionary movements, whatever their ultimate success, inevitably involve, but also a serious threat to the nation's cultural heritage and prestige through the isolationism against which, a generation earlier, Welhaven had taken the field. It is no doubt arguable that the difficulties experienced by many now brought up on Nynorsk in appreciating the classics written even in their grandfathers' time is a misfortune, that some Norwegian writers have been frustrated by their self-imposed determination to fashion a new instrument before using it and that they who did successfully use it have been scanted at home and abroad of the reputation that but for its strangeness would have been theirs. Much of this, however, can be only hypothesis. All the consequences of the Tower of Babel must be accepted; and, this done, it must also be accepted that a Garborg, Duun or Aukrust showed himself master of a language as copious, effective and adaptable as any other and, with it, enriched the heritage his predecessors were thought to menace.

The Landsmaal controversy and the names just cited by a natural transition lead on to the second distinguishing feature of modern Norwegian literature when it is surveyed as a whole, a feature predominant in the second half of the period under consideration, as the public function of authorship was characteristic rather of the first half; and that is, to use that vague term again, the prominence of the 'country interest'.

Synnøve Solbakken, Big Lad, Brand and *Peer Gynt* remind us that it was there from the very start. For a span of years it lay over-shadowed beneath the urban or bourgeois colouring of typical works like *The Lifer, Garman & Worse, Pillars of Society, Dangerous People, The Flags are Out,* though it may be noted that even in the 'seventies and 'eighties the authors of these occasionally laid their scenes in the country (*The Family at Gilje, Snow, Rosmersholm, Tora Trondal, Magnhild,* for instance). After 1890 there is, however, a striking shift of focus. It is the natural corollary of the reaction then setting in, the revolt against *tendens,* social criticism, the canvassing of 'problems'—a revolt, it may be worth recalling here, in which the Riksmaal writers took the lead. In its pure form, the reactionary 'movement' did not amount to much. But this element in it endured. There are traces of it in the works of some of the remaining veterans—in Bjørnson's last fiction and plays, most notably in Garborg after his revivification by his native Jæren; and with only trivial, specious exceptions, all the more distinguished new writers were born and bred in the country and set the scene of their most characteristic work there.

The setting itself can be the subject of artistic treatment, in self-contained poems or as lyrical insets of prose and verse amid narration or speculation that at the time are the author's greater concern; it may indeed be no more than the chance *mise-en-scène* for an action transferable with no loss to a town. What is truly significant is the presentation in depth and from within of the ethos of the countryside and the 'soul of the peasant', not as a curio, but as an essential—even *the* essential—constituent of the national life. Depth, purposiveness and authenticity varied greatly, of course, from artist to artist. Humorists like Aanrud and aesthetes like Vilhelm Krag make their contribution; on the one hand we have Kinck in a great fraction of his work dedicating himself entirely to the elucidation of this ethos; on the other Hamsun, the consummate painter of the scene, disdaining 'purpose', denying the typical, fascinated by the tramp and waster with whom it would be grotesque to associate any word like ethos—yet writing *Growth of the Soil*.

As the natural corollary of the *renouveau* of 1890 this enhanced preoccupation with the life of the country had its parallel in the other literatures in which a similar shift of focus—often subsumed as 'Neo-Romanticism'—was simultaneously announcing itself. *Heimatdichtung*, in its origins a by-product of the older Romantic revolt, took on a new lease of life everywhere. It would be idle to deny that, side by side with a vast deal of shoddy sentimentality, humour and theatricality, much fine work can be ranged under this heading or the less happy one of 'peasant-literature'. We have our Hardy, and other distinguished names can be put alongside his—Jókai, Verga, Grazia Deledda, the Danes Pontoppidan and J. V. Jensen, Hauptmann, Blasco Ibañez, to give but a few. Even with most of these, however, stories and evocations of country life made up only a part, sometimes only a small part, of their output, and its whole bulk was usually insignificant by comparison with that of writing properly to be designated by other terms. Norway has had the distinction, shared perhaps only with the Flanders of Gezelle, Buysse, Streuvels and Timmermans, of making over a long range of years its rural literature, in all its ramifications, truly central and, through the genius and talents of its dedicated exponents, a worthy counterpart to the literature of the earlier generation that had won it world-wide fame.

GENERAL NOTES

PAGE 1

1 And far from populous: in 1814 the total number of inhabitants was just under one million; the largest town, Bergen, had less than 20,000 inhabitants and Christiania, the capital, little more than half that.

2 The outstanding politician and economist of his generation Anton Martin Schweigaard (1808–70) adjured his fellow-countrymen in words which boded ill to the advancement of the arts: 'Work as much, enjoy as little as you can.'

3 A consequential effect of this was the absence of diplomatic representatives in Christiania, which contributed not only to the sense of isolation and inferiority, but also to the provinciality of the capital.

PAGE 2

1 S. Laing, *Journal of a Residence in Norway* (1836), p. 458; Laing's is one of the best books in our language written by an eyewitness about conditions in a foreign country.

2 For 128 years it was called after the Danish king, *Universitas regia Fredericiana*; until 1948 it was the only university in the country.

PAGE 3

1 The Napoleonic troubles had reduced their numbers and the wealth of those who survived.

2 An early enactment of the Storting (1824) abolished, on the death of the holders, the titles of nobility still in existence; there were then two counts and six barons.

3 The decisive engagements were the abolition of the lord-lieutenancy (*de facto* 1856, *de jure* 1873), the formation of a disciplined opposition party (the Venstre or Left, 1869) and the successful impeachment by Parliament of the prime minister and his Cabinet, which ensured parliamentary government (1884). After 1884 political agitation was mainly concerned with the achievement of complete independence, finally ensured by the dissolution of the Union with Sweden in 1905.

4 The comprehensive term Bonde (plural Bønder) is often objected to in Norway, and 'peasant', almost always a pejorative in English, is even more misleading. 'Country interest' is a more

satisfactory term, since it can connote not only all, from the day-labourer to the substantial farmer, who made their living directly from the land, but also the allied fishermen-crofters of the coastal villages and those rural shopkeepers, schoolteachers, inferior clergy and minor officials whose sympathies lay with their agricultural neighbours. The latent strength of the country interest resided in the distribution of parliamentary seats, guaranteed by the constitution, two rural for one urban.

PAGE 4

1 As members of Det norske Selskab, founded in Copenhagen in 1772.

2 Like their opponents, however, they never constituted a coherent political party or even an association.

PAGE 5

1 Wergeland made his position quite clear in a speech he made at Eidsvold in 1834: '*Our* Norway and the Norway of antiquity seem like two severed half-rings which fit most closely together; the age between like the spurious solder we have to break so as to fuse the genuine halves' (*Digterverker og Prosaiske Skrifter*, v, 1884, 165).

2 It ought to be said, however, that the finest of Wergeland's poetry is not much coloured by *tendens*. Even if his long imaginative poems, *Jøden* and *Jødinden*, may have helped to raise the ban against Jewish immigration into Norway, he mostly kept his serious poetry and his propaganda distinct.

3 Cf. O. J. Falnes, *National Romanticism in Norway* (New York, 1933).

4 E.g. Johan Christian Dahl (1788–1857), Thomas Fearnley (1802–42), Adolf Tideman (1814–76), Hans Gude (1825–1903).

5 E.g. Ole Bull (1810–80) and Halfdan Kjerulf (1815–68); cf. Landstad's *Norske Folkeviser* (1852–3) and Lindeman's *Ældre og nyere norske Fjeldmelodier* (1853–67).

PAGE 6

1 *Norske Folkeeventyr* (1st ed. 1842–4); *Norske Folkeeventyr, ny Samling* (1871); *Norske Huldreeventyr og Folkesagn* (1st ed. 1845–8).

2 The most eminent of them was Peter Andreas Munch (1810–63) and his greatest work *Det Norske Folks Historie* (1852–63).

PAGE 7

1 This was a progressive phenomenon; some students of a subject in which it is difficult to obtain certainty believe that cultivated Norwegian speech came nearest to cultivated Danish speech actually during the first years of the independent Kingdom.

2 *Prøver af Landsmaalet i Norge* (1853), *Ervingen* (1855) and *Symra* (1863).

3 Aasen himself, though a figure of fun to look at, was generally respected for his learning and integrity; the conservative university offered him a professorship, which his modesty made him decline.

PAGE 8

1 On the linguistic question see A. Sommerfelt, *Written and Spoken Word in Norway* (1942); D. A. Seip, *Norsk Sproghistorie* (1920) and, in an abbreviated form, *En litn Norsk Språkhistorie* (1946). The most important influence in the development of Riksmaal from Danish was that of Knud Knudsen (1812–95). It is estimated that today one-third of schoolchildren receive their instruction in Nynorsk.

2 He wrote to Ibsen in 1867: 'Hold fast ved Danmark, hold fast . . . Danmark er for os Kulturen' (*Gro-Tid*, II, 1912, 26). It was he who defiantly coined the term Riksmaal.

3 E.g. Belgium at roughly the same epoch.

PAGE 9

1 Asbjørnsen may be reckoned to the Party of Intelligence and had nothing to do with Landsmaal; but his (tactfully managed) fidelity to the spoken sources of his tales obliged him to bring in words and turns of phrase unknown to the stiff official style.

2 First cousin of the historian Peter Andreas Munch, who in his turn was the uncle of the painter Edvard Munch.

3 He was also the first to receive (1860) a parliamentary pension for his services to literature (*digtergage*).

4 *Kong Sverres Ungdom* (1837), *Donna Clara* (1840), *Salomon de Caus* (1854), *En Aften paa Giske* (1855), *Lord William Russell* (1857), *Hertog Skule* (1864).

5 The only writer of such in any degree remembered is the schoolmaster Mauritz Christopher Hansen (1794–1842), who mainly turned out wild concoctions in the debased style of the German Lafontaine, but also ventured occasionally on delineations of contemporary manners.

6 The bibliography by P. Botten Hansen of 1867, *La Norvège littéraire*, reveals the poverty of the soil.

PAGE 10

1 L. K. Roksund, 'Europeisk Litteratur i Norge i 1. Halvdel av 19. Århundrede', *Edda*, LIII (1953), 248, is based on the not very typical correspondence between S. O. Wolff and N. M. Aalholm in the period 1830–60.

2 Cf. F. Bull, 'Balzac et la Norvège', *Hommage à Balzac* (Paris, 1950), p. 111. I have listed only the great names here; the Gothic novel and what Jonas Lie was to call 'Red Indian' stories, of foreign origin, were widely disseminated.

3 Neither then nor later do the classics as literature seem to have roused much interest in Norway; and the Sagas, though 'required reading' on many a book-list, left less of a mark on imaginative writing than might have been expected: in the forty years between *Arnljot Gelline* and Sigrid Undset's début virtually none.

4 For the effect of the Moderne Gjennembrud's great promoter Georg Brandes, see pp. 29 ff., 56 ff. Brandes, rightly considering them as the most eminent of its exponents, kept a close contact with most of the major Norwegian authors; vol. IV of his *Brevveksling med nordiske Forfattere*, ed. F. Bull (1939), is therefore of the greatest interest.

PAGE 11

1 It is true, however, that a critical spirit, at variance with the starry-eyed pietas of the National Romanticists, had already coloured a good deal of Ibsen's and Vinje's writings and appeared here and there also in Bjørnson's, while Camilla Collett's pioneer work might well have been written under the impulse of the Moderne Gjennembrud.

PAGE 12

1 It is remarkable how small an impact was made on belles-lettres by the great political event of the time, the severance of the Union with Sweden which brought the country to the verge of war. The Great War, however, was felt as a doomsday, and the deep divisions it wrought in the country appeared in the imaginative literature of the time (cf. pp. 201, 207 ff. above).

2 The Danish critic Clemens Petersen, in 1868 (*cit.* K. Hamre, *C. Petersen og hans Forhold till Norsk Litteratur*, 1945, p. 24).

PAGE 13

1 H. Beyer, too, struggles in the chronological snare when he says (*History of Norwegian Literature*, 1956, p. 162) that Vinje 'may

appear to be a typical representative of the transitional years around 1850–60'.

2 The *Amtmand* (now styled *fylkesmann*) corresponds to the French *préfet*. He is the salaried representative of the government in a large district, with wide executive powers and great prestige.

PAGE 14

1 As indicated, Camilla Collett had as good as no native models to help her. She knew, as one might expect, the novels of George Sand, who is mentioned in *Amtmandens Døttre* (though she does not seem greatly to have admired the novels until later), and the 'feuilleton-literature' of other foreign authors, such as the Dane Thomasine Gyllembourg. There is nothing to show that she knew *Wuthering Heights* or *Jane Eyre*. Only the title of her book has much in common with Fredrika Bremer's widely read *Präsidentens Döttrar* (1834).

PAGE 15

1 His copious journalism up to that date had all been written in Riksmaal. On Vinje's language there is a study in German by V. Waschnitius, 'Vinjes Sprachentwicklung', *Edda*, XIV (1920), 161.
2 One of his most unamiable traits was the disparagement of his contemporaries once they achieved fame. There were good grounds for being critical of Bjørnson's peasant stories, but he elected to treat *Arne* just as a practical joke on the public and meted out the same treatment to Ibsen's *Brand*, most infelicitously comparing it with *The Dunciad*! (Cf. *Skrifter i Samling*, I, 323 and II, 181). When *Peer Gynt* appeared, so congenial, one would think, to Vinje for its *milieu* and satirical approach, he could simply do nothing with it: *Dølen* passed it by in silence.
3 *Britain and the British* (Edinburgh, 1863).

PAGE 16

1 It came out originally as a supplement to *Dølen* early in 1861, but was also published separately as a book in the same year; the 'Journey' was undertaken on foot from Christiania to witness the coronation of King Charles at Trondheim.
2 His other lengthier imaginative work was *Storegut* (*Big Lad*, 1866), an experiment in a 'folk-epic' or rather a cycle of connected poems revolving round a rustic champion from the time of the Napoleonic troubles. Vinje had small powers of construction or of projecting characters, and, as a whole, *Storegut* must be reckoned a failure.

PAGE 17

1 It may be of interest to list the first ten recipients of the prize: Sully-Prudhomme, Mommsen, Bjørnson, Mistral, Echegaray, Sienkiewicz, Carducci, Kipling, Eucken, Selma Lagerlöf.
2 'Den bedste Del af hans Væsen er nedlagt i hans Værker' (G. Brandes, *Samlede Verker*, III, Kjøbenhavn, 1900, 406); 'Hans liv var hans bedste digtning.—Og det, i sin livsførelse at realisere sig selv, mener jeg er det højeste, et menneske kan naa til' (Ibsen, centenary edition, XVII, p. 476).
3 Not to mention his signal services as a man of the theatre, as director of the Bergen Theatre 1857–9, of the Christiania Theater 1865–7, of the Møllergate Theatre in Christiania 1871–2, and as producer of his own plays for many years later.

PAGE 18

1 W. M. Payne, *Bjørnstjerne Bjørnson 1832–1910* (Chicago, 1910), p. 11.
2 *Ibsen and the Temper of Norwegian Literature* (1960), p. 88.
3 The beginnings of this are well described in K. Hamre, *Clemens Petersen* (Oslo, 1945), pp. 20 ff.; the first translation into English was *Synnøve Solbakken* as *Trust and Trial* (1858), without the author's name.

PAGE 19

1 In collected editions Bjørnson had a tale he entitled 'Min første Fortælling'; it is not 'Aanun', but 'Thrond', presumably drafted earlier and extensively revised before its publication (in two differing versions) in 1857. Others also were rewritten after their original publication. The *Samlede Digter-Verker* (vol. 1) go back to the earliest printed versions.
2 At one time or another Bjørnson read Blicher, Auerbach and George Sand, but it is doubtful whether he had done so by 1856; there were curiously few examples of peasant-tales by Norwegians before this date, and they were negligible as models.
3 If a translation is needed it might run *Sunniva of Sunnyside Farm*. The English title of 'En glad Gut' was 'Ovind' (1869).
4 It is Riksmaal, naturally diversified by a few dialect words and expressions. Bjørnson wrote one poem, 'Nils Finn', for *Halte Hulda*, in Landsmaal and turned the tale 'Farligt Frieri' into it, but eventually became one of its strongest opponents. Cf. D. A. Seip, *Edda*, V (1916), 1.

PAGE 20

1 Letter to Botten Hansen of 13 March 1857 (in Bjørnson's *Gro-Tid*, I, 1912, 2). The Copenhagen *Dagblad* stigmatized Bjørnson's language as 'en malabarisk Dialekt' (*cit.* C. Collin, *Salmonsons Konversationsleksikon*, III, 1915, 245). Ibsen remembered the expression in *Peer Gynt* when he presented a lunatic whose endeavour it is to bring back the speech of the Malabaris to that of the primeval orang-outang, in its elaborate context an obvious smack at the Landsmaal fanatics (cf. Archer's translation IV, 185 f.).

2 †'Blakken', first printed in 1868, a story about a horse, scarcely counts.

PAGE 21

1 They were first acted in 1857 (Christiania Theater) and 1862 (Møllergate Theatre, Christiania) respectively. The first has a long stage history in several countries; the second was a failure from the start.

2 On Bjørnson's drama see H. Noreng, *B. Bjørnsons dramatiske Diktning*; M. Lamm, *Modern Drama*, Eng. trans. (Oxford, 1952), p. 76, and B. W. Downs, 'Bjørnson and Tragedy', *Scandinavica*, I (1962), 17. His conversion from Scribe is attributable to the criticisms of Hermann Hettner and P. L. Møller.

3 Originally planned as two plays, it was published in 1864 and produced at the Christiania Theater in a greatly revised version on 29 March 1867.

PAGE 22

1 Written and published in 1862; Parts I and III were first acted at Trondheim on 30 September 1863, Part II had to wait for its production till 1885 (4 March, Christiania Theater).

2 *Samlede Digter-Verker*, VIII, 215, 216.

PAGE 23

1 The poems alluded to in this paragraph are to be found in *Samlede Digter-Verker*, IV, 310, 220, 367, 403 respectively.

2 *Ibid.* VIII, 245.

3 One might adduce as examples of the best he could do in this vein 'Frida, jeg vidste . . .', 'Jeg reiste forbi . . .' or 'Aften er stille . . .' (*ibid.* pp. 250, 318, 282).

PAGE 24

1 Structurally *Arnljot Gelline* resembles them too, each being a series of separate 'romances', differing in mood and (except for Runeberg's poem) also in metre.

2 As there was no second *Arnljot Gelline*, so the later editions of *Digte og Sange* were the original one only slightly expanded: a handful of lay hymns ('Salmer', *Samlede Digter-Verker*, III, 461 ff.) are a curious novelty. There is a further collection, *Bjørnsons Samlede Digter* (1927), and an admirable selection, *Digte og Sange i Utvalg*, ed. F. Bull (1957), but no complete edition. For criticism see F. Bull, 'Bjørnsons Lyrikk', *Studier og Streiftog* (1931).

PAGE 25

1 First acted, at the Royal Theatre, Copenhagen, on 23 November 1865. It was a great success both in the theatre and as a book.

2 Edvard Brandes in the 'Festskrift', *Bjørnstjerne Bjørnson* (Copenhagen, n.d.), p. 18.

3 It was begun in 1866 at latest, but completed after Bjørnson had fallen under the spell of Grundtvig in the summer of 1867.

PAGE 26

1 'En sangers kall profetens er' (*Samlede Digter-Verker*, VIII, 379).

2 *Cit. ibid.* III, ii.

PAGE 27

1 Grundtvigianism was essentially Danish. Bjørnson, a foreigner, chose the moment of Grundtvig's death (1872) to exhort the Danes, still smarting under their defeat in 1864, to drop their hostility to the Germans and, together with the other northern peoples, to embrace a kind of pan-Germanism. This kindled the so-called *Signalfejde* (Signal-Feud), from the nautical metaphor to the effect that Denmark should reverse her signals, her sailing-orders. Whatever his religious beliefs, Bjørnson could never have recovered the ground he then lost. See H. Beyer, 'Bjørnsons Religion', *Fra Holberg til Hamsun* (1934).

2 *Cit.* R. Thesen, 'B. Bjørnson og Georg Brandes', *Edda*, XXXVIII (1938), 37, ex *Verdens Gang* of 12 February 1902.

3 Bjørnson's political activity, spectacularly begun with speech and journalism during his Bergen days, had received a set-back through the unpopularity it incurred when he moved to Christiania in 1859—reflexions of which may be discerned in *Sigurd the Bad*—and for several years after that been kept in stern check.

PAGE 28

1 His power in internal politics waned after this; but he concerned himself increasingly with foreign affairs, as the advocate in the world's press of Dreyfus, oppressed racial minorities and international arbitration. These causes left no trace on his plays or fiction.

2 It was first given in German, at Hamburg on 11 October 1883; for the Norwegian *première* in 1886 (Christiania Theater) it was extensively revised.

PAGE 29

1 On this altercation, which takes its name from Hans Jæger's novel *Fra Christiania-Bohêmen* (1885), see p. 102 above.

2 Bjørnson came to mitigate his rigour, as *Mary* testifies.

3 See R. Thesen, 'Bjørnstjerne Bjørnson og Georg Brandes', *Edda*, XXXVIII (1939), 39.

4 It served as the Introduction to the courses printed as *Hovedstrømninger i det 19de Aarhundredes europæiske Litteratur* (6 vols. 1872–90), though oddly omitted from the English translation.

PAGE 30

1 The sentence, though carefully worded, has often been misunderstood. Brandes, a Romantic at heart, claimed, not that all literature should be realistic 'problem-literature', but rather that a ferment of ideas and problems within a corpus of literature kept the whole from decay.

2 On this see G. Ahlström, *Det moderna Genombrottet i Nordens Litteratur* (Stockholm, 1947).

3 *Cit.* H. Fenger, *Den unge Brandes* (1957), p. 54.

4 Printed in *Georg og Edv. Brandes Brevveksling med Nordiske Forfattere* (ed. M. Borup, IV, i, Copenhagen etc., 1939), p. 1.

PAGE 31

1 *Artikler og Taler*, II (1913), 334.

2 *Samlede Digter-Verker*, IV, 488. Bjørnson acknowledged that every book Brandes wrote had increased his insight and extended his ideas and that he had transformed the literary consciousness (*bevidsthed*) of the north (G. Gran, *A. L. Kielland og hans Samlid*, 1923, p. 131).

3 Through Ernst Sars and his circle of friends, with whom he became intimate in the early 'sixties. See A. Krogvig and E. Skavlan, *Fra Norge paa Syttiarsdagen* (1912); also P. Amdam,

Edda, LX (1960), 254. Later in life Bjørnson was to declare: 'Spencer and Bain were my favourites among the philosophers, as Darwin and Huxley were my liberators.'

4 Not yet, of course, in the special sense adopted by the school of Zola.

5 They were not exactly revolutionary, since they carried on the rather tenuous tradition of serious anti-heroic drama that had originated with Lillo and Diderot in the eighteenth century and had, in German literature, attained the status of a sub-genre, 'das bürgerliche Trauerspiel'. (Ibsen had a high regard for its two chief exponents, Hebbel and Ludwig.)

6 The following plays by Augier (alone or in collaboration) were produced at the Christiania Theater: *Beau Mariage, Ceinture Dorée, Diane, Les Effrontés, Fils de Giboyer, Les Fourchambault, Gabrielle, Gendre de M. Poirier, Madame Caverlet, Pierre de Touche.* Balzac's *Mercadet* was done there in 1869.

7 *En Fallit* was set up in the summer of 1874, but not published until after its stage production, which took place in a Swedish translation at Nya Teatern, Stockholm, on 19 January 1875 and in the original ten days later at the Christiania Theater. It proved, in the many countries in which it was given, perhaps the author's most popular play, mainly for the complete wholesomeness of its moral.

PAGE 32

1 *Redaktøren* was finished and printed, after a lengthy incubation, in 1874; its composition took place concurrently with that of *En Fallit*. The first stage production was, in Swedish, on 17 February 1875, at Stockholm, and the original text was published a few days later.

PAGE 33

1 The production at the Norwegian National Theatre on 11 September 1902 is the first I have discovered.

PAGE 34

1 The others are †*Leonarda* (1879); †*Det ny System* (1879); †*Laboremus* (1901); *Paa Storhove* (1902); *Daglannet* (1904); †*Naar den ny vin blomstrer* (1909); †*Over Ævne*, Part II (1895).

PAGE 35

1 There is an extensive literature on Richter's death and Bjørnson's treatment of it. Cf. particularly I. Arctander, 'Statsminister Ole

Richters Død', *Samtiden* (1930), pp. 13 ff. and 305 ff., and F. Bull, 'Ole Richter, Bjørnstjerne Bjørnson og Paul Lange', *Mennesker* (Oslo, 1938), pp. 64 ff.

2 It was first acted in Swedish at Nya Teatern, Stockholm, in 1886, in the original both in Copenhagen and at the National Theatre of Christiania in 1899.

PAGE 36

1 *Samlede Skrifter*, III (Kjøbenhavn, 1900), 408.

2 Their more generally acknowledged forerunners Wedekind and Strindberg came into this field in 1891 (*Frühlings Erwachen*) and 1898 (*Till Damaskus*) respectively.

PAGE 37

1 *The Quintessence of Ibsenism* (1922), p. 187. Shaw may not have had much direct knowledge of Bjørnson's writing, but may well have heard, early in his career, about it from William Archer. Stage-debates on matters of principle were nothing new (*Troilus and Cressida, Le Misanthrope*, also *Kjærlighedens Komedie*).

2 A brief chronology may be of service here: 1855, Camilla Collett's pioneer *Amtmandens Døttre*; 1868, Bjørnson's *Fiskerjenten*; 1871, Brandes's inaugural lecture and Zola's first *Rougon-Macquart* novel; 1874, Lie's *Lodsen og hans Hustru*; 1880, Kielland's *Garman & Worse*; 1884, Bjørnson's *Det Flager*.

PAGE 38

1 He did not, however, shrink from alluding to masturbation and venereal disease in *På Guds Veje*.

2 Zola's novels, of course, have some of these characteristics too. The mark of Dickens, a household god throughout the world, who had a pervasive influence on all writers who combined story-telling with social purpose, is not so plain as it is on certain passages in Kielland's or Lie's novels. Bjørnson's trick of bringing in characters already figuring in other works need not be attributed to the example of Thackeray. An interesting parallel might be drawn between the author of *Det flager* and the author of *Tono-Bungay*, another disciple of Herbert Spencer.

3 His religious speculations owed much to Unitarian divines in the U.S.A.

PAGE 39

1 That of the earlier novel lends its name to the English translation, *The Heritage of the Kurts*, in showing how the manor-house they turned into a school had become the property of Tomas Rendalen and his mother, and gives scope for Bjørnson's notions about heredity. It has been much praised for the archaizing pastiche of its style.

PAGE 42

1 So far did morality sink into the background that his last play, *Når den ny Vin blomstrer*, might easily be turned into a rather distasteful musical comedy with the title 'Rutting Time'.

PAGE 43

1 *Norma*, a political squib in dialogue form, parodying Bellini's opera and printed in the students' magazine *Andhrimner* in 1851, might rank as a seventh. It and *St John's Night* are among translations in T. Jorgensen, *In the Mountain Wilderness* (Northfield, Minn., 1957), while *Early Plays of Henrik Ibsen*, trans. A. Orbeck, (New York, 1921), comprises *Catiline*, *The Warrior's Barrow* and *Olaf Liljekrans*, which were likewise omitted from Archer's collection.

PAGE 44

1 *Gildet paa Solhaug* was the first play by Ibsen to be acted abroad (Dramatiska Teatern, Stockholm, 4 November 1857). *Olaf Liljekrans* and *Sancthansnatten* were not printed till 1902 and 1909 respectively. *Fru Inger til Østerraad* was printed in 1857; the final spelling of the title was adopted for the considerably revised second edition, of 1874.
2 Its five acts are in prose throughout, except for a fragment of a song in Act I.

PAGE 45

1 Published April 1858 and produced at the Møllergate Theatre, Christiania, on 24 November 1858. Helgeland is the name now given to the district south of the Saltenfjord; a precise localization was, however, not intended, merely an indication of the extreme verge of human habitation in the tenth century. Parallels to Ibsen's story are to be found in the *Vølsungasaga* and, more particularly, the *Laxdøla Saga* and Oehlenschläger's recent tragedy of *Kiartan og Gudrun* (1848). *Hærmændene paa Helgeland* and Bjørnson's

somewhat similar *Halte-Hulda* (of the same year) were written in complete independence of one another. Ibsen modelled his style on Danish translations of the Sagas. His linguistic development is admirably summarized by T. Knudsen, *Scandinavica*, I (1963), I.

2 He attributed the 'weightier content' which his life received to his marriage (June 1858); it would perhaps be more just to refer it to his engagement in the year *Hærmændene* was begun, since it was Susannah Ibsen who served as his model for Hjørdis.

PAGE 46

1 A rudimentary form of it of course is present in most plays, where the opening passages give the spectator some idea of the existing relationships between the main characters (the *donnée*).

2 Works covering a great span of time like *Brand*, *Peer Gynt* or *Kejser og Galilæer* are hardly dependent on the analytic technique. Elsewhere, too, the generalization I have made calls for certain reservations (notably *Gengangere* and *Rosmersholm*).

3 *Emne* meaning matter, material, stuff, the more accurate translation would be The Stuff of Kings, Royal Stock or The Scions of Royalty. The play (five acts, prose, with interspersed songs) was published in October 1863 with 1864 on the title-page and produced at the Christiania Theater on 17 January 1864, to be given eight times, a respectable figure for the time and place. *Kongs-Emnerne* came in the year following Bjørnson's *Sigurd Slembe*, which also conformed to Hettner's requirement; in a sense it winds up the sequence of Bjørnson's historical cycle.

PAGE 48

1 A prose draft of *Svanhild* (first published in 1909, translated in the Oxford Ibsen, II, 203 ff.) was begun in 1860.

2 It made both critics and the general reader uncomfortable, and was not thought fit for theatrical representation until 1873, when (24 November) it was put on at the Christiania Theater, in a slightly revised form.

PAGE 49

1 The parable of love and tea, to be found in *Amtmandens Døttre* (1879 ed. I, 197) and brilliantly worked up by Falk (Centenary Edition, V, 202; Archer-Herford, I, 386).

2 For this there was no model in Norwegian literature, but two Danish authors, much admired by Ibsen, had successfully experimented with the form, J. L. Heiberg and Paludan-Müller.

PAGE 50

1 The removal of the scene in Act IV of *Peer Gynt* to North Africa adds to the exuberance and spaciousness of the rest. The legendary Peer Gynt, about whom Ibsen derived much of his knowledge from Asbjørnsen's tales, hailed from the Gudbrandsdal. For the legends see *Edda*, xxx (1930), 120 and 680.

2 *Brand*, first planned and partly written as a narrative poem, was published in 1866; Act IV, by itself, was given at the Christiania Theater that summer, the whole, in a Swedish translation, first at Nya Teatret, Stockholm, on 24 March 1885.

3 Ibsen denied that he had drawn a portrait of Kierkegaard himself (as is obvious enough) or had even read his writings. But the Danish philosopher's main tenets, much 'in the air' of Norway at the time, must have been known to him.

PAGE 51

1 *Peer Gynt* was written, at high speed, in Italy in 1867 and published on 14 November of that year. It was first acted, at the Christiania Theater, on 24 February 1876, with the incidental music that Grieg had been commissioned to compose for the occasion. During the nineteenth century it had only sporadic performances, but the less cumbrous stage-mechanics of the twentieth century gave it a fresh lease of life.

PAGE 52

1 Some believed the satire to be more pervasive, that Ibsen in the waster Peer was typifying the national character, and took umbrage accordingly.

2 The subject began to interest Ibsen soon after his arrival in Italy in 1864. Work on it was seriously taken in hand in 1870 and completed in 1873. Divided into two parts of five acts each, all in prose, it was published in the autumn of that year; it had to wait for something like a full stage production till 1903 (National-theatret, Christiania).

3 *Ibsen* (1962), p. 45. Each word carefully weighed, the claim is not as extravagant as it sounds, especially if Goethe's *Faust* is relegated to the eighteenth century.

4 This interest goes some way to accounting for the immediate success of *Kejser og Galilæer* as a book: 4,000 copies, a very considerable figure in the northern book-market at that time, were sold in the first two months; it may also explain the fact that it

was the first drama of Ibsen's to be translated into English (by C. Ray, 1876).

5 Arne Garborg's *Henrik Ibsens 'Keiser og Galilæer'* (2nd ed. Christiania, 1874), p. 61.

PAGE 53

1 On them see O. Svendsen and P. G. de la Chesnais, *Edda*, XXXIII (1933), 198, and XXXVII (1937), 7, respectively, as well as the Introductions in the Centenary and Oxford editions.

2 An exception has sometimes been adduced with the later 'De sad der, de to', which indeed Ibsen marked as a preliminary study for *Bygmester Solness*; the completed play is only faintly connected with the essentially static situation indicated in the poem. None of the poems, in fact, suggests dramatic possibilities.

3 Until the Centenary Edition (vol. XIV) included everything that could be retrieved at the time, successive editions were substantially the same as the first, augmented by a very few items written after 1871. A full discussion of the poetry is in H. Dahl, *Bergmannen og Bygmesteren* (1958). There are English translations by F. E. Garrett (1912) and R. A. Streatfield (1902).

PAGE 54

1 It was written late in 1859 or 1860.

2 Garrett's translation is in *Lyrics and Poems from Ibsen* (1912), p. 23. The two following poems *ibid.* pp. 5 and 16, the last composed as an epilogue to the collected *Digte*. It need scarcely be said that the 'he' is Ibsen in his exile.

PAGE 56

1 'Til min Ven Revolution-Taleren!' written in 1869. Garrett's translation, p. 34.

2 For certain resemblances between *Faust* and *Peer Gynt*.

3 Cf. his letter to Brandes of 4 April 1872 (Centenary ed. XVII, 30).

PAGE 57

1 G. Brandes, *Samlede Skrifter*, V (1900), 12.

2 After this time Ibsen hardly ever wrote verse again. There is an anecdote illustrating his revulsion from poetry told by Gunnar Heiberg (*Salt og Sukker*, 1924, p. 52): when one night, half-seas-over, he was walking through the streets of Rome with Heiberg and had a poem of his own quoted to him, his reaction was to roar out: 'Vers! Vers! Bare Vers.'

3 Finished in the spring of 1869, published on 30 September and produced (Christiania Theater) on 18 October. It was the year in which the Venstre party was taking shape and the leadership of the Opposition passing from the 'peasant' Ueland (represented in the play by the sitting member Lundestad) to the lawyer Sverdrup. The political bias is clear and surprising. Not only is the new political force which the 'hero' calls into being shown as a mere racket—so that the word 'Youth' becomes in effect a term of abuse—but his contemptible self was seen to be an amalgam of three liberal leaders, the grandiloquent Bjørnson, the heiress-hunting Richter and the agile Sverdrup. Its first production accordingly had a very stormy reception, and Bjørnson was beside himself with fury. The play has always been immensely popular in Norway.

PAGE 58

1 Begun in October 1875, completed in July 1877, published on 11 October and produced (Royal Theatre, Copenhagen) on 18 November of that year. It was highly successful in print and on the northern stages and produced a veritable furore in Germany.
2 Aune and his predicament are given a certain prominence and are sympathetically treated. But Ibsen had no design of setting up a proletarian versus a bourgeois morality. He quickly provided Aune with a counterpart in the scoundrelly carpenter Engstrand of *Ghosts*. J. Korg, *George Gissing* (1965), p. 121, makes a valuable double point in noting that when Gissing read Ibsen (about 1888) 'perhaps *Pillars of Society*, *The Wild Duck* and *Ghosts* suggested to him that it was possible to pursue a criticism of society without espousing the cause of the poor'.

PAGE 59

1 'He is parochial, and not of a very large or a very distinguished parish. He is, in that parish, a frequenter chiefly of the hospital and the asylum' (G. E. B. Saintsbury, *The Later Nineteenth Century*, 1907, p. 326).
2 It is interesting that Ludwig Anzengruber was developing the Volksstück in much the same direction as Ibsen just at this time (*Das vierte Gebot*, 1877). Its distinguishing features were the realistic setting, the multiplicity of the personages, usually from the circles of moderately substantial *commerçants* or farmers and, many of them, involved in 'sub-plots', the opportunities given for spectacle and music, as well as the sound morality pretty

plainly inculcated—all as in *Pillars of Society*. One may note that, side by side with the better-known products of the *école de bon sens* in France and Ostrovsky in Russia, experiments were made in the eighteen-seventies for freeing drama from its routine theatricality in countries as widely dispersed as Poland, Italy, Portugal and the Netherlands. A parallel to Anzengruber may be discerned in Henry Arthur Jones, who, hailed a few years later as a pioneer, exemplifies in *The Silver King* (1882) the transition from an English variety of Volksstück to realistic modern drama, dealing with 'problems'. For the technique of Ibsen's later plays see P. F. D. Tennant, *Ibsen's Dramatic Technique* (1948) and J. Northam, *Ibsen's Dramatic Method* (1953).

PAGE 60

1 Published 4 December 1879; produced at the Royal Theatre, Copenhagen, seventeen days later.

PAGE 61

1 See p. 56 above.
2 Centenary Edition, XIV, 449.

PAGE 62

1 *Ibid.* XVII, 449.
2 Ibsen knew the book in Georg Brandes's Danish translation of 1869; Camilla Collett's feminism was also well known to him through her writings and personal intercourse.
3 Written from June to October 1881 and published in December 1881. The first performance was given (in the original text) at the Aurora Hall, Chicago, on 20 May 1882. The following year it was taken into the repertory of the Swedish actor-manager Lindberg, who gave it at the Møllergate Theatre in Christiania on 17 October 1883. The French title *Revenants* renders 'Gen-gangere' better than *Ghosts*.

PAGE 63

1 More might be made of this than is commonly done. Often presented from the start as a doomed melancholic, Osvald is, like his father in youth, a *charmeur*, and his mother's eagerness to preserve in him the joy of life which she is conscious of having by her austerity helped to pervert in his father is thereby explained and adds a nuance to the personal philosophy she has worked out for herself.

2 Bjørnson, long estranged by the 'ambush in the Muses' grove', as he designated *De Unges Forbund*, gallantly leapt to Ibsen's side. But the chief Liberal paper of Christiania, *Dagbladet*, cut his defence of *Gengangere* down to a minimum.

PAGE 64

1 Written with great speed and enjoyment in the spring and summer of 1882; published on 28 November of that year and produced on 13 January 1883 at the Christiania Theater.
2 *Cit.* Koht, *Henrik Ibsen* (1928), II, 199.

PAGE 65

1 Elster had had the historical drama *Eystein Meyla* (which remained in manuscript) acted for one performance in 1863 and during that decade turned out articles and translations for the newspapers; Lie too was involved in journalism in the eighteen-sixties and published a thin volume of unremarkable verse, *Digte*, in 1866.

PAGE 66

1 Bjørnson was for a time its Norwegian co-editor.
2 'Solskyer' (first printed in the Norwegian *Nordisk Tidsskrift* for 1877) presents another tragic case of conscience, in a somewhat higher stratum of rural society.
3 *Farlige Folk* came out after its author's death; it was immediately translated into German (*Gefährliche Leute*).
4 Elster heard Brandes lecture in Copenhagen in 1873, and some letters passed between the two; but they never 'met'.

PAGE 67

1 It is said to be modelled on Christiansund.

PAGE 68

1 This was the feature that perhaps most endeared Elster to Kielland, who rightly saw him as his most obvious precursor. (Lie, it may be observed, a believing Christian, kept clear of this field altogether.)
2 Letter to Elster of 21 August 1879 (M. Borup, *Georg og Edv. Brandes Brevveksling met nordiske Forfattere*, IV, i, Copenhagen, 1939, 379). Elster was a pioneer in translating Turgeniev into Danish. His taste and position in the history of literature are further indicated by his other translations—all appearing in the

Christiania *Aftenblad*, 1867–9—from Spielhagen, Fritz Reuter, Wilkie Collins. The admixture of melodrama in an otherwise realistic story-with-a-purpose is characteristic of Spielhagen.

PAGE 70

1 During this time appeared, besides the novels *En Malstrøm* (1884), *Maisa Jons* (1887) and *Onde Magter* (1890), also †*Trold* (*Ogres*, 2 vols. 1890 and 1891); *Otte Fortællinger* (1884) is mostly old stuff. Other books not mentioned elsewhere are the novels *Naar Sol gaar ned* (1895), *Faste Forland* (1899), *Ulfungerne* (1903) and *Østenfor Sol, Vestenfor Maane* (1905); a second collection of *Digte* (1889) and three equally negligible plays, *Lystige Koner* (1894), *Lindelin* (1897) and *Wulffie & Co.* (1900). The English versions of *Livsslaven* and *Kommandørens Døttre* are entitled *One of Life's Slaves* (1895) and *The Commodore's Daughters* (1892) respectively; eight tales from the first collection of *Trold* and three others by Lie were translated by R. N. Bain as *Weird Tales from the Northern Seas* (1893).

2 But his wife prodded him into reading current French fiction during the eighteen-eighties.

3 The disclaimer may be taken with a grain of salt. As a young man Lie was credited with the almost unbelievable feat of knowing most of Wergeland's monstrous *Skabelsen-Mennesket-Messias* off by heart.

4 Camilla Collett in her turn enthusiastically hailed *The Pilot and his Wife* for carrying on her feminist mission (*auct.* Garborg, *Jonas Lie*, p. 192).

PAGE 73

1 Lie's conscientiousness is well illustrated in the letter he wrote to Ragna Nielsen about *Niobe* (17 January 1894): 'The book is directed at the whole difficult period—the decade of the disturbance over Christiania's "Bohemia" [cf. pp. 102 f. above]. In the distress of the time all literature is filled with the cry of the children. But the decade would not be thoroughly sifted if the mothers' despair and grief were trodden underfoot beneath the heel of silence. The entire cultural atmosphere of our country and the decade would be missed or become a one-sided, untruthful tradition for posterity if art did not take *that* side too.'

PAGE 76

1 Its tenor was anticipated in the short story 'Slagter-Tobias' (first printed in *Nyt Tidsskrift*, 1882, p. 513, and included in *Otte*

Fortællinger, 1885) which succinctly describes the hand-to-mouth existence, on the brink of famine, of a rural proletarian and his family. It is grim, but not uniformly depressing: Tobias is a plucky fellow, occasional kindnesses are done him, and, it is reported, he finally makes good in the stockyards of Chicago.

2 Lie was accused of plagiarizing another novel of a bastard preyed upon by his mother, Daudet's *Jack* (1876); he declared on his honour in a public letter (Christiania *Dagblad*, 1883, no. 226) that when he wrote his book he had never read Daudet's book.

PAGE 77

1 Norwegian *Slave* = convict; *livsslave* is one under sentence of penal servitude for life.

2 He acknowledged its existence, however, and called it by that name (letter to Hegel of 15 April 1880).

PAGE 78

1 This was caused by the *Sædelighedsfejden*, the row about marital morals, when Lie threw in his lot against the rigorous sexual puritanism and intolerance preached by Bjørnson, who was enraged by the strong hint conveyed in Lie's *Maisa Jons* that the heroine, a poor seamstress, would have been better off in every way if she had not preserved her chastity for her brute of a husband.

2 *Samtiden*, LV (Oslo, 1946), 240.

3 One marvels at J. Wiehr's statement in *Journal of English and Germanic Philology* (XXVIII, 1929, 42): 'Lie was never a moralist.'

PAGE 79

1 *Ibsen and the Temper of Norwegian Literature* (1960), p. 97. The reference to Nordland envisages the poetry of Petter Dass (1647–1707). The claim that Lie wrote the 'first love novels' passes over *The Sheriff's Daughters*.

PAGE 80

1 At this critical time, when Alphonse Daudet appeared the rising star of modern prose literature, both were impressed by *Fromont jeune et Risler aîné*.

PAGE 81

1 His personal contacts with Georg Brandes were slight; their correspondence did not begin till 1880.

2 By unusual good luck we have Kielland's bookshop-accounts (G. Gran, *A. L. Kielland og hans Samtid*, 1923, p. 147); he bought several copies of Mill's books, clearly to give away. He acquired also Herbert Spencer's *Education*, works by Spinoza, Hartmann, Bostrøm, Darwin, Haeckel and German biblical critics, as well as some general histories of thought. There is no evidence that he knew Buckle, who would have delighted him.

3 Stavanger had a population of about 20,000 at this time.

4 The novels are: *Garman & Worse* (1880), *Arbeidsfolk* (1881), *Else* (1881), *Skipper Worse* (1882), *Gift* (1883), *Fortuna* (1884), *Sne* (1886), *Sankt Hans Fest* (1887), *Jacob* (1891).

PAGE 82

1 Kielland wrote two *proverbes*, of little interest, included in *For Scenen* (1880). The first of these 'Paa Hjemveien' actually preceded the *Novelletter* by a few months (*Nyt Tidsskrift*, III, 1878). Ten years later he turned out a number of plays which had some success on the stage, but fall infinitely below the level of his fiction. I cannot recollect that he mentions Musset anywhere.

2 'Erotik og Idyl' and 'Balstemning' are in the first collection of *Novelletter*, 'Torvmyr' and 'En Skipperhistorie' in the *Nye Novelletter*. Almost all Kielland's Novelletter are translated by W. Archer or R. L. Cassie in *Tales of Two Countries* (1891) and *Norse Tales and Sketches* (1896) respectively.

PAGE 83

1 Letter to G. Brandes of 6 November 1884 (*Samlede Verker*, XII, p. 172).

2 W. Keilhau, *Det Norske Folks Liv og Historie*, x (Oslo, 1935), 167, rightly observes that it also provided the 'almost too obvious' model for Thomas Mann's *Buddenbrooks*.

3 *Mutatis mutandis* it is Stavanger; but the name is never given.

PAGE 85

1 Kielland also noted this phenomenon when writing the much harsher *Arbeidsfolk* and very frankly put it down to the pull against doctrinaire *tendens* which his projection of the actual scene continually exerted.

2 The English term is used.

PAGE 86

1 1771–1824.

PAGE 87

1 A right-minded professor of Hygiene and Pharmacology had declared that subversive books like *Arbeidsfolk* should have a warning label attached, and Kielland obliged him with this title, which is also a saturnine pun; 'Gift' means 'Poison', but also 'married', and the story of the book is in good part concerned with a disastrous marriage.

2 As Stavanger had notably experienced in a great crash of 1882.

PAGE 89

1 This was an incident in the 'Bohême-fejden' described on pp. 102 f. Kielland had refused to involve himself in it and thereby lost much radical support.

2 The Affair (1885–7) is admirably summarized by Gran (*op. cit.* pp. 222 ff.). One of the most influential speakers against Kielland was Lars Oftedal, member of Parliament for Stavanger and holder of a benefice in that city. His character and activities (with which Knut Hamsun dealt faithfully in his pamphlet *Lars Oftedal*, 1889) were very much the same as those of Morten Kruse in *Sankt Hans Fest*. Kielland had the last laugh (but suppressed it) when, from fear of exposure, Oftedal, in 1892, was driven publicly to confess to infamous practices with young girls under his charge. (Cf. E. Ryngestad in *Samtiden*, LXXIV, 381.)

3 He renounced it when Kielland's was refused.

PAGE 90

1 Cf. O. Storstein, 'Hvorfor kunde ikke Kiellands Produktivitet overleve 80-årene?', *Edda*, XXXI, 241.

2 The distinguished Swedish critic Lamm, who elaborates the parallel (already drawn by Georg Brandes) between *Jacob* and *Au Bonheur des Dames*, thinks that Kielland, if he continued to write, could now only do so in Zola's manner and realized that it did not suit him (*Festskrift til Francis Bull*, Oslo, 1937, p. 170).

PAGE 91

1 *Samlede Verker*, VI (1949), 166.

2 *Ibid.* I (1949), 377.

PAGE 92

1 *Sne* is the only novel unconnected with the rest. Even *Arbeidsfolk*, where the scene is never laid in Stavanger, figures Delphin, Fanny Garman's paramour, among the Christiania bureaucrats, and Lauritz Seehus, one of the emigrants to America in the end,

is the man loved by the unhappy Henriette in *Skipper Worse*. *Gift, Fortuna* and *Sankt Hans Festen* are very closely linked through Abraham Løvdahl, whose progressive deformation is a prominent theme in all. Even in *Jacob*, which deals with a different social stratum from the other 'contemporary' novels, Bankchef Christensen plays as important a part as in *Fortuna*. Cf. A. M. Sturtevant 'The Chronology of Events in Kielland's Novels', *Scandinavian Studies and Notes*, xii (Menasha, 1933), 101.

2 Letter to Bjørnson of 22 May 1890.

3 In Elster he recognized a precursor; he venerated Bjørnson for his loyalty and courage, and stood in (hushed) awe of Ibsen ('Mesteren' in *Tilskueren*, xii, Copenhagen, 1896, 502). He acclaimed Strindberg's *Röda Rummet* (cf. F. Bull, 'Kielland og Strindberg' in *Samtiden*, lviii, 1949, 96 ff.) and loved Jacobsen as a man and the author of *Pesten i Bergamo*. Georg Brandes excepted, however, he owed nothing to his northern contemporaries. His women characters (Wenche, Dr Løvdahl's wife, in *Gift*, unloved by her husband, deceived in her lover and defeated in her efforts to save her son from the constrictions of convention, is the most fully drawn, but her fate remains secondary to the theme) mostly have a hard time of it, apart from old 'bodies' like the mothers of Jacob Worse and Morten Kruse; but he was no campaigner for the Woman's Cause from whom Camilla Collett could derive great joy.

PAGE 93

1 One of the plays, the unsuccessful *Fjeldmennesker* (*Highlanders*, 1889), was written in collaboration with Erik Skram.

PAGE 94

1 Strindberg and his plays were well known in Copenhagen around 1890.

2 Refused by more eminent theatres, it was briefly presented at Bergen and the Dagmar Theatre of Copenhagen when new. It was revived at the Norwegian National Theatre in 1910 and again in 1937 and 1962.

3 So great that, it is said, Amalie Skram's radical friends, for fear of compromising their party, tried to dissuade her from publishing until after the next general election.

4 Even Kielland thought fit (though privately) to compare the two: he never could stomach Fru Skram's vulgarity of manners and expression.

PAGE 95

1 Published in the collection *Kjærlighed i Nord og Syd* (1891).

2 The phrase was first used in Arne Garborg's review of *Constance Ring* (*Nyt Tidsskrift*, IV, 1885, 377) and, by an extreme extension, has been applied to Amalie Skram herself. On the latter point there is no evidence at all. E. Øberg (in *Samtiden*, LV, Oslo, 1946, 418) declares (what others have hinted at) that Amalie Skram had much sexual experience outside wedlock. It is interesting to note that her first piece of journalism (in *Bergens Tidende*, no. 41, 1877) was a review of Jacobsen's novel *Fru Marie Grubbe* (1876), the heroine of which affords a psycho-pathological 'case' akin to Constance Ring's; and also that her husband-to-be, Erik Skram, in the novel *Gertrude Coldbjørnsøn* (1879), rather gingerly presented a woman who bolted after the nuptial night. At the relevant time Amalie Skram could not know Tolstoi's *Kreutzer Sonata*. Bjørnson's *Magnhild* (1877) had presented a wife who finds her husband repulsive.

PAGE 96

1 At the end of her life, Amalie Skram's 'imperative' weakened. She thought Scandinavian-Teutonic convention made too much of love as a prerequisite of successful marriage and that 'they order this matter better in France' (B. Krane, *Amalie Skram og Kvinnens Problem*, 1951, p. 58).

2 It first appeared in *Nyt Tidsskrift*, I (1882), 557, and was reprinted in the volume *Forraadt* (1892), where it is dated 1883. Lie's *Lifer* (see pp. 76 f. above) came a little later.

3 To Venner is the name of a ship, S. G. Myre a name on a shop-front.

4 An odd one too. Lucie is a Christiania Tivoli-walker, and she dies wretchedly. But before that she is made in every sense an honest woman, her death is attributable in no way to her prostitution and her (intermittent) unhappiness in the married state mainly to her husband's unjustified jealousy.

5 A sequel to *Afkom* was intended, but never written.

PAGE 97

1 In an obituary notice (*Den 17de Mai*, 13 March 1905) Garborg wrote: 'Ho var den einaste som heilt ut var det me den tid alle vilde vera, naturalist. Men ho var det paa sin eigen maate, kunde ikkje herme.'

2 A. Tiberg, *Amalie Skram som Kunster og Menneske* (Kristiania, 1910), p. 79.

3 Like Zola, Amalie Skram had a strong puritan strain; but hers is firmly grounded in the Old Testament; sin and the requital of sin meant more to her than genetics.

PAGE 99

1 First printed anonymously in *Fedraheimen*.

PAGE 100

1 He does not throw her over, however; he reappears as an unhappily married clergyman in *Mannfolk*.
2 The story's being laid sufficiently far back in time to represent Vinje as still alive has no significance.

PAGE 102

1 The original text was re-issued, with an introduction, by O. Eidem (Oslo, 1950). Jæger defined 'Bohême' as 'the world of the homeless'.
2 In the 1950 edition, I, 215.

PAGE 103

1 When a collection of his writings, *Kampen for Tilværelsen* (*The Struggle for Existence*, 4 vols. 1919) was in contemplation, it was considered prudent to have it printed in Copenhagen; but no steps were taken against its importation into Norway. For the vicissitudes of the book cf. A. Thuesen, *Krohg's 'Albertine'* (Oslo, 1926). Krohg's veridic exposures undoubtedly contributed to the abolition of police control over prostitutes in 1893.
2 The history of this sub-chapter in Norwegian literature is as tangled and bedevilled with semi-irrelevances as Jæger's novel and his defence before the Supreme Court (included in the republication of *Fra Kristiania-Bohêmen*, 1950). It is not identical, but obviously interlocked with the *Sædelighedsfejde*, sparked off by Bjørnson's *Hanske* (September 1883, cf. p. 28 above) and warmed up again by his lecture on Monogamy and Polygamy, first delivered in November 1887, where the categorical imperative is 'one man, one woman (his wife)'; the position he had taken up made it extremely difficult for him to intervene in the row over *Fra Kristiania-Bohêmen* and *Albertine*, though it came to touch on the principle of free speech to which normally he would have given energetic support. As, on the one hand, this became a political issue (see pp. 88 ff. above), notably in the debates on granting a state pension to Kielland, who had, as it happened, provided

the first specimen of 'prostitution-literature' with *Else* (late 1881), so, on the other hand, *En Hanske* is related to the 'wife–husband' debates begun with Ibsen's *Dukkehjem* (1879) and *Gengangere* (1881) and given a new twist by Amalie Skram's *Constance Ring* (1885) and her subsequent novels; among these *Lucie* (1888) can be reckoned a direct contribution also to the *Bohême-fejde*. Garborg had said his say also in the earlier phase of these debates with the short story 'Ungdom' ('Youth') (autumn 1884, included in *Forteljingar og Sogur*), which made fun of the stern thesis advanced in *En Hanske*. Garborg took the ill-advised step of complaining to the ministry of Justice that no prosecution had been instituted against him for *Mannfolk*; he consequently lost his position in the government audit department.

3 Fanny Holmsen's story is told separately in *Hjaa Ho Mor* (1890), a novel coming between *Mannfolk* and *Trætte Mænd*. (It was first published in the Danish translation *Hos Mamma* in 1889.) Fanny Holmsen is also broken by Gram's imbecility, finds that she detests her husband, fails to nerve herself to the suicide she intended and takes to religion. One of Garborg's weakest performances, *Hjaa Ho Mor* was most enthusiastically received in Germany.

4 'De trætte gaar til Præsten' (*Skrifter i Samling*, III, 226).

5 *Ibid.* I, 328.

PAGE 104

1 Before the Christiania Studentersamfundet he had given the lecture 'Betegner den moderne Naturalisme i Poesien et Fremskridt eller et Forfald' in 1881; in 1891 he wrote a series of articles for the Christiania newspaper *Dagbladet* on 'Den idealistiske Reaktion'.

2 *Die Überwindung des Naturalismus* (1891).

3 See p. 146 above.

4 Garborg wrote a play, *Uforsonlige* (*Irreconcilables*, 1888) around a political situation analogous to the actual parliamentary crisis of the time, dealing with the salving of the government party by careful manoeuvring and the consequent rout of honest radical journalists. A little too diffuse, it embodies its theme in an interesting and satisfying manner; but, it was too 'actual' to be acted.

5 George's *Progress and Poverty* (1879, translated into Norwegian, 1886) advocated a redistribution of wealth through a single tax on land. Garborg's advocacy of physiocratic principles did not begin until a little later, but his first essays on both Nietzsche and Tolstoy date from 1890.

PAGE 105

1 He rather grotesquely justifies this under the proviso that no pleasure of any kind is involved.

PAGE 107

1 They are connected with the Christiania novels too: Daniel Braut of *Bondestudentar* and *Mannfolk* is the new parish priest who joins in the persecution of Paulus Hòve.

2 *Lærar* or *Lærer* is more narrowly used to designate a lay-preacher at private gatherings. The play had to wait for production until 1914 when there was a Landsmaal theatre, Det norske Teatret, to present it.

PAGE 108

1 Garborg based his case on extensive theological reading; the weightier of his articles he printed together in *Den burtkomne Messias* (*The Lost Messiah*, 1908, not in the collected editions), in which the main conclusion was that all the Churches had denied Christ and that the difference between Roman Catholicism and Protestantism was the difference between Purgatory and Hell.

PAGE 110

1 At this time, at any rate, Garborg did not know the *Divina Commedia* except by hearsay. Such literary influences as may be traced in *I Helheim* were those of the *Draumkvæde* and other pre-Christian poetry of the north. On the theme see Y. Agren, *Edda*, LXVIII (1958), 271.

2 How influential it was, outside the linguistic field, is not easy to assess; it was certainly in no wise comparable in effect with Bjørnson's. A considerable portion only reached a comparatively small public, which certainly listened to him, but even within it there were many whom his radical propaganda on all fronts, including republicanism, repelled.

3 For a similar reason most of the dialogue of *Uforsonlige* must be accounted Riksmaal too.

PAGE 111

1 He was somewhat singular in his camp for maintaining that the Danish connexion had been to Norway's advantage.

2 *Fedraheimen* (1878), *Den 17de Mai* (1894) and *Syn og Segn* (1895).

3 In which he showed himself familiar with linguistic controversies simultaneously taking place in Flanders, Finland and other countries.

4 Either singly or in collaboration he was responsible for translations of the *Odyssee*, *Ramayana*, *The Merchant of Venice* and *Macbeth*, *Georges Dandin*, *Jeppe paa Bjerget* and *Den politiske Kandestøber*; he helped A. M. S. Arctander with his Landsmaal translation of Goethe's *Faust*.

5 Fundamentally the issue was decided in the schools, where Landsmaal was made permissive already in 1879, and in the Teachers' Training Colleges with their strong peasant-clientele, where it was made a compulsory subject in 1892.

6 This has already begun to happen.

PAGE 112

1 The artificiality of Aasen's language is disconcertingly illustrated by Garborg himself, when, already in possession of his mature faculties, eager and brought up entirely in a part of the country whose locutions were closely akin to those on which Aasen drew, it took him a whole summer to learn it (J. A. Dale, *Arne Garborgs Språk og Stil*, p. 31, quoting from Garborg's *Knudaheibrev*).

2 They were greatly helped by a man of very different provenance and background from theirs, Moltke Moe (1859–1913), the son of Asbjørnsen's colleague Jørgen Moe; he became the first professor of Norske Folkemaal in the University of Christiania in 1886.

PAGE 115

1 Something about the Landsmaal theatre is said on p. 138 above.

PAGE 116

1 Written in the spring and summer, published in November, of 1884. In the copious preliminary notes, a wild duck does not figure. The first production was at Bergen, 9 January 1885. Friends and foes alike were baffled and, for the most part, repelled. It was not until well on into the twentieth century that it was frequently acted or esteemed as a masterpiece.

2 *The Master Builder* would come under fire next. But there is no reason why Solness's work-room and assistants should not be as untidy and shabby as those of many a high-class solicitor near Lincoln's Inn Fields; his wife's drawing-room is 'prettily furnished', the house stands in its own grounds; whether the community be that of a country town or a suburb of Christiania, its owner is a not inconsiderable member of it. A rapid perusal of Ibsen's stage-directions would show that, outside *Vildanden*, all the personages of his modern plays live 'in easy circumstances'.

PAGE II7

1 We have here one of numerous key-words or phrases which are, unhappily, untranslatable. The word Hjalmar uses (*uvedkommende* or interlopers) is that which occurs in the Norwegian equivalent to 'No admittance except on business'.

PAGE II8

1 R. Lothar, *Henrik Ibsen* (2nd ed. 1902), p. 126.

PAGE I20

1 Begun, first as *Hvide Heste*, in the late spring of 1886, finished and published that autumn—two years later, it may be noticed, than the resolution of the political crisis. After long absence, Ibsen visited Norway in the summer of 1885, staying mainly at Molde (which was to provide the setting for *Fruen fra Havet*); there he met the Swedish poet Count Snoilsky, who gave him suggestions for the character of Rosmer.

PAGE I2I

1 These words are taken from one of the few public speeches Ibsen made, to a Working Men's Association at Trondheim on 14 June 1885. There can be no doubt of Ibsen's fundamental sympathy with Rosmer, ideals and all.
2 H. Jæger, *Life of Henrik Ibsen*, Eng. trans. (1890), p. 230.
3 On a postcard to some inquiring schoolboys (*cit.* Centenary Edition x, 338).

PAGE I22

1 Somewhat oddly, it may appear today, early English critics of Ibsen often likened him to Thackeray: both, writing in a 'bourgeois' society, were exposers of shams and hypocrisies (a reason why Thackeray is highly esteemed in Russia). Since *Vanity Fair* was reasonably well known on the continent, it seems to me not wildly improbable that Ibsen took his heroine's name from Becky Sharp. It may be worth mentioning that this love-story was written well before its author met Emilie Bardach, who is often held responsible for the erotic element in *Hedda Gabler* and *Bygmester Solness* (cf. p. 244 below).

PAGE I25

1 *Fruen fra Havet* was written in the summer of 1888, published in November that year and simultaneously produced on 12 February 1889 at the Christiania Theater and the Hoftheater, Weimar.

2 An actual case like Ellida Wangel's, which may in part have come to Ibsen's notice, was described in William Preyer's *Ein merkwürdiger Fall von Fascination* (1895).

3 *Hedda Gabler* was written in the late summer and early autumn and published just before Christmas, 1890, the earliest performance being that which Ibsen himself attended at the Residenztheater, Munich, on 31 January 1891.

PAGE 126

1 This is sometimes disputed; but in one of his preliminary notes Ibsen marked it as an overriding factor; it is touched on very early in the play, and the later discreet hints would be mere mystification if one were not to assume the reality.

2 *Lille Eyolf*, written between June and October and published on 11 December 1894, was given a performance by English amateurs at the Haymarket Theatre, London, before publication, the first professional production being that at the Deutsche Theater, Berlin, on 12 January 1895.

PAGE 127

1 The last two chapters of *The Quintessence of Ibsenism*, first published in 1892, were added in the edition of 1913.

2 Written mostly in the summer of 1892 and published on 12 December. The earliest performances were by English amateurs at the Haymarket Theatre, London, on 7 December 1892 and by a company of Danish professionals at Trondheim on 19 January 1893.

PAGE 128

1 The most disturbing of these *revenants* was Laura Kieler, a friend of twenty-five years ago, whose mischances had provided material for *Et Dukkehjem*. On this see B. M. Kinck, 'Henrik Ibsen og Laura Kieler', *Edda*, xxxv (1935), 498, summarized in my *Study of Six Plays by Ibsen* (1950), pp. 125 and 184.

2 The best known of these love-affairs was that with young Emilie Bardach, who suggested traits for Hedda Gabler and the Hilde Wangel of *Bygmester Solness* (cf. B. King, 'Ibsen and Emilie Bardach', *Century Magazine*, New York, 1923, p. 803); there were about the same time other flirtations, as Fru Ibsen chose to consider them. For Hamsun's programme see pp. 148 f., above.

1 To be sure, the excursionists in *Naar Vi Døde Vaagner* have strayed rather far afield and the last short act of snow-strewn fir-wood by night, with its mobile stage-set, in *John Gabriel Borkman*, has as much superficial romanticism as one could wish for.

2 *John Gabriel Borkman* was written in the summer and autumn of 1896 and published on 15 December; the first performances were in London (English amateurs at Haymarket Theatre), 14 December 1896, and Helsinki (Swedish-speaking professionals), 10 January 1897.

1 There are several parallels between *John Gabriel Borkman* and *Vildanden*, which was originally planned to centre on Hjalmar's ambition to redeem the family name, tarnished through the conviction of his father and (no doubt) his 'betrayal' by an associate who continued to prosper like Grossere Werle.

2 There is more than one suggestion that Hilde should be regarded as pathologically deranged. On Solness, in the agitation wrought in him by Hilde, the verdict perhaps might just be that 'the balance of his mind was disturbed'.

1 Ibsen's habitual two-year cycle of work having been interrupted by the celebrations of his seventieth birthday in 1898, *Naar Vi Døde Vaagner* was written between February and November 1899, first acted, in London, on 16 December and published on 19 December of the same year. The earliest professional performance was at Stuttgart on 26 January 1900.

1 Some play is made with the fact that when he saw a performance of *Brand* for his seventieth birthday, Ibsen wept (e.g. by A. Fibiger, *Henrik Ibsen en Studie over Guds-Linien i hans Liv*, Copenhagen, 1928, p. 18). Tears can be a sign of repentance; but 'what a genius I had then' is no palinode.

2 The title-page called *Naar Vi Døde Vaagner* 'en dramatisk Epilog': whether it is an epilogue to Ibsen's whole life's work or to the trilogy *Solness–Borkman–Naar Vi Døde Vaagner* is disputed. What Ibsen meant when he said he would go on to something 'quite new' is unascertainable; he suffered his first stroke immediately after the publication of *Naar Vi Døde Vaagner*.

PAGE 133

1 The playhouse was actually built and (with a Danish troupe) run for the first season by the Swedish impresario Strömberg, who then handed it over to a syndicate of Norwegian backers. Strömberg had previously inaugurated (1816) a short-lived experiment at Trondheim. This had been the first regular professional theatre in the country. From the end of the eighteenth century onwards, there had been amateur theatricals on an extensive scale in the principal towns, and Danish strollers had begun to tour the country, as they did throughout the nineteenth century. It was to these that Ibsen (at Skien) and Bjørnson (at Molde) owed their first acquaintance with the stage. Strömberg's house in the Theatergate, Christiania, was soon burned down and its place taken in 1837 by a new building in Bankpladsen.

PAGE 134

1 Plays by Holberg, Wessel, P. L. Heiberg, Hauch, etc., were included in the repertoire of the Christiania Theater, but may be said to have got there via Copenhagen. On Andreas Munch see p. 9 above.

2 P. Botten Hansen, *La Norvège littéraire* (1867). The earliest in his list should be singled out *honoris causa*, *Fjeldeventyret* (1824), a musical comedy with much Norwegian local colour by Henrik Anker Bjerregaard.

PAGE 135

1 Its coach was Knud Knudsen, the philologist who through a long life (1812-95) successfully laboured to regularize and codify the Riksmaal emerging from the old Dano-Norwegian.

2 It could not, and did not, attempt to vie with the Copenhagen house's great tradition in opera and (most notably) ballet, whose history in Norway is scrappy and insignificant until the twentieth century.

3 At this time the translations were preponderantly of Parisian boulevard successes; comparable German plays were gradually coming in, and the proportion of new Danish plays slowly diminished. It may be of interest to note that in this not untypical season of 1867-8 the stock company presented fifty-eight plays, alternating on the usual continental repertory system; they were exactly divided between one-acters and longer plays; 45 had been given before, either 'carries-over' from the preceding season or 'revivals'.

PAGE 136

1 The outstanding success during all its seventy-one years was N. Rolfsen's 'Christmas Play', *Svein Uræd* (1890), with song, dance and spectacle, which was given fifty times in the first year of its production.

2 Bjørnson wrote no play while he was engaged at Bergen.

PAGE 137

1 Even at the end of its time, the average 'run' of a production was less than ten performances, just about double what it had been in 1863, when there was a public for no more than four nights a week.

2 In its first season it made up its repertoire as follows: three plays by Holberg, four by Ibsen (including *Gengangere* and *Naar Vi Døde Vaagner*, never done at the Christiania Theater), four by Bjørnson, Heiberg's *Harald Svans Mor* (*première*) and one play each by Hulda Garborg and the foreigners Shakespeare, Hostrup, Moser, Halm (*Voldemar*), Villetard & Belot, Sardou, Drachmann, Benzon and Hartleben; four of the latter were taken over from the Christiania Theater.

3 It might be noted, however, that the Christiania Theater had given Russian plays (Gogol, Turgeniev) before 1890.

4 His father, before the days of his puritanism, had done the same with Offenbach's *Belle Hélène*.

PAGE 138

1 Christiania Theater did in fact mount Aasen's *Ervingen* when it was relatively new.

PAGE 139

1 Hamsun's *Ved Rigets Port* proved a false dawn.

PAGE 140

1 Helge Krog (born 1889) might be bracketed with him.

2 Even the more liberal National Theater did not put on his most celebrated play, *Balkonen*, until twenty-three years after its publication.

3 A pioneer in this was the otherwise negligible playwright G. A. Dahl (1855–87), in his *Eva* (1879, produced as *Fru Faber* in 1881).

PAGE 141

1 *Cit.* E. Skavlan, *Gunnar Heiberg* (1950), p. 255. An innate moralism, none the less, appears in the definition: Heiberg could not leave 'mankind' out of it.

2 Needless to say, there was no love lost between these two cudgel-players. Bjørnson publicly opposed a state-grant to Heiberg and (not unjustifiably) stigmatized *Kjærlighetens Tragedie* as 'profound twaddle' (*dybsindig vås*).

PAGE 142

1 'Om at være i sandhet', speech to Studentersamfundet, 31 October 1877.

PAGE 143

1 This in itself naturally caused no indignation: but invented behaviour of the dead man's family cast a slur on those of Ibsen and Bjørnson (whose 'cases' plainly provided the starting-point) which was quite unjustified, especially with regard to the former, who at the time had protested energetically at the interferences with their private concerns which they were powerless to repel.

2 *Cit.* A. Schouw, *Samtiden*, XLVIII (1937), 463.

PAGE 144

1 Christen Dreyer Collin (1857–1926), professor of European Literature at Christiania from 1914, the friend and biographer of Bjørnson, was a champion of Tolstoy and of British moralists such as Carlyle, Ruskin and Herbert Spencer. His *Kunsten og Moralen*, which first brought him to the public eye, is dated 1894.

PAGE 145

1 The title is the only link with *Kjærlighetens Komedie*. In *Kjærlighetens Tragedie* there is no verse, champagne takes the place of tea, it is not at all an attempt to show what would have happened if Svanhild had in fact accepted Falk.

2 What must be construed as attempts at poetry are even more disastrous: e.g. the preposterous fustian with which Hadeln thinks fit to console a man whose wife has just committed suicide: 'Vær stolt Erling Kruse. Sæt et Kors paa din dør. Et blodig Kors. For Kjærligheten har hjemsøkt dit hus.'

PAGE 147

1 Except to the limited extent that Garborg used Landsmaal for presenting the lives of the *intelligentia*.

2 One of the chief grumblers at this time was Carl Nærup (1864–1931), later to become an influential reviewer and a notable defender of the young school that had come to maturity when he published his *Skildringer og Stemninger fra den yngre Literatur* in 1897. A more conservative critic of his generation was Hjalmar Christensen (1869–1925), who also ventured unsuccessfully into original writing (cf. *Unge Nordmænd*, 1893, and *Vort litterære Liv*, 1902).

PAGE 148

1 *Röda Rummet* (1879) and some of the short stories that followed had already become fairly well known, to Kielland especially.

2 There the great poetic tradition from the beginning of the century had never been broken and still had one of its most eminent representatives in Holger Drachmann. Nevertheless after their long predominance in Norway Danish belles-lettres had come to the 'receiving-end' where imaginative literature was concerned; in the quarter-century after *Brand*, it is said, ten Norwegian books were read in Denmark to one Danish book read in Norway.

3 This vast and complicated subject is exhaustively treated in H. Beyer, *Nietzsche og Norden* (2 vols. Bergen, 1958–9). Brandes began his propaganda for Nietzsche with a course of lectures on him in Copenhagen in 1888.

4 All the major authors, with the exception named, rejected Nietzsche's teaching, especially that of the Superman, for whom, in *John Gabriel Borkman*, Ibsen coined the equivalent Super-Scoundrel (*over-skurk*), though he strongly objected to dismissing Nietzsche as a mere devil (H. Beyer, *Nietzsche og Norden*, II, 1959, 29).

5 After several short-lived pioneers, *Samtiden*, founded in 1890 and still flourishing today, was the first lasting literary forum in the country; its editor Gerhard Gran was an open-minded don, but it was not the intention that *Samtiden* should be an *avant-garde* organ.

PAGE 149

1 Bjørnson, who believed the most strongly in literature as an applied art, was the most leniently treated and, in general, kept the allegiance of *les jeunes* most firmly, even when he poured public scorn on them. Interpreting the term very variously, all the men of the 'nineties professed to adore *vitality*, and of that quality they rightly saw in him the supreme exemplar.

2 Reproduced in T. Hamsun (ed.), *Paa Turné* (1960), facing p. 96.

PAGE 150

1 *Fra Gutt til Mann* (1932) and *Oplevelser* (1934).

PAGE 152

1 The evanescence of his reputation is attested by his complete omission from the last part of Halvorsen's great *bibliographie raisonée*, published in 1904. On the other hand it should be recorded that, writing as late as 1946 (*Samtiden*, LV, 241), Sigrid Undset referred to him as, of recent times, 'Norges største dikter' *tout court*; her criteria are not very clear, but, significantly, one of them is what links Vogt with the literature predominant in his youth, a concern for the oppressed and unjustly treated. In the essay referred to, Sigrid Undset does not mention Obstfelder.

PAGE 153

1 The low-toned quality, skirting bathos so closely as to prompt parody, is not confined to love-poems: cf. the beginning of 'Adieu':

> Min svibel er syg.
> Den hænger med hodet.
> O gid jeg kunde gjæte dine tanker, hyazinth!
> Ønsker du mindre vand?   (*Samlede Skrifter*, I, 65)

2 The poems here referred to are on pp. 46, 10, 67 and 20 respectively of *Samlede Skrifter*, I.

3 It is clear that as reproductive beings women were altogether abhorrent to Obstfelder; there could be no stronger antidote to desire than the prose-poem 'Bugen' ('The Belly', *ibid.* p. 75); the heroine of *Korset* laments that women have breasts.

4 Maeterlinck's *Aveugles* and *Princesse Maleine* had appeared in Danish translations in 1891 and 1892 respectively.

5 From *Korset* (*Samlede Skrifter*, II, 56).

PAGE 154

1 Vol. I (1890), 460.

2 Vilhelm Krag was the pioneer in Norway in the composition of prose-poems, which had been invented in France (Baudelaire's *Petits Poèmes en Prose*, 1869) and given renewed popularity by the impressionistic technique of Maeterlinck and Georges Rodenbach.

PAGE 155

1 His biographer in *Norsk Biografisk Leksikon* hazards that his most important poem is 'O Sørland, du min Moderjord', which he significantly calls a hymn to that district.

2 See pp. 108 ff. and 112 ff. above.

3 Vogt, Krag and Obstfelder (as well as the other authors discussed in this chapter) wrote in the traditional literary language: of Obstfelder, indeed, one may say that he was the last Norwegian author of eminence to write pure Danish.

PAGE 156

1 Four acts, prose, not acted till 1928.

PAGE 158

1 Egge's *Minner fra Barndom og Ungdom* (1948), p. 207.

2 'En Ensom' was published in the volume *Noveller* (1892).

PAGE 159

1 The title is taken from the hooting of an owl off-stage, which symbolizes the hero's sickness of mind.

2 His first novel was *Jon Graff* (1891). *Frank Hjelm, Historien om en Hjemløs* (1912) is largely autobiography. Thomas, like Vilhelm, took to the celebration of the Sørland.

3 With 'Den moderne Litteratur og dens Forhold til Sædeligheden'.

4 It was extensively rewritten for production (unsuccessful) at the National Theatre in 1909.

5 It might be said that Krag was playing Rostand to Obstfelder's Maeterlinck.

PAGE 160

1 Troops wear armour, but use firearms.

PAGE 161

1 The word used in the Norwegian translation of Numbers xvi. 9 corresponds to copper, which may, of course, profoundly affect the interpretation.

PAGE 162

1 The three centuries when Norway was a Danish colony had been commonly swept aside as a period of sterile degradation until the historian Ernst Sars had begun a work of rehabilitation, notably in his *Udsigt over den Norske Historie* (1873–91). Kristofer Janson (1841–1917) had published a historical novel in Landsmaal *Fra Danske Tidi* in 1875.

2 Cancelliraad was a title accorded to meritorious civil servants. Weydahl is a fictitious character.

PAGE 163

1 Norwegian literature of this kind, in Landsmaal and in Riksmaal, is no worse in these respects than the parallel products abundant in other countries at this time, the German-speaking lands, for instance, or Scotland with its 'kailyard school'.

2 He wrote another novel, to some extent autobiographical, *Mot Kveld* (1900), in which his best qualities are drowned in fantastic, even apocalyptic pictures and in much seriously meant, but unconvincing 'psychology'.

3 Aanrud's fiction and plays are published as *Samlede Verker* (3 vols. 1943). He wrote no novel.

PAGE 164

1 'Simon Venaasen' and 'Ane-Petter' were published in *Fra Svipop til Venaasen* (1892); the other two stories are 'Hvorledes Vaarherre fikk Høiet til Asmund Borgemellem' and 'Brødre i Herren' in *Fortællinger* (1891).

2 *Hanen* is an apocalyptic play about the fate of some of the characters after death, when they fare much better than parsons and professors of divinity. It takes its title from the golden cock which, much to his annoyance, the heavenly authorities have set up outside the lodge of their porter, Peter, to keep him reminded of his own back-sliding.

3 A minor humorist of the time was Jacob Hilditch (1864–1930), the first of whose collections of tales, *Under Norsk Flag*, came out in 1889 and whose great popularity is mainly sustained by *Trangviksposten*, a most amusing 'spoof' small-town newspaper, which he issued for seven years (1900–7). The very prolific Jacob Breda Bull (1853–1930), whose fiction was collected as *Samlede Folkelivsbilleder og Nutidsromaner* (12 vols. 1937–8), began as a humorist, but, after his anti-Ibsenite play *Uden Ansvar* (1890), took himself seriously as a playwright, poet and fiction-writer of strongly reactionary views and very humble quality.

PAGE 165

1 Hamsun, however, was not only helpful, but sympathetic towards the tougher brethren, though he can hardly be said to have made common cause with them. The robuster poets who came forward fifteen or twenty years later met with his approval.

2 For the sake of his overflowing vitality, both were devoted admirers of Bjørnson. He was the only older Norwegian author for whom Hamsun had a good word. Kinck was on terms of friendship

with him, with Lie (and with Hamsun); he admired the work
of Garborg and Amalie Skram and always put Ibsen *hors concours*;
but his work owed nothing to any of these.

PAGE 166

1 It is remarkable (and significant) how little Kinck, Italy being
one of his 'subjects', has to say about the antique Romans. He
and Hamsun completely ignore religion *as* religion.

2 'Bondekulturen', *Artikler* (1939), p. 110.

3 There are the extraordinary diatribe against the theatre and the
drama in *Segelfoss By* (*Samlede Verker*, x, 1934, 278 ff.) and the
sentence towards the end of *Markens Grøde* quoted p. 187 above.

4 An instance of his avoidance of sharp transitions is the extraordinary skill with which, dealing for the most part with un-
educated people, he transferred—and faithfully enough—their
racy or vulgar expressions into his own Riksmaal through the
various devices of *oratio obliqua*.

PAGE 167

1 Most of his best short stories are contained in *Flaggermusvinger*
(1895), *Fra Hav til Hei* (1897) and *Trækfugle og Andre* (1899)
and of lyrics in the posthumous *Mands Hjerte* (1927).

2 J. Bukdahl, with his 'folkist' prejudices, declared: 'Hans E.
Kinck ... was the central figure of modern Norway. No one tells
us more of Norway as a nation, more about its unique and precious
qualities ...' (*American-Scandinavian Review*, xv, 1927, 589). This
essay may be found a useful corrective to any strictures passed in
my account.

3 It is an indication of his contemporary reputation at home that
thirty years had to elapse before any book of his went into a second
edition; except in the Netherlands, where J. de Vries made
manful propaganda on his behalf, he was scarcely known outside
Scandinavia. Hamsun had a big international following, especially
in Germany and Russia, even before the award of the Nobel
Prize to him.

4 'Driftekaren' might in general be more properly rendered as 'The
Drover'; but this word in English suggests sheep and oxen, with
which Vraal has nothing to do, whereas much stress is laid on his
horse-coping, which has the same dubious associations for
Norwegians as for us.

PAGE 168

1 Kinck avowed that his chief models for Vraal were an old Norwegian crowder and—Victor Hugo (E. Beyer, *H. E. Kinck*, 1956, p. 441).

2 *Agilulf den Vise*, taken from one of the tales in Boccaccio's *Decamerone*, was published in 1906 and produced, for nine performances, at the National Theatre, Christiania, in 1909. *Driftekaren* was not acted until 1938.

PAGE 169

1 *Paa Rindalslægret* (*In the Rindal Encampment*, 1925) is an epilogue to *Driftekaren*.

2 *Sus* and *Hugormen*.

PAGE 170

1 Letter to his closest friend Steen Konow cited by A. H. Winsnes, *Litteratur Norsk Historie*, v (1937), 448.

2 The enormously heavy emigration from the Norwegian countryside to America during the second half of the nineteenth century is frequently alluded to by authors both in Landsmaal and Riksmaal (e.g. by Kielland in *Arbeidsfolk*); but it did not provide the subject of any work by a major writer before Bojer's *Vor egen stamme* (1924).

PAGE 171

1 There is a lot of highly allusive talk about a yellow-hammer, evidently intended to stand for the doctor's deceased wife, but it provides no enlightenment.

2 K. Elster (*Illustreret Norsk Litteratur Historie*, v, 2nd ed. 1934, 132) sees this pillage as a manifestation of the peasants' desire for a 'richer life' than theirs; it isn't exactly obvious.

3 *Sneskavlen* is placed in the eighteen-seventies when both a more militant democracy was 'breaking through' and the nation's centre of gravity was shifting from the countryside to the towns. Towards the end of the trilogy a new generation of officials, better trained and more humane, perhaps, takes over from the old; but no hope is suggested that they will effect a bridge between their own culture and that of the *administrés*.

PAGE 172

1 The limitations of this sociologist's purview are most disconcerting. Except in *Doctor Gabriel Jahr* (1902)—where the restricted section presented offers no more grounds for hopefulness than the

rest of his work—metropolitan society is reflected only as some-one's distant memory; places like Stavanger or Trondheim might not exist. That Norway had a working administrative or educational system, a church, merchant princes, artists, explorers and *savants* could hardly be inferred. Industrial enterprise enters into *Herman Ek*, culminating in large-scale machine-breaking.

PAGE 173

1 Kinck constantly uses the terms 'rase', 'stam', 'nation', 'folk' and 'ætt' (to be rendered perhaps by 'breed'). In a private letter of 1904 (*cit.* E. Beyer, *Hans E. Kinck*, 1956, p. 250) he makes the damaging admission that he does not know what 'rase' and 'raseinstinkt' really are; they may be just 'gale gloser', meaningless vocables.

2 *Storhetstid* (1922) is the title of three closely related studies intended to combat the claims made by Fredrik Paasche and Sigrid Undset that at the 'Time of Greatness' Norway was a fundamentally Christian country. Like several of his contemporaries, Kinck was lenient to the Danish domination, generally denounced throughout the nineteenth century; the damage to the national spirit, he held, had been done earlier. It may be noted that he wrote no tales or plays on the national past.

3 The most substantial of these are collected in *Stammens Røst* (1919); Kinck was in sympathy with some Italian writers who later supported fascism—a parallel trait to Hamsun's approval of nazism—but he turned strongly against Mussolini's braggart chauvinism.

PAGE 174

1 A. H. Winsnes in *Norsk Litteratur Historie*, v (1937), 301.

PAGE 175

1 Ch. II, with a little of ch. I, was printed in the Copenhagen magazine *Ny Jord* for November 1888. The whole was published in volume form in 1890. Before *Sult* Hamsun, under his original name of Kn. Pedersen, had published (in 1877 and 1878) three pieces of fiction, not included in any collection.

PAGE 177

1 Nagel speaks of 'Blods subjektive Logik', a phrase that like much else in Hamsun's books anticipates D. H. Lawrence.

2 If 'influences' are looked for, they should be sought first in Dostoievsky and in Strindberg, whose recent novel *I Hafsbandet*

shows more points of resemblance to *Mysterier* than death by drowning. Hamsun highly admired these two and looked on Strindberg as the Rousseau of his age, a conservative revolutionary. In an often quoted passage in *Prager Presse* (9 January 1922, *auct.* Berendsohn, p. 163) Thomas Mann declared that Dostoievsky and Nietzsche had no disciples among their own countrymen to equal Hamsun. For the relationship with Nietzsche see H. Beyer, *Nietzsche og Norden* (especially II, 94 ff.). The hero of *Pan*, with his moments of ecstasy, his self-sufficiency and ruthlessness, is certainly a person of whom Nietzsche would have approved; and Nagel of *Mysterier* has some of Glahn's characteristics and is conspicuous for that *generositas* which Nietzsche attributed to his Superman; Kareno, in *Ved Rigets Port*, bases his diatribes against utilitarian philosophers on Nietzschean principles. The clearest echo from Nietzsche is found in the poem 'Sven Herlufsens Ord' (*Samlede Verker*, V, 1934, 398):

> Og du vil vite hvordan Piken holdes elskovsvarm
> og hvordan hun skal hindres fra at løpe?
> Saa ofte du omslynger hende en Gang med din Arm
> omslyng hende fire med din Svøpe.

It may be remarked that, for all his sympathies for Germany, Hamsun had only a defective knowledge of its language: an interpreter had to officiate at his interview with Hitler in 1943. English he knew well, while detesting Anglo-Saxon civilization. He had a good word for Whitman and even Emerson, and the mixture of colloquialism and 'classical' English he detected in Mark Twain (on whom he wrote an article in three numbers of *Ny illustreret Tidende*, 22 March–5 April 1885) may well have affected his own idiosyncratic style. In the rather vague praise he bestows on French psychological novelists ('Psykologisk Literatur', *Paa Turné*, 1960, pp. 45 ff.), he was thinking of the Goncourts and probably also of Huysmans and Bourget in his first phase. He admired Oriental quietism, though talk about Buddha is 'tøv'.

PAGE 178

1 It is not likely that the title was to make explicit reference either to the Danish periodical which gave Hamsun his start, or to Turgeniev's novel, commonly translated as *Virgin Soil*.
2 It is represented by Professor Gylling, disciple of Mill and Spencer.

PAGE 179

1 *Ved Rigets Port* went through the relatively high number of twenty-one performances, when produced at Christiania Theater, 28 October 1896; *Livets Spil* and *Aftenrøde*, produced there on 3 December 1896 and 17 October 1898 respectively, had sixteen and eleven performances. *Livet Ivold* was produced at the National Theatre, 26 November 1910, and done fourteen times. *Munken Vendt* was apparently not acted till 1926 (at Heidelberg).

2 Produced as 'en billedbok fra Kaukasia' and performed twelve times at the National Theatre 1903/4.

PAGE 180

1 The heroes of *Hunger*, *Mysteries* and *Pan* had come near to the type, but the first two resent their factual homelessness and long to have done with it, and Lieutenant Glahn, the acme of virility, has (except perhaps in the postscript) nothing that would suggest the appellation of a tramp.

2 Hamsun seems to have written some verse from his early days, but it was only about 1900 that he took it up seriously. If *Munken Vendt* is left out of account, his published verse-output was small. The *Dikte* of 1921 are mainly made up of items from *Det Vilde Kor*, often revised, not always for the better.

3 *Cit.* J. Landquist, *Knut Hamsun* (1929), p. 62.

PAGE 181

1 *Samlede Verker*, v (1934), 392.

2 *Ibid.* pp. 400, 403, 404 and 407.

PAGE 182

1 His fatal hatred of England was for Napoleon's 'nation of shopkeepers'—and of tourists. No less than tourists, he (like Kinck) abominated those who made their living by them, and for that reason 'Swiss' was one of the strongest terms of abuse in his vocabulary.

PAGE 185

1 The parallel with Scott's *Jernbyrden* (see p. 197 above) is striking. Jan Vibe in the earlier book is a local Hercules, much more deeply implicated in the concerns of his friendlier neighbourhood and the misfortunes of its inhabitants than the completely one-ideaed Isak. Scott may score with the incidents that these involve, Hamsun with the momentum of the whole.

PAGE 187

1 W. Worster's translation, *Growth of the Soil* (1920), p. 405.

2 *Sidste Kapitel* (1923), more tightly constructed than usual, has no strongly marked wanderer-type, but, set round a sanatorium, it deals with a group of men and women who are certainly uprooted; the heroine, in her mating with a yokel of the neighbourhood, finds something of the same peace which was Sellanraa's. But it is not suggested that she should be taken as a model.

PAGE 188

1 See O. Øyslebø, *Hamsun gjennom Stilen* (1964).

PAGE 190

1 They wrote most interesting recollections of this time: Egge with *Minner* (1948–55) and Bojer with *Læregutt* (1942) and *Svenn* (1946). So did Vilhelm Krag (*Dengang vi var tyve Aar*, 1927) and Vogt (*Fra Gutt til Mann*, 1932, and *Oplevelser*, 1934).

PAGE 191

1 In *Hjærtet* (1907) the two motifs are combined.

PAGE 193

1 And also for a metaphysical coherence, particularly in *Den Store Hunger* (1916), the 'Hunger' of the title being the restless craving of a meditative engineer who, for the sake of the 'hymn' in his heart, goes through manifold experiences, from poverty to riches and back again to poverty, in order to find simple, true values and the peace they give.

PAGE 194

1 The title is ambiguous, in that it points both to a popular demonstration, ending in a procession of boats in which the hero meets his death by drowning, and to the 'onward march of the people' in its current obsession with (mostly futile) parliamentary politics.

PAGE 196

1 Bojer also wrote plays of a varied character—one even about the elder Brutus; but, though they honestly earned their royalties, the best of them are stiff and conventional by contrast with Egge's.

PAGE 197

1 E.g. *Kari Kveldsmat,* 1913.
2 Jernbyrden was originally the burden or ordeal of (red-hot) iron, by which, under medieval law, accused persons could seek to establish their innocence. The torture of the girls (convicted poisoners) in *The Ordeal* is part of their sentence.

PAGE 198

1 Enok Ruben is Jan Vibe's son, and *Enok Rubens Levnetsløp* (1917) covers some forty years from about 1775. The hero is involved in the peasants' revolt associated with the name of Olav Lofthus, about which Scott had collected a good deal of fresh material.
2 I. Ross, 'Lidt om Kvindernes Bidrag til den norske Litteratur fra 1814 til 1896' (*Samtiden,* XIV, 1903, 77) gives an account of some of the minor literary figures of that time, such as Hanna Winsnes (1789–1872), Marie Colban (1814–84), Bolette Gjør (1835–1909), Elise Aubert (1838–1909).

PAGE 199

1 To them should be added another pair of women authors, Alvilde Prydz (1848–1922) and Anna Munch (*née* Dahl, 1856–1932), whom the general public and the reviewers held in respectful esteem also during the earlier years of the twentieth century, though their amateurish manner and their explicit devotion to 'the ideal' (often religious) showed that they belonged to an older generation. Alvilde Prydz made her début as far back as 1880; *Gunvor Thorsdatter til Hærø* (1896, translated into English as *The Heart of the Northern Sea*) and the cycle conflated as *To Mennesker* in 1918 are accounted her best works. Anna Munch made her mark with *Kvinder* (1889), in which she polemicized against Maupassant and Zola; she reached her peak with *Glæde* (1904).
2 This boy was christened Ove, abbreviated to Ve; the title is a dubious pun, Ve meaning woe.

PAGE 200

1 Based on her lifelong experiences as a teacher in elementary schools, she also wrote realistic stories of proletarian life in Christiania (e.g. *Barnets Tjenere,* 1910), sometimes tinged with left-wing sympathies. Her *Eventyr* (1925), *Nye Eventyr* (1926), *Nordlandsnat* (1927) and *Det Gråner mot Høst* (1928) are collections of folk-lore in the manner of Asbjørnsen and Moe.

PAGE 202

1 Unless it be as a writer for children with her seven-volume series *Peik- og Fjeld-musernesbøker* (completed 1917–18). Her first novel was *Jomfruen* (1914); before that she had published clever, generally humorous short stories after the manner of Aanrud (*Fnugg*, 1909, and *Den Kjærligheten*, 1913).

PAGE 203

1 Another curious fact is the enhanced prestige and influence of Swedish writers at this time: Strindberg, Heidenstam, Selma Lagerlöf, Fröding, Karlfeldt particularly.

2 Uppdal contemplated, but did not execute, a sequel, and Falkberget, many years after his first, produced a second cycle, *Nattens Brød* (four titles, 1940–59).

PAGE 204

1 It is a remarkable accident that between them the four distinguished novelists of their generation cover virtually the whole of Norwegian social history after the Viking Age: Sigrid Undset the 'Gothic' centuries, Falkberget mainly the seventeenth century and the eighteenth century, Duun the nineteenth century and Uppdal his own time.

2 This is the proper title of the first volume published (1911) after Uppdal had conceived of the cycle as such; it was preceded by *Ved Akerselven* (1910), which was later extensively revised to fit into the series as *Vandringa*. (Similar alterations to the same end were ultimately made in others of the earlier constituents.) Uppdal's earliest publications were two volumes of verse, 1905.

PAGE 205

1 It was begun with *Galgberget* in 1930. 'Kulten' is a kind of allegorical nickname.

2 Gorky was first translated into Danish in 1901 and into Norwegian in 1902; he was known both to Uppdal and to Falkberget. The proletariat had been fully presented in Lie's *Livsslaven* and Sivle's *Streik* and had irrupted into Bjørnson's *Fallit* and *Over Ævne II* and Kielland's *Garman og Worse*; the four volumes of Andreas Haukland (1873–1933) about Ol-Jørgen (1902–5) prefigure Uppdal's *milieu* most plainly.

PAGE 206

1 *Cit.* H. Wildenvey, *Vingehesten og Verden* (1937), pp. 317 f.

2 Its spontaneity is not in question, but instigations for it have been found in Heine, in the English classics he knew well and, more plainly, in the fine poets which the 1890 *renouveau* threw up in Denmark (Holstein, Stuckenberg) and Sweden (Fröding, Karlfeldt) and in Knut Hamsun, whose *Wild Chorus* carried him away when he turned poet.

PAGE 207

1 He then took up a strong pro-German attitude, but later was radically 'Left' in his partisanship and turned so violently against nazism and Hitler that he was sent to a German concentration camp from 1942 to 1945. His attacks on Christianity were equally violent, and he is the only Norwegian to have stood trial for blasphemy, his acquittal no doubt justifying the conferment on him in 1952 of a Knighthood in the Order of St Olav.

2 And its impeccable Riksmaal, for which he has been an ardent fighter against the prestige and, what he considers worse, the contaminations of Nynorsk.

PAGE 208

1 See pp. 112 f. above.

BIBLIOGRAPHICAL APPENDIX

All books published in Norway since 1814 are listed in *Norsk Bok-fortegnelse* (formerly *Norsk Bog-Fortegnelse*, 1848–); H. Pettersen, *Bibliotheca Norvegica* (4 vols. 1899–1924) has, as vol. IV, a catalogue of books by Norwegian authors printed in foreign countries, including translations, and, as vol. II, a catalogue of books and papers relating to Norway printed outside Norway; J. B. Halvorsen and H. Koht, *Norsk Forfatter-Leksikon* (4 vols. 1885–1907) contains not only bibliographical details of all books by Norwegian authors up to the time the successive parts were issued, but also their contributions to the principal newspapers and other periodicals, references to the foremost reviews of their works, together with valuable biographical matter; R. Øksnevad compiled a series of special bibliographies dealing with the Norwegian reception of foreign literature (e.g. *Det Britiske Samvelde og Eire i Norsk Litteratur*, 1949) and another listing the literary articles in a number of Christiania newspapers, also an exhaustive *Norsk Litteraturhistorisk Bibliografi 1900–1945* (1957).

The fullest Norwegian encyclopaedia is *Aschehougs Konversasjons-Leksikon* (18 vols. 1954–61). The *Norsk Biografisk Leksikon* (ed. E. Bull *et al.* 1923–) is nearing completion.

A. Bugge *et al. Norges Historie* (13 parts, 1907–17) concentrates on political history; parts 12 and 13, by J. E. Sars, cover the period 1814–1905; E. Bull *et al. Det Norske Folks Liv og Historie* (11 parts, 1929–38) gives much more space to social and economic history and the history of the arts; parts 9, 10 and 11, by W. Keilhau, cover the period 1814–1938. Shorter histories are A. Holmsen and M. Jensen, *Norges Historie* (2 vols. 1949) and, in English, K. Gjerset, *History of the Norwegian People* (2 vols. New York, 1927), K. Larsen, *A History of Norway* (Princeton, 1948) and T. K. Derry, *Short History of Norway* (1957). G. Gathorne-Hardy, *Norway* (1925) gives political, social and cultural history from the earliest days in an admirably succinct account. The title of the copiously illustrated *Norsk Kulturhistorie* (ed. A. Bugge *et al.* 5 vols. 1938–42) indicates its scope. For the nineteenth century in particular W. C. Brøgger (ed.), *Norge i det nittende Aarhundrede* (1900), and W. Konow and K. Fischer, *Norway: official publication for the Paris Exhibition* (1900) should be consulted. The sections, maps and illustrations relating to Norway in

R. Millward, *Scandinavian Lands* (1964) present the geographic, demographic and economic background.

The fullest literary history is that by F. Paasche *et al. Norsk Litteraturhistorie* (6 vols. 1924–55, now in process of revision); vols. IV and V (the period 1848–1914) are by F. Bull and A. H. Winsnes, respectively, vol. VI by P. Houm. A shorter, more popular presentation is that of K. Elster (jr), *Illustreret Norsk Litteratur Historie* (2nd ed. 6 vols. 1934–5). H. Beyer, *Norsk Litteratur Historie* (1963), with an admirable bibliography of 59 pages, is the revision and expansion by E. Beyer, of the first edition (1952), of which *A History of Norwegian Literature* (American-Scandinavian Foundation, 1956) is a translation and adaptation by E. Haugen, the bibliography being confined to works available in English. Other accounts in English are J. Jorgenson, *History of Norwegian Literature* (New York, 1933), I. Grøndahl and O. Raknes, *Chapters in Norwegian Literature* (1926), and E. Bredsdorff *et al. Introduction to Scandinavian Literature* (1951, the Norwegian chapters by R. Popperwell). J. W. McFarlane, *Ibsen and the Temper of Norwegian Literature* (1960) comprises studies of nine outstanding literary figures, a chapter on Nynorsk literature and a select bibliography of translations into English. In French there is J. Lescoffier, *Histoire de la Littérature Norvégienne* (1952).

The most important Norwegian periodicals for literary criticism and history are *Samtiden* (1890–), *Syn og Segn* (1894–) and *Edda* (1914–); there are many valuable articles on literary and cultural topics relative to Norway in the *Nordisk Tidskrift för Vetenskap, Konst och Industri* (1878–) published by Letterstedtska Föreningen of Stockholm. A full list of Norwegian periodicals is given in H. L. Tveterås, *Norske Tidsskrifter intill 1920* (1940).

Camilla Collett's collected *Skrifter* appeared in 11 volumes, 1892–4. On her see L. Heber, *Camilla Collett* (1913), A. Benterud, *Camilla Collett* (1947), and E. Steen's two books, *Diktning og Virkelighed* (1957) and *Den lange Strid* (1954).

Vinje's *Skrifter i Samling* (1921) were supplemented by a sixth volume (1927) containing his previously unpublished, only play *Olaf Digre*. On him see H. Koht, *A. O. Vinje* (1909), and J. A. Dale, *A. O. Vinje* (1960).

CHAPTER 2: BJØRNSON

For a full bibliography down to 1932 see A. Thuesen, *Bjørnson-bibliografi* (5 vols. 1948–57): for later matter consult H. Beyer, *Norsk Litteratur Historie* (1963), pp. 496–9. Bjørnson's imaginative writings are collected in *Samlede Digter-Værker* (9 vols. 1919–20) and frequently reprinted; the edition used here is that of 1927. Supplementary are his *Artikler og Taler* (2 vols. 1912–13, with a valuable study of Bjørnson's public life by the historian Ernst Sars) and several selections from his enormous correspondence. All Bjørnson's longer and much of his shorter fiction is translated in *The Novels of Bjørnstjerne Bjørnson* (13 vols. 1895–1909, with an introduction by E. Gosse).

Major biographical and general studies are: F. Bull in vol. IV (rev. ed. 1963, pp. 487–705) of F. Paasche *et al. Norsk Litteraturhistorie*; G. Gran, *Bjørnstjerne Bjørnson, Høvdingen* (1910); C. Collin, *Bjørnstjerne Bjørnson hans Barndom og Ungdom* (rev. ed. 1923); J. Lescoffier, *Bjørnson la seconde Jeunesse* (Paris, 1932); P. Amdam, *Den unge Bjørnson* (1960). In English: G. C. M. Brandes, *Henrik Ibsen, Bjørnstjerne Bjørnson* (1899); W. M. Payne, *Bjørnson 1832–1910* (Chicago, 1910); and H. B. Larsen, *Bjørnson, a Study in Norwegian Nationalism* (New York, 1944). A valuable survey is provided by H. Noreng, 'Bjørnson Research', in *Scandinavica*, IV (1965), I.

CHAPTERS 3 AND 7: IBSEN

The fullest bibliographies are H. Pettersen, *Henrik Ibsen 1828–1928* (1928), and I. Tedford, *Ibsen Bibliography 1928–1957* (1961).

The complete centenary edition (*Hundreårsutgave*) of Ibsen's *Samlede Verker* (21 vols. 1928–57, including letters, articles and speeches and an iconography) has thorough introductions and critical apparatus by its editors F. Bull, H. Koht and D. A. Seip. The most complete English translation is still by William Archer and associates, *Collected Works of Henrik Ibsen* (12 vols. 1907–12), which will be superseded by the Oxford Ibsen (ed. J. W. McFarlane, 1960–), where each volume includes also translations of the draft-material, full lists of English translation and criticisms, together with an introduction by the editor.

The standard biography is H. Koht, *Henrik Ibsen eit Diktarliv* (rev. ed. 2 vols. 1954; English translation of the 1st ed. 1931). On Ibsen's family life see especially *De Tre* (1948, translated as *The Three Ibsens*, 1952) by his daughter-in-law Bergljot Ibsen. General works on Ibsen in English are Bernard Shaw's *Quintessence of Ibsenism* (enlarged ed. 1913); H. J. Weigand, *The Modern Ibsen* (1925); I. Zucker, *Ibsen the Master Builder* (1930); M. C. Bradbrook, *Ibsen the Norwegian* (1946); B. W. Downs, *Ibsen: the Intellectual Background* (1946); J. Lavrin, *Ibsen an Approach* (1949); also F. L. Lucas, *The Drama of Ibsen and Strindberg* (1962).

CHAPTER 4: ELSTER AND LIE

Elster's *Samlede Skrifter* were published in two volumes (rev. ed. 1903–4). There are two good essays on him: F. A. Gödecke, in *Nordisk Tidskrift*, v (Stockholm, 1883), 388, and I. Holm, in *Samtiden* (1941), p. 127. Lie's belles-lettres were collected in the Standardutgave (*Samlede Digterverker*, ed. V. Erichsen, 1920–2) and some of his correspondence in *Jonas Lie og hans Samtidige* (ed. C. Nærup, 1916). There is a good biographical memoir by his son, Erik Lie, *Jonas Lie en Livskildring* (1933); Herman Jæger's entry *sub verbo* in *Norsk Biografisk Leksikon* is exemplary. *Jonas Lie en Udviklingshistorie* (2nd ed. 1893) by his friend and contemporary Arne Garborg is still valuable; C. O. Bergström, *Jonas Lies Väg till Gilje* (Swedish, 1949), gives a very thorough account of his life and work to 1883 and contains an admirable bibliography. Cf. also H. Midbøe, *Jonas Lies Ungdom* (1964), and *Jonas Lies Utvikling* (1965). For the English reader there are chapters on Lie in A. Gustafson, *Six Scandinavian Novelists* (New York, 1940), and in J. W. McFarlane, *Ibsen and the Temper of Norwegian Literature* (1960), pp. 25 and 197 respectively.

CHAPTER 5: KIELLAND AND AMALIE SKRAM

Kielland's books, essays and letters are assembled in *Samlede Verker* (12 vols. 1949–50). Though more material has subsequently come to light, *Alexander L. Kielland og hans Samtid* (1922) by the literary historian Gerhard Gran, a friend and contemporary, remains valuable for its picture of the cultural and political environment, and O. Storstein, *Kielland på Ny* (rev. ed. 1949), is good on the history of Stavanger while Kielland lived there. See on him also N. L. Bæhrendtz, *Kiellands litterära Genombrott* (Udevalla, 1952), and F. Bull, *Omkring A. Kielland* (1949).

There is a collection of Amalie Skram's imaginative writings, *Samlede Værker* (9 vols. Copenhagen, 1905–7). The biography and bibliography by B. Bjerkelund in *Norsk Biografisk Leksikon*, xii (1958) are capital. *Amalie Skram og Kvinnens Problem* (1951) and *Amalie Skrams Diktning* (1961) are two elaborate studies by the psychiatrist Borghild Krane.

CHAPTER 6: GARBORG AND OTHER LANDSMAAL
AUTHORS OF HIS TIME

For Garborg's bibliography see T. M. Andersen, *Garborg-Litteratur 1866–1942* (1943–5). His belles-lettres and some autobiographical fragments are collected in *Skrifter i Samling* (8 vols. 1944). All his life he was a copious contributor to newspapers and magazines: a selection from his articles on public and on cultural affairs he published himself as *Politikk* (1919) and *Straumdrag* (1920) respectively; there is also his *Tankar og Utsyn, Artikler* (ed. J. A. Dale and R. Thesen, 2 vols. 1950). A collection of his letters, *Mogning og Manndom* (same editors) appeared in 1954. The series (Nynorsk) by R. Thesen, *Arne Garborg fra Jærbu til Europear* (1933), *Arne Garborg Europearen* (1936) and *Arne Garborg fra Europear til Jærbu* (1939) are capital biography and comment. There is a useful study in English: I. Lillehei, *A Study in the Language and the main Ideas of Arne Garborg's Works* (n.p. 1914). Cf. also J. A. Dale, *Garborgs Språk og Stil* (1950).

Valuable studies by a veteran expert in Landsmaal language and authors are collected in O. Midttun, *Menn og Bøker* (1963). On Landsmaal literature in the eighteen-seventies see V. Skard, *Fra Dølen til Fedraheimen* (1949); for the drama, J. A. Dale, *Nynorsk Dramatikk i hundre År* (1964).

On Mortensson Egnund see K. Langen, *Ivar Mortensson Egnund* (1958). Sivle's belles-lettres are collected in *Skrifter* (3 vols. 1909–10); there are studies of him by Anders Hovden, *Per Sivle ei Livssoge* (1939) and by B. Birkeland, *Per Sivle* (1961, with a full bibliography). On Tvedt see O. Midttun, in *Syn og Segn* for 1927 and A. Espeland, *Jens Tvedt glimt* (1939). Løland's *Skrifter i Samling* were published in 4 vols. 1941–2; on him see O. Bakken, *Rasmus Løland* (1938).

A further study of Landsmaal authors in Garborg's time should comprise the following: Bolette Christine Pavels Larsen, *née* Lund (1874–1904), the daughter of a lawyer from Sogndal, who wrote *Smaoe Skjeldringa* (*Little Sketches*, 1897) in that dialect; Vetle Vislie (1858–1933), a peasant's son of Skafså in Telemark, after 1897 teacher or headmaster in teachers' training colleges; Rev. Anders Hovden (1860–1943), son of a crofter-fisherman from Ørsta, author of hymns in Landsmaal; Karen Hulda Bergersen (1862–1934), daughter of an attorney from Stange in Hedmark, who became Fru Garborg and on whom see J. A. Dale, *Hulda Garborg* (1961); Rasmus Olai Steinsvik (1863–1913), son of a peasant of Dalsfjord, primarily a journalist; and Hans Andreas Seland (1867–1949), son of a peasant from Flekkefjord. All the men, it will be observed, were sons of the soil; the ladies were middle-class converts.

CHAPTER 7: IBSEN AFTER 1882

See chapter 3.

CHAPTER 8: THE NORWEGIAN THEATRE: GUNNAR HEIBERG

For the history of the Norwegian theatre: T. Blanc, *Christiania Theaters Historie 1827–1877* (1899); B. Lorentzen, *Det første norske Theater* (1949), which deals with the Bergen venture of 1850; P. Gjesdahl, *Centralteatrets Historie* (1964); A. Rønneberg, *National-theatret gjennem femti Aar* (1949); O. Dalberg, *Det norske Teatret 1913–53* (1953); N. Sletbak (ed.), *Det norske Teatret* (1963); Ø. Anker, 'Scenekunst gjennom 150 år', in *Dette er Norge*, III (1963), 161 ff. Anker has also published valuable lists (1956) of all the plays given at the Christiania Theater throughout its existence and at the Møllergate Theatre, Christiania, 1852–63.

For Heiberg: twelve of his plays are collected as *Samlede dramatiske Verker* (4 vols. 1917–18) and his most important articles in *Pariser-breve* (1900), *Set og Hørt* (1917,) *Ibsen og Bjørnson paa Scenen* (1918), *Franske Visitter* (1919), *Norsk Teater* (1920), *1905* (1923), *Salt og Sukker* (1924). *I Frihetens Bur* (a satirical play about marriage) was completed in 1910, but only posthumously published. On him see E. Skavlan, *Gunnar Heiberg* (1950).

CHAPTER 9: THE NEW MEN OF THE 'NINETIES

There are collected editions or extensive selections from the writers discussed in this chapter as follows: Aanrud's *Samlede Verker* (3 vols. 1943; short stories and plays—he wrote no novels); Andersen's *Samlede Fortællinger* (3 vols. 1916); Vilhelm Krag's *Skrifter* (4 vols. 1930; belles-lettres only); *Thomas Krag Mindeudgave* (9 vols. 1915–17); Obstfelder's *Skrifter*, ed. S. Tunold (3 vols. 1950); Vogt's *Et Liv i Dikt* (1st ed. 1930).

On Aanrud consult A. Bolckmans, *Stories of Hans Aanrud* (Bruges, 1960) and P. Hallberg, *Harmonisk Realism* (1963), which deals with other peasant-literature as well; on Andersen, C. Gierloff, *Tryggve Andersen* (1942); on Obstfelder, J. F. Bjørnsen, *Sigbjørn Obstfelder*,

Mennesket, Poeten og Grubleren (1959), A. Hannevik, *Obstfelder og Mystikken* (1960, with bibliography), and two essays in English: C. C. Schoolfield, 'Sigbjørn Obstfelder, a Study in Idealism' (*Edda*, LVII, 1957, 163), and J. W. McFarlane, in his *Ibsen and the Temper of Norwegian Literature* (1960, p. 104).

A. Örbeck, *Norway's Best Stories* (American-Scandinavian Foundation, 1927) includes specimens of Aanrud, J. B. Bull, Hilditch and T. Krag.

CHAPTER 10: KINCK AND HAMSUN

For Kinck there is no bibliography, collected edition or translation into English. His earliest poem was of 1889, his earliest novel of 1892, and he continued to publish until the year of his death. The first novel to show his best powers was *Sus* (1896), which, incorporating its sequel, *Hugormen* (1898), was reissued, slightly altered, as *Herman Ek* in 1923. The most important of his writings not mentioned elsewhere are the novel *Præsten* (1905) and the prose plays of modern Norwegian life *Mellem Togene* (1898) and *Paa Ekre'rnes Gaard* (1913). On him see: E. Beyer, *Hans E. Kinck* (1956); J. Bukdahl, 'Hans E. Kinck', *American-Scandinavian Review*, XV (1927), 589; B. M. Kinck, *Hans E. Kinck: Grunnmotiver i hans Diktning* (1941); D. Lea, *H. E. Kincks Livssyn* (1949); A. H. Winsnes, *Hans E. Kinck og vår Tid* (1954) and his criticisms of Beyer's study in *Edda*, LIX (1959), 178.

There is as yet no comprehensive edition, bibliography or study of Hamsun's writings. The latest completed edition of his belles-lettres, *Samlede Verker*, is in fifteen volumes (1954–6). There is also a collection of *Artikler* (1939). Admirable on the material available at the time of their publication are J. Landquist, *Knut Hamsun hans Levnad och Verk* (Swedish, 1929) and W. A. Berendsohn, *Knut Hamsun* (German, 1929); the copious notes in the latter comprise much bibliographical information. *Knut Hamsun* (1959) by Knut's son Tore Hamsun and *Regnbuen* and *Under Gullregnen* (1959) by his widow Marie Hamsun are full of biographical detail. T. Braatøy's *Livets Cirkel* (1954) is a psycho-analytical study. In English: H. A. Larsen, *Knut Hamsun* (1922).

CHAPTER 11: THE NEW CENTURY

For several of the authors referred to in this chapter there are as yet no monographs of great critical importance. The admirable paragraphs devoted to Øverland and Aukrust in Paasche *et al.* *Norsk Litteraturhistorie* are in vol. v (P. Haum), the rest in vol. IV

(A. H. Winsnes). For studies of particular points refer to the bibliography in the second edition (1963) of Beyer's *Norsk Litteraturhistorie*.

The best of Egge's fifty-seven books are reprinted in *Samlede Verker* (6 vols. 1949), and there are similar collections of Bojer's *Samlede Verker* (10 vols. 1927–33) and Scott's *Romaner i Utvalg* (some of them revised, 12 vols. 1945–6). On these see R. S. Jystad, *Peter Egge og hans Trønderromaner* (1949), P. G. la Chesnais, *Johan Bojer, sa Vie et ses Œuvres* (1930) and A. Beisland, *Gabriel Scott, en Sørlandsdikter* (1949) respectively.

Ragnhild Jølsen's five novels were bundled together in two volumes as *Samlede Skrifter* (1923). On her see A. Tiberg, *Ragnhild Jølsen i Liv og Digtning* (1909) and, on Fru Roll Anker, E. Kielland, *Nini Roll Anker i Liv og Arbeid* (1948).

There is a collection of Duun's *Skrifter* (12 vols. 1949) and, on him, R. Thesen, *Mennesket og Makterne* (1942), and D. Håkonsen, *Olav Duun* (1949); on Falkberget, E. Døhl, *Bergstadens Dikter* (1936), and R. Thesen, *Johan Falkberget og hans Rike* (1959). The only collections of Uppdal's writings are his *Dikt i Utval* (1960) and two volumes of journalism, *Uversskyer* (1917) and *Andadrag* (1918); on him see O. Salumsmoen, *Kristofer Uppdal, Domkirkebyggeren* (1960).

Wildenvey's *Samlede Digte* or *Samlede Dikt* have gone through many editions, since 1927, and there is also a volume of his *Prosa i Utvalg* (1929); on him see K. Haave, *Herman Wildenvey, Poeten, Kunstneren* (1952). Olaf Bull's *Samlede Dikte* and *Dikt i Utvalg* first came out in 1934 and 1950, respectively; T. Greiff, *Olaf Bull, Taper og Seirer* (1952), and E. Ofstad, *Olaf Bulls Lyrikk* (1955) are comprehensive studies. For Øverland, *Samlede Dikt* (3 vols. 1947), *Noveller i Utvalg* (1939), and O. Gelsted, *Arnulf Øverland* (Copenhagen, 1946) are available. *Eldringen* (1924) and *Viljan og Lagnaden* (1946) are selections from Ørjasæter's verse. Aukrust's *Dikt i Samling* (1942) include work not published in his lifetime; on him see H. Groth, *Olav Aukrust, Problematikk og Utvikling* (1948).

INDEX

Bold figures indicate main entries

Aanrud, Hans, 139, 157, **163 f.**, 189, 193, 252, 260, 267 f.
Aasen, Ivar Andreas, 7 f., 16, 111, 138, 211, 217, 242
Ammers Küller, Jo van, 201
Andersen, Hans Christian, 10, 81 f., 209
Andersen, Tryggve, 157, **161 f.**, 189, 200, 251 f., 267, 269
Andersen Nexø, Martin, 205
Anker, Nini Roll, 198, **200 ff.**, 269
Anzengruber, Ludwig, 21, 230 f.
Archer, William, 137, 225
Asbjørnsen, Peter Christen, 5 f., 9, 209, 217
Aubert, Élise, 259
Auerbach, Berthold, 19
Augier, Émile, 30, 31, 33, 34, 37, 136, 224
Aukrust, Olav, **208**, 212, 268 f.

Bain, Alexander, 224
Balzac, Honoré de, 10, 92, 218, 224
Barrès, Augustin-Maurice, 12
Belot, Adolphe, 247
Benzon, Carl Otto Valdemar, 247
Bergen, theatre at, 43 n., 44, 134 f., 136, 138, 140 n., 163 n., 220, 267
Bergson, Henri, 208
Bismarck, Otto von, 55
Bjerregaard, Henrik Anker, 25, 246
Bjørnson, Bjørn, 19 n., 137
Bjørnson, Synnøve, 12 f., 19, 20
Bjørnson, Bjørnstjerne Martinius, 8, 10 ff., 14 n., **17 ff.**, 56, 57, 58, 61, 64, 66, 68, 79, 81, 102, 105, 109, 135, 136, 137, 139, 141 f., 146, 158 n., 181, 190, 203 n., 206, 209 f., 213, 219, 220 ff., 226 f., 230, 232, 238, 239, 246, 247, 248, 249, 252 f., 260, 263 f.
'Aanun', 20
'Absalom's Hair', 42
Arne, 19, 219
Arnljot Gelline, 16, 23 f., 109
articles and speeches, 17, 264
Bankruptcy, A, 31 f., 58, 260
Between the Battles, 21
Beyond our Powers (I), 27, 35 ff.

Beyond our Powers (II), 36, 136
Captain Mansana, 37
'Dust', 27, 42
Editor, The, 28, 32 f.
Fisher Lass, The, 25 f., 31
Flags are Out, The, 29, 38 f.
Gauntlet, A, 28, 239
Geography and Love, 35
King, The, 28, 31, 33 f., 136 f.
King Eystein, 21
King Sverre, 21
Leonarda, 28, 37
Limping Hulda, 21, 227
Magnhild, 37, 212, 238
Mary, 40 ff.
Mary Stuart in Scotland, 21
'Monogamists and Polygamists', 29, 239
'Mother's Hands', 41 f.
Newly Wed, The, 25 f., 31
New System, The, 28, 39
On God's Paths, 39 f.
'Ovind', 220
Paul Lange and Tora Parsberg, 28, 35, 136
poems and songs, 20, 22, 23
'Rail Road and the Churchyard, The', 20
Sigurd the Bad, 21 f., 227
Sigurd the Crusader, 21
Synnøve Solbakken, 12 f., 19, 20
'Thrond', 220
Blicher, Steen Steensen, 19
Boccaccio, Giovanni, 254
'Bohêmefejden', 29, 102 f., 147, 158, 233, 236, 239
Bojer, Johan, 157, 190 f., **193 ff.**, 203, 254, 258, 269
Bokmaal, *see* Riksmaal
bønder (peasants) and their politics, 3, 166, 212 f., 215 f.; *see also* Landsmaal, *Venstre*
Bourget, Paul, 256
Braaten, Oskar Alexander, 203 n.
Brandes, Georg Cohen Morris, 17, 29 ff., 36, 39, 56 ff., 81, 146, 148, 150, 158 f., 218, 222 f., 249

Bremer, Fredrika, 209, 219
Brontë, Charlotte, 14, 200
Brontë, Emily, 14
Bull, Jacob Breda, 206 n., 252, 268
Bull, Olaf Jacob Martin Luther, **206**, 269
Burckhardt, Jacob, 174
Bymaal, *see* Riksmaal
Byron, George Gordon, *lord*, 10, 30, 97, 181

Caine, Thomas Henry Hall, 194
Carducci, Giosuè, 18
Chekhov, Anton, 82, 94
Christensen, Hjalmar, 249
Christiania
    Christiania Theater, 133 ff., 140, 220, 246 f., 267 *et passim*
    Møllergate Theater, 43 n., 135, 220, 267
    National Theatre, 137 f., 143, 163 n., 247
Colban, Marie, 259
Collett, Jacobine Camilla, 10, **13 f.**, 49, 70 f., 79, 95 f., 97, 149 n., 198, 199, 219, 231, 263
Collin, Christen Christian Dreyer, 144, 152, 248
Collins, William Wilkie, 233
Cooper, Fenimore, 70

Dahl, Gustav Adolph, 247
D'Annunzio, Gabriele, 147
Dante Alighieri, 241
Darwin, Charles, 15, 224
Daudet, Alphonse, 234
Decadencee, literary, 104, 147, 152
De Foe, Daniel, 160
Delius, Frederick, 140
Denmark, political and cultural relations between Norway and, 2, 4, 6, 7, 8, 9 f., 133 ff., 148, 209, 219, 241, 246, 249, 251, 255, 261
Dickens, Charles, 10, 70, 92, 225
Dietrichson, Lorentz Henrik Segelke, 209
Dostoievsky, Fedor, 12, 146, 165, 172, 255 f.
Drachmann, Holger Henrik Herholdt, 150, 156, 165, 181, 247, 249
Dumas, Alexandre (*senior*), 10
Dumas, Alexandre (*junior*), 30, 136

Duun, Ole Julius, **203 f.**, 207, 212, 260, 269
Dybfest, Arne, 157, **158**, 189

Egge, Peter, 139, 157, **190 ff.**, 196, 203, 258, 269
Eliot, George (*pseud.*), 78
Elster, Kristian Mandrup, **65 ff.**, 79, 232 f., 237, 265
Elster, Kristian (*junior*), 66 n., 263
Emerson, Ralph Waldo, 256
Euripides, 64
Expressionism, literary, 36, 225

Fahlstrøm, Johan *and* Fru Fahlstrøm, 138
Falkberget (*or* Falkberg), Johan Petter, **203 f.**, 260, 269
Feuerbach, Ludwig, 30
Feuillet, Octave, 136
Finne, Gabriel, 157, **158 f.**, 189
Friele, Christian Frederik Gottfried, 32
Fröding, Gustaf, 12, 260

Galsworthy, John, 36, 92, 201
Garborg, Arne, 11, 98, **99 ff.**, 113, 146, 155, 190, 212, 213, 229, 238, 239 ff., 266
    articles, 111, 266
    Free-Thinker, A, 99, 239
    Haugtussa, 108 f., 155
    Henrik Ibsens Keiser og Galilæer, 99, 229
    Hjaa Ho Mor, 240
    In Hel's Abode, 109 f., 241
    Irreconcilables, 240, 241
    Ivar Aasen, 111
    Lost Father, The, 106 f., 108, 109
    Lost Messiah, The, 241
    Men-Folk, 100 ff., 103, 239, 241
    Peace, 105 ff.
    Peasant Students, 100 f., 103, 104, 241
    Returned Son, The, 108
    Teacher, The, 107, 113, 241
    Tired Men, 103, 110
Garborg, Hulda (*née* Bergersen), 99 n., 138, 198, 247, 266
George, Henry, 104, 110, 240
Gissing, George, 101, 230
Gjør, Bolette, 259
Goethe, Johann Wolfgang, 56, 111, 242
Gogol, Nikolay Vasilyevich, 247
Goldschmidt, Meïr Aron, 15

Goncourt, Jules *and* Edmond de, 256
Gorky, Maxim (*pseud.*), 205, 260
Gotthelf, Jeremias (*pseud.*), 19
Gran, Gerhard, 249, 265
Grimm, Jakob *and* Wilhelm, 9
Grundtvig, Nicolai Frederik, 10, 27, 208, 222

Hamsun, Knut, 11, 128, 139, 148 f., 157, 165 ff., **174 ff.**, 189, 191, 194, 196 n., 197, 207, 209 ff., 213, 236, 252 ff., 268
    articles and lectures, 128, 148 f., 256, 268
    At the Gates of the Kingdom, 178 f., 189, 256, 257
    August, 187
    Benoni, 182
    But Life is Alive, 187
    Children of the Age, 184 f.
    Editor Lynge, 178
    Evening Glow, 179, 257
    Growth of the Soil, 185 ff., 191, 197, 213, 257
    Hunger, 148, 175, 255, 257
    In Fairy-Tale Land, 180, 182
    In the Grip of Life, 179
    Lars Oftedal, 236
    Last Chapter, The, 258
    Last Joy, The, 183 f.
    Monk Vendt, 179 f.
    Mysteries, 175 ff., 256, 257
    New Ground, 178
    On Overgrown Paths, 175 n., 182
    Pan, 175, 177 f., 256, 257
    Play of Life, The, 179, 257
    poems, 180 f., 257
    Queen Tamara, 179
    Ring Closed, The, 187
    Rosa, 182
    Segelfoss Town, 184 f., 253
    Tramps, 187
    Under the Autumn Star, 183
    Victoria, 180
    Wanderer plays on muted Strings, A, 183
    Wild Choir, The, 180 f., 207
    Women at the Pump, The, 188
Hansen, Mauritz Christopher, 217
Hansson, Ola, 114, 181
Hardy, Thomas, 34, 75, 78, 106, 191, 192, 194
Hartleben, Otto Erich, 247

Hauch, Johannes Carsten, 134, 246
Hauge, Hans Nielsen, 86
Haukland, Andreas, 260
Hauptmann, Gerhart, 164
Hebbel, Christian Friedrich, 224
Hegel, Georg Wilhelm Friedrich, 52
Heiberg, Gunnar Edvard Rode, **140 ff.**, 146, 150, 203, 229, 247 f., 267
    articles, 267
    Artists, 140
    Aunt Ulrikke, 141
    Balcony, The, 144, 145
    Big Lottery Prize, The, 140
    Gert's Garden, 140, 145
    Harald Svan's Mother, 247
    In Freedom's Cage, 267
    I Will Defend my Country, 143, 145, 203
    King Midas, 141 f., 145
    Love's Tragedy, 144 f., 248
    Lying in State, 143, 248
    Popular Assembly, The, 140
Heiberg, Johan Ludvig, 10, 54, 56, 227, 246
Heiberg, Johanne Luise, 54
Heidenstam, Carl August Verner von, 148, 260
Heine, Heinrich, 15 f., 92, 261
Hertz, Henrik, 10, 56
Hettner, Hermann, 46, 221, 227
Hilditch, Jacob, 252, 268
Hjemstavnsdiktning, 161, 163, 213
Holberg, Ludvig, 15, 111, 134, 136, 179, 246, 247
Holm, Viggo, 247
Holstein, Ludvig Detlev, 261
Homer, 15, 111
Hostrup, Jens Christian, 247
Hovden, Anders, 266
Hugo, Victor, 31, 254
Huxley, Thomas Henry, 224
Huysmans, Joris-Karl, 104, 256

Ibsen, Bergljot, 19 n., 264
Ibsen, Henrik Johan, 8, 10 f., 13, 17 f., 22, 25, 27, 28, 29, 30, 37, **43 ff.**, 68 n., 70, 71 f., 96, 99, 105, **116 ff.**, 134, 136, 139, 142, 145, 146, 149, 156, 158, 168, 179 f., 190, 207, 209 f., 219, 224, 226 ff., 242 ff., 246, 247, 264
    articles, speeches and letters, 264
    Brand, 47, 49 f., 99, 219, 227, 228

Ibsen (*cont.*)
Catiline, 43 f., 226
Doll's House, A, 28, 58, 60 ff., 72, 231,
    244
Emperor and Galilean, 52 f., 56, 99, 227,
    228 f.
Enemy of the People, An, 11, 46, 58, 64,
    232
Feast at Solhaug, The, 44, 226
Ghosts, 29, 58, 60 ff., 96, 120, 136,
    230, 231, 247
Hedda Gabler, 120, 122 ff., 125 f., 179,
    243 f.,
John Gabriel Borkman, 120, 127 ff.,
    245, 249
Lady from the Sea, The, 72, 123 ff., 127,
    130, 149, 243 f.
Lady Inger, 44, 226
League of Youth, The, 27, 57, 72, 136
Little Eyolf, 120, 123 f., 126 f., 145,
    244
Love's Comedy, 25, 47 ff., 55, 136, 227
Master Builder, The, 120, 127 f., 229,
    242, 243, 244, 245
Norma, 226
Olaf Liljekrans, 44, 226
Peer Gynt, 49 f., 51 f., 99, 156, 168,
    219, 227, 228, 229
Pillars of Society, 38 ff., 141, 158, 230 f.
poems, 53 ff., 207, 229
Pretenders, The, 22, 46 f., 49, 227
Rosmersholm, 71 f., 118, 120 ff., 145,
    149, 243
St John's Night, 25, 44, 226
Vikings in Helgeland, The, 45 f., 226 f.
Warrior's Barrow, The, 44, 226
When We Dead Awaken, 127 ff., 131 f.,
    245, 247
Wild Duck, The, 116 ff., 120, 142, 230,
    242 f., 245
Ibsen, Sigurd, 19 n., 43 n.
impressionism, literary, 11, 165, 175, 189
Ingemann, Bernhard Severin, 10

Jacobsen, Jens Peter, 238
Jæger, Hans Henrik, **102**, 158, 239
Jæger, Henrik, 102 n.
James, William, 208
Janson, Kristofer Nagel, 251
Jølsen, Ragnhild, 198, **199 f.**, 259, 269
Jones, Henry Arthur, 231
Joyce, James, 188

Karlfeldt, Erik Axel, 260
Kielland, Alexander Lange, 11, 29, 38,
    80 ff., 96, 104, 139, 146, 156,
    158 n., 162, 189, 194, 210 f.,
    234 ff., 239 f., 249, 260, 265
Else, 87, 91, 92, 96
essays and letters, 265
Feast of St John, The, 88 f., 91 f., 236 f.
Fortuna, 87, 91 f., 156, 237
Garman & Worse, 83 ff., 91 f., 235, 260
His Majesty's Bailiff, 139
Jacob, 89 f., 237
Novelettes and New Novellettes, 81 ff.,
    235
Poison, 87, 236, 237
proverbes, 235
'Skippers' Yarn, A', 82 f., 87
Skipper Worse, 85 ff., 91 f., 162, 236
Snow, 87 f., 237
Two Novelettes from Denmark, 81
Working Men, 87, 89, 92, 235, 236 f.,
    254
Kierkegaard, Søren Aabye, 10, 27, 92,
    228
Kinck, Hans Ernst, 11, 157, **165 ff.**, 175,
    180, 189, 194, 211, 252 ff., 268
Agiluf the Wise, 168, 254
Anny Porse, 169 f., 173
articles, 253, 255
Avalanche Broke, The, 171 ff., 254
Between the Processions, 180, 268
Emigrants, 170 f., 172, 254
Herman Ek, 169, 254, 255, 268
Horse-Coper, The, 167 ff., 171, 172,
    180, 253 f.
In the Rindal Encampment, 254
Last Guest, The, 169, 174
Parson, The (Præsten), 268
People of the Renaissance, 174
poetry, 167, 268
Quill Driver, A, 174
short stories, 167
Time of Greatness, The, 255
Towards Carnival, 174
Kipling, Rudyard, 12, 147, 196
Kjær, Nils, 203 n.
Kleist, Heinrich von, 21
Knudsen, Knud, 217, 246
Krag, Thomas Peter, 157, **159 ff.**, 169,
    189, 200, 251, 267 f.
Krag, Vilhelm Andreas Wexels, 149, **154
    ff.**, 189, 205 f., 213, 250 f., 258, 267

Krog, Helge, 203 n., 247
Krohg, Christian, **102 f.**, 239

Labiche, Eugène Marin, 136
Lagerlöf, Selma, 12, 163, 260
Laing, Samuel, 214
Landsmaal, 7 f., 14 f., 52, 110 ff., 155
    217, 219, 220, 221, 242, 248, 261,
    263, 265 ff.
Landstad, Magnus Brostrup, 216
Larsen, Bolette Christine Pavels, 266
Laube, Heinrich, 136
Lawrence, David Herbert, 255
Lie, Jonas Lauritz Idemil, 11 f., 38,
    68 ff., 83, 93, 105, 139, 146, 162,
    190, 198 f., 210 f., 232, 233 f., 260,
    265
    Adam Schrader, 69
    Barque 'Fremtiden', The, 69
    'By Lake Enare', 69, 78
    Commandant's Daughters, The, 70, 71,
      233
    Dyre Rein, 70
    Evil Powers, 77, 233
    Family at Gilje, The, 69, 70 f., 162
    Faustina Strozzi, 69
    Go Ahead, 69, 79, 195
    Grabow's Cat, 69, 139
    letters, 265
    Lifer, The, 69, 76 f., 79, 233, 234, 260
    Life Together, 70, 72, 79
    Maisa Jons, 233, 234
    Niobe, 70, 73 ff., 79, 190, 233
    Ogres, 77, 78, 233
    Pilot and his Wife, The, 69, 76, 233
    plays, 69, 139, 233
    poems, 232, 233
    Rutland, 69
    Thomas Ross, 69
    Visionary, The, 69, 78
    When the Iron Curtain Falls, 70
Lie, Thomasine, 68 n., 69 n.
Lincoln, Abraham, 54
Lindeman, Ludvig Mathias, 216
Løland, Rasmus, **114**, 266
Ludwig, Otto, 224
Lytton, Edward George Earle Bulwer,
    lord, 10

Maeterlinck, Maurice, 12, 147, 153,
    156 f., 169, 250
Mallarmé, Stéphane, 147

Mann, Thomas, 235
Marryat, Frederick, 70
Masefield, John, 203 n.
Maupassant, Henri de, 82, 259
Mill, John Stuart, 29, 61, 62, 81, 225
    256
Moderne Gjennembrud, det, 29 f., 81,
    146, 218; *see also* Brandes
Moe, Jørgen, 5 f., 209, 242
Moe, Moltke, 242
Molière, 111, 136
Möller, Peder Ludvig, 221
Moreto y Cavana, Agustín, 136
Mortensson Egnund (*previously* Morten-
    sen), Ivar, **112 f.**, 208, 266
Moser, Gustav von, 136, 247
Munch, Andreas, 9
Munch, Anna, 259
Munch, Edvard, 102 n., 152, 154, 217
Munch, Peter Andreas, 216, 217
Musset, Alfred de, 82, 235

Nærup, Carl, 249
National Romanticism, 5 ff., 8 f., 20, 44,
    49, 52, 134, 174
Naturalism, literary, 31, 38, 75, 76 ff.,
    96 ff., 104, 240; *see also* Zola
Neo-Romanticism, literary, 12, 128, 147,
    149 ff., 189, 198, 213
Nietzsche, Friedrich, 12, 104, 146, 148,
    165, 249, 256
Normann, Regine Serine, 198, **200**, 259
Nynorsk, *see* Landsmaal

Obstfelder, Sigbjørn, 139, 149, **152 ff.**,
    154, **156 f.**, 159, 189, 250 f., 267 f.
Oehlenschläger, Adam, 10, 21, 24, 26,
    56, 136
Oftedal, Lars, 236, 266
Ørjasæter, Tore, **207 f.**, 269
Osborne, Lloyd, 193
Oslo, *see* Christiania
Øverland, Arnulf, **206 f.**, 261, 268 f.

Paludan-Müller, Frederik, 10, 56, 227
Pinero, Arthur Wing, 126, 136, 145
Pirandello, Luigi, 117
Portaas, Herman Theodore, *see* Wilden-
    vey
Porto-Riche, Georges de, 145
Proudhon, Pierre Joseph, 30
Prydz, Alvide, 259

Ramm, Minda (*later* Kinck), 167 n.
Realism, literary, 11, 31, 57, 65, 190, 198
Reuter, Fritz, 233
Richter, Ole Jørgensen, 35, 224 f., 230 f.
Riksmaal, 8, 217, 219, 220, 251, 253, 261
Rilke, Rainer Maria, 152 n.
Ring, Barbra Mathilde, 198, **202**, 260
Rodenbach, Georges, 153
Rolfsen, Nordahl, 156, 247
Romanticism, literary, 10 f., 57, 65, 127; *see also* National Romanticism, neo-Romanticism
Rostand, Edmond, 12, 251
Runeberg, Johan Ludvig, 24, 222

'Sædelighedsfejden', 29 f., 234
Sagas, Norse, 45, 113 n., 226
Sainte-Beuve, Charles Augustin, 29
Sand, George (*pseud.*), 19, 30, 219
Sardou, Victorien, 37, 136, 247
Sars, Johan Ernst Welhaven, 223, 251, 264
Schiller, Friedrich, 10, 21 f., 136
Schönthan, Franz von, 136
Schweigaard, Anton Martin, 54, 215
Scott, Gabriel (*pseud.*), 157, 190 f., 193 n., **196 ff.**, 257, 259, 269
Scott, Sir Walter, 10
Scribe, Augustin Eugène, 10, 21, 44, 45, 136
Seland, Hans Andreas, 267
Shakespeare, William, 21, 22, 44, 46, 70, 111, 136, 179, 206 n., 247
Shaw, George Bernard, 37, 127, 225
Sheridan, Richard Brinsley, 136
Sivle, Per, **113 f.**, 260, 266
Skram, Bertha Amalie (*née* Alver), 11, 77, 80, **93 ff.**, 139, 145, 146, 190, 198, 237 ff., 265
Skram, Erik, 93 n., 237, 238
Sophocles, 46, 64
Spencer, Herbert, 142, 224, 225, 256
Spielhagen, Friedrich, 233
Steinsvik, Rasmus Olai, 266 f.
Sterne, Laurence, 15
Stevenson, Robert Louis, 193
Storm, Theodor, 82
Strauss, David Friedrich, 81
Strindberg, August, 10, 147, 148, 158 f., 172, 208, 225, 249, 255 f., 260
Strömberg, Johan Peter, 246

Stuckenberg, Viggo Henrik Fog, 261
Sudermann, Hermann, 126, 136, 145
Sue, Eugène, 105
Sundt, Eilert Lund, 20
Sweden, political and cultural relations between Norway and, 1 f., 4, 143, 148, 203, 209, 260, 261

Taine, Hippolyte, 29, 81
Tegnér, Esaias, 10, 24
tendens and literature with a purpose, 5, 11, 26 ff., 31 ff., 58, 67, 87 f., 146, 165, 166, 187, 189, 194
Thackeray, William Makepeace, 92, 243
Tolstoy, Lev, *count*, 12, 18, 97, 104
Turgeniev, Ivan, 42, 68, 146, 232
Tvedt, Jens, **114**, 266
Twain, Mark (*pseud.*), 256

Undset, Sigrid, 78 f., 200, **202**, 210, 260
Uppdal, Kristofer Oliver, 203, **204 f.**, 207, 260, 269

Vālmīki, 111
Venstre (political party of the Left), 27 f., 88 f., 215, 230; see also *bønder*
Villetard de Prunières, Charles Edmond, 247
Vinje, Aasmund Olafsen, 7, 10, 13, **14 ff.**, 20, 110, 112, 211, 218 ff., 263
Vislie, Vetle, 266
Vogt, Nils (of Bergen), 150 n.
Vogt, Nils Collett, **149 ff.**, 154, 155, 189, 250, 258, 267

Wedekind, Frank, 225
Welhaven, Johan Sebastian Cammermeyer, 6, 8 f., 13 n., 23, 54, 56, 111
Wergeland, Henrik, 4 ff., 8, 9, 13 n., 174, 209, 216
Wessel, Johan Herman, 246
Whitman, Walt, 256
Wiers-Jenssen, Hans, 203 n.
Wildenvey, Herman (*pseud.*), **205 f.**, 207, 269
Winsnes, Hanna, 259
Winther, Christian, 10

Zola, Émile, 64, 76 f., 92, 94, 97, 146, 184, 225, 236, 259